TIM RUTHERFORD-JOHNSON

The Music of Liza Lim

W<small>ILDBI</small>RD

Published 2022 by Wildbird Music Pty Ltd

www.wildbirdmusic.com.au
mail@wildbirdmusic.com.au

Copyright © Tim Rutherford-Johnson 2022

All rights reserved. No part of this book may be reproduced or transmitted in any form or by any means, electronic or mechanical, including photocopying, recording or by any information storage and retrieval system, without prior permission in writing from the publisher.

Cover design and typesetting by Philippa Horn

Musical examples typeset by Pete Readman

Printed and bound in Sydney by Ligare Pty Ltd

 A catalogue record for this work is available from the National Library of Australia

WB-B-221

Contents

Introduction		1
1	Music for solo instrument	9
2	Music for chamber ensemble	48
3	Music for voice	87
4	Music for installations	125
5	Music for orchestra and large ensemble	140
6	Music for the stage	185
Chronology		232
Further Reading		234
List of Works		235

This one's for Liza, in friendship and admiration

dream's glimmer forms
returning, again, again

to a birthing ground
whose voices
shimmer
like new rain

Patricia Sykes, 'latitude of gain',
from *Mother Tongue*

Introduction

Liza Lim is one of Australia's most internationally renowned composers. Her works are performed regularly around the world, and she has been commissioned by major organisations in Europe, North America and her home country. She has been a featured composer at numerous festivals and was composer-in-residence for the Sydney Symphony Orchestra in 2005 and 2006. Among her awards are the Paul Lowin Prize for Orchestral Composition (2004), the Don Banks Award for Music (2018) and the Happy New Ears composition prize from the Hans and Gertrud Zender Foundation (2021).

Lim was born in Perth on 30 August 1966 to Chinese-Bruneian parents. After a series of moves between Australia and Brunei while she was young, her family settled in Melbourne, where she began high school as a boarder at Presbyterian Ladies' College. Having taken piano lessons in Brunei she took up violin at PLC, where there was also a focus on contemporary music and classroom composition; among her classmates was the soprano Deborah Kayser, who became a close friend and one of her most inspirational performers. At around this time Lim became 'switched on' to sound and began to hear sounds in the environment not in isolation but as colours, shapes, melodies and rhythms (Speak Percussion 2016). Encouraged by her teachers, at fifteen Lim began private composition lessons with Richard David Hames, then a teacher at the Victorian College of the Arts (he later became a distinguished corporate philosopher). She also took lessons with Riccardo Formosa, himself a student of Franco Donatoni. Lim took her undergraduate degree at VCA, where she majored in violin – Hames had left the faculty by the time she arrived, and composition was no longer taught.[1] After graduating she studied in Amsterdam, the Netherlands, for six months in 1987 with Ton de Leeuw at the Sweelinck Conservatory, and took a small number of private lessons with Brian Ferneyhough in The Hague. Her postgraduate studies were at the University of Melbourne (MMus, 1988) and the University of Queensland (PhD, 2002). She taught at the University of Melbourne from 1988 to 1992, and in 1995 was a visiting lecturer at the University of Western Sydney. From 2008 to 2017 she was Professor of Composition at the University of Huddersfield, UK, where she also directed the university's Centre for Research in New Music (CeReNeM). In 2017 she was appointed Professor of

Composition at the Sydney Conservatorium of Music, the University of Sydney, where she leads the Composing Women program and in 2019 became the inaugural Sculthorpe Chair of Australian Music.

A significant moment in Lim's early career came during her last year at VCA, in 1986, when some of her student colleagues formed ELISION, a group that has since become possibly Australia's leading new music ensemble. Lim was involved with the group from the start, contributing to and conducting a work at the ensemble's second-ever concert – *Blaze* for countertenor and six musicians, a student work written in a post-Boulezian style. Soon after this, ELISION commissioned the work that was to become the first in her official catalogue, the thirty-minute *Garden of Earthly Desire* (1988–9), a kaleidoscopic mix of inspirations from Hieronymus Bosch, Italo Calvino, tarot cards and puppet theatre for an unusual ensemble of eleven instruments that included mandolin, electric guitar and harp. ELISION toured the piece in Europe, introducing Lim's music to an international audience and attracting the attention of her eventual publishers, Casa Ricordi. Since *Garden*, Lim's story has been closely entwined with ELISION's (the ensemble's artistic director, Daryl Buckley, is her husband). She has written many works for the group, whose virtuoso players and collective fearlessness and spirit of adventure have allowed her musical ideas to develop rapidly and without inhibition.

A second important moment came with the ISCM (International Society for Contemporary Music) World New Music Days in Hong Kong, in 1988. This was the first time this annual festival had taken place in East Asia, and only the seventh time in sixty-five years that it had been staged outside Europe. Events like the ISCM attracted many of the leading figures within the world of new music – especially in an era when it was still relatively uncommon to take a transcontinental flight. At the festival the new music specialist Arditti Quartet played an early piece of Lim's called *Pompes funèbres* (after the 1948 novel by Jean Genet).[2] She also attracted the attention of Germany's Radio Bremen, who commissioned her next piece, *Voodoo Child* (1989) for soprano and ensemble, for the station's Pro Musica Nova festival. It was first performed there in 1990 by Ensemble Avance with the soprano Ingrid Schmithusen.

Voodoo Child sets two stanzas from Sappho's poem *To a Young Girl*, and was soon followed by Lim's first opera, *The Oresteia* (1991–3). *The Oresteia* combines texts by Sappho and Aeschylus, and was written in collaboration with Barrie Kosky (b. 1967), a recent graduate of the University of Melbourne, and today a leading international opera director. As well as Kosky, others involved in producing *The Oresteia* included the choreographer and dancer Shelley Lasica (b. 1961) and the stage designer and architect Peter Corrigan (1941–2016); the opera was performed by ELISION and conducted by the Italian conductor Sandro Gorli (b. 1948). It is unusual for a composer to have a work of this scale so early in their catalogue, but Lim says that the experience of working with puppet theatre in *Garden of Earthly Desire* led quite naturally – helped by the combination of naivety and ambition that groups of young artists like this can inspire – to the idea of writing a chamber opera.

Through Corrigan, Lim met the interdisciplinary artist Domenico de Clario, with whom she made a series of site-specific installations that dominate her work of the mid-1990s: the seven-night Easter week vigil *Afterward: From a Tower (a translation)* (1994); *Bardo'i-thos-grol* (1994–5), also performed over seven nights; and the pair of dawn-to-dusk meditations, performed in autumn and spring, that make up *The Cauldron: Fusion of the Five Elements* (1996). Coloured lamps were installed by de Clario to create lighting for each performance based on Hindu or Taoist philosophies, drawing audiences into a meditative consciousness of breath, the seasons, the passage of celestial bodies, and so on. These environments were partnered in Lim's music by performances of extended duration and a strong emphasis on improvisation.

Although the collaborations with de Clario are extreme cases, Lim often asks her performers to play outside their usual comfort zones. The opera *The Oresteia* (1993) and *Mother Tongue* (2005) for soprano and ensemble, both written for ELISION, both require the soprano to play a cello while singing. *Tongue of the Invisible* (2010–11) for Musikfabrik requires extended passages of improvisation; the opera *Tree of Codes* (2016) for the same ensemble requires all of its players to appear in costumes as part of the scenography, blurring the line between musical accompaniment and on-stage action. *Extinction Events and Dawn Chorus* (2018) for Klangforum Wien asks its solo violinist to make her entrance draped in a large sheet of cellophane. Later, the violinist engages in some play-acting with the percussionist before they both use wind-wands (swirling wooden instruments a little like bull-roarers) to mimic the sound of tropical fish.

Fundamental to Lim's musical imagination is an interest in the physical relationship between a performer and their instrument. Many of her solo pieces have been written in close consultation with their first performers, with discussions taking place around new playing techniques and sonic possibilities. The fruits of such discussions often then become the basic compositional material for the piece itself.

Lim has also drawn inspiration from ELISION's unique sonic signature. Throughout its existence, the group has featured instruments not typically found within a contemporary music ensemble. Buckley's electric guitar has been at the heart of the group from the start; its other members and regular players have included a harpist, a *koto* player, a Hardanger fiddler, two singers, a saxophonist and a recorder player. Likewise, Lim has frequently made use of instruments from different cultural and historical contexts in her works for ELISION and for other ensembles. *The Oresteia* features a *baglama saz*, a long-necked Turkish lute, but it is in *Koto* for eight musicians (1993) that Lim first directly addresses instrumental music from outside the Western tradition. After this, a Hardanger fiddle (a Norwegian folk violin with four or five sympathetic strings below the usual four) is used in *Philtre* (1997) and *Winding Knots: 3 Knots* (2014); a Baroque cello is used in *Street of Crocodiles* (1995); *Indonesian angklung* (a tuned bamboo percussion instrument) and Chinese *erhu* (a two-stringed fiddle) feature in *The Alchemical Wedding* (1996); an *erhu* also features in *Yuè Lìng Jié* (1997–2000), as does as a Japanese *koto* (a type of zither); the koto also appears as a solo instrument in Sixteen touches of the zither (1999) and *Burning House* (1995); a didgeridoo is given a solo role in *The Compass* (2005–6); and so on.

Introduction   3

Between 2002 and 2004, Lim took a break from composition around the birth of her son. She returned with the orchestral piece *Ecstatic Architecture* (2004), commissioned by the Los Angeles Philharmonic for the inaugural season at Walt Disney Concert Hall, Los Angeles, a building designed by Frank Gehry, whose boldly gestural architectural style was an inspiration for Lim's piece. This was at this point Lim's most high-profile commission (and her first to come from North America), yet she was never fully satisfied with it, and it is effectively withdrawn from her catalogue. It is notable that before her break she withdrew another orchestral work, *The Tree of Life* (2001), and she has spoken since of the creative difficulties she was having at this time.[3] It was a pair of smaller, more modest works that indicated the future path of her music.

In the Shadow's Light for string quartet and *The Quickening*, for soprano and *qin* (a Chinese zither similar to a Japanese *koto*) were written for the 2005 Festival d'Automne à Paris, along with the much larger *Mother Tongue*. This generous group of commissions, spearheaded by the Festival's musical co-director Joséphine Markovits, energised and enabled a new phase in Lim's creative life. Both *In the Shadow's Light* and *The Quickening*, Lim writes in her programme note,

> inhabit a dream-world where things are not grasped directly, where sensations are filtered through different kinds of veils. These veils might be experienced as a tangle of submerged pathways through which one senses the movement of creatures on the surface above; perhaps as a trance of saturated light coming from a place beyond, or as oscillating interference patterns created by intersecting lines and arising from the coupling and uncoupling of sonic elements. (Lim 2004)

The 'oscillating interference patterns' of intersecting lines recall quite consciously the cross-hatched and dotted patterning found in much Aboriginal Australian art. The visual illusion – known as 'shimmer' – created by these patterns is believed to connect paintings with ancestral spirits. It serves as something like an aura that surrounds ritual forms (dances, body markings, music, paintings) and through which those forms might be interpreted in shamanic dreams. In *In the Shadow's Light* and *The Quickening*, shimmer is used metaphorically to the suggest the tactile awareness of the string quartet and *qin* players; it may also be applied to 'the quickening' – the term for a mother's first, fluttering sensations of her baby in her womb.

It was with the ensemble work *Songs Found in Dream* (2005), however, that Lim began to engage directly with Aboriginal art, and particularly the art of the Yolngu people of Arnhem land in northeastern Australia. *Songs Found in Dream* was, she has said, 'a "turning point" in terms of finding a new aesthetic voice' (conversation with the author). In 2006, Lim was keen to research the singing traditions of Yolngu women in relation to a concert series she was curating as part of the Adelaide Festival. She was invited to spend a week with the Yunupingu clan, where she was a guest at funeral ceremonies for a female cultural leader who had recently died; on her arrival she exchanged some of her hair (to make the brushes that would paint the coffin) for red ochre, whose silvery sheen when rubbed on her skin would protect her from bad spirits.

Coming into direct contact with Aboriginal cultural practices like these introduced Lim to 'a cultural economy of hiddenness', and 'involved a perspectival shift in my work from the horizontal construction of Chinese knowledge … to a much more vertical idea of structure made up of different layers of transparency/viscosity/opacity' (Lim 2009). By this, Lim refers to the various layers of knowledge that structure Aboriginal culture. Each of these layers, and thus the plural meanings of an object or image, is made accessible in turn through acts of initiation designed to keep them secret and sacred. The shimmer pattern, for example, may appear as a surface effect, but to the initiated it is the manifestation of underlying spiritual and cultural forces. This idea of veiled and secret knowledges that may be uncovered through deliberate and ritualised experience is explored explicitly in the series of works that Lim wrote subsequent to this encounter, including *Shimmer Songs* (2006) for ensemble; *Ochred String* (2008) for oboe, viola, cello and bass; *Pearl, Ochre, Hair String* (2010) for orchestra; and *Invisibility*. Typically, its traces may also be found in works predating her experience of Yolngu culture – for example, in the Japanese calligraphic notation she used in *Burning House* (1995) for singing *koto* player, which required her to engage with a knowledge system with which she was unfamiliar – and it reverberates in later works that deal with alternate ways of knowing, including *Winding Bodies: 3 Knots* (2014) for ensemble, *The Turning Dance of the Bee* (2016) for six musicians and *An Elemental Thing* for solo woodblock (2017).

From 2007–8, Lim lived in Berlin as part of the DAAD (Deutscher Akademischer Austauschdienst) artist-in-residence programme. For this year her focus was not her shimmer-inspired pieces, but the composition of her third opera, *The Navigator*. This again represented a coming together of collaborators and other influences. The opera's libretto was written by the Australian poet Patricia Sykes, with whom Lim had previously worked on *Mother Tongue* (2005) for soprano and ensemble. The partnership with Barrie Kosky was also renewed for the work's first productions at the Brisbane Festival and Melbourne International Festival of the Arts. Once more the music was composed for ELISION, and several of the group's players gained new solo and ensemble works extracted from the piece (*Wild Winged-One* (2007) for trumpet, *Weaver of Fictions* (2007) for alto Ganassi recorder, *the long forgetting* (2007) for tenor Ganassi recorder, and *Sensorium* (2007) for countertenor, Baroque harp, viola d'amore and harpsichord). *The Navigator* also makes reference to Wagner: Lim has said that hearing the prelude to *Tristan and Isolde* in 2004, towards the end of her two-year break from composing, helped her fall 'in love with music again' (Leonard 2008). Both the *Tristan* story and disguised moments of the music itself feed into her own opera.

Although Lim has continued to write works for ELISION, after *The Navigator* she noticeably widened her circle of musical collaborators. Most significant among these has been the Cologne-based ensemble Musikfabrik, for whom Lim has composed two major works, *Tongue of the Invisible* and her fourth opera *Tree of Codes*, as well as solo pieces for bassoonist Alban Wesly (*Axis Mundi*, 2012–13), euphonium player Melvyn Poore (*Green Lion Eats the Sun*, 2014–15) and bassist Florentin Ginot (*The Table of Knowledge*, 2017).

As well as these compositions, an important outcome of Lim's extended collaboration with Musikfabrik has been another change in perspective, similar to that gained from her encounter with Yolngu culture in 2006. In this case, the change was to how Lim viewed collaboration itself. This emerged from her participation in research by the music scholars Eric Clarke and Mark Doffman that used *Tongue of the Invisible* as a case study in forms of 'distributed creativity' (see Clarke, Doffman and Lim 2013). Realising that the composer–performer relationship she had fostered up until now was one in which the performer was generally cast as an artisan, 'providing building blocks for the architectural vision of the composer' (Lim 2013b), Lim began to seek instead a new mode of collaboration that was more reciprocal, and that gave greater weight to the flux and metamorphosis of a process rather than to the creation of stable building blocks. This approach informed Lim's solo works for members of Musikfabrik, as well as *An Elemental Thing* (2017) for woodblock, for Eugene Ughetti of Australian group Speak Percussion.

Inspired by the work of the British anthropologist Tim Ingold, and in particular his essay 'The Textility of Making' (2010), Lim refers to this approach as a 'mycelial' model of collaboration, a reference to the (often large) networks of branching and converging threads through which fungi absorb nutrients from their environment. The ecological metaphor has proved resonant to Lim's works since around 2015: there are suggestions of it in the animal-human hybrids of *Tree of Codes* and the notions of interconnectedness explored in the violin concerto *Speak, Be Silent* (2015), but it comes to the fore in the concerto for *sheng* and ensemble *How Forests Think* (2016), named after Eduardo Kohn's extra-human anthropology of the Ecuadorian rainforest (2013), and in *Extinction Events and Dawn Chorus*, Lim's most important work of this decade.

At the University of Sydney, Lim leads Composing Women, a development programme set up in 2016 to foster and empower women composers through scholarships, workshops, mentoring and professional partnerships. At the same time, her most recent works have engaged directly with aspects of women's experience: the orchestral *Annunciation Triptych* (completed at the time of writing), which celebrates female spiritual icons from Ancient Greek, Christian and Muslim traditions; and *Sex Magic* (2020) for contrabass flute, electronics and kinetic percussion, written for the American flautist Claire Chase. As with every other phase in Lim's career, this is both a new direction and an aspect of her work that has been present throughout, traceable through the themes of motherhood and fertility in *The Quickening* and *Inguz* (1996), the divine eroticism of *The Alchemical Wedding* (1996) and *Tongue of the Invisible*, and all the way back to the settings of Sappho in her very first works.

Lim regards her compositional practice as one of continuous and evolving research. Each of her compositions seems to derive from a new well of inspiration – her programme notes are full of references to advanced theories in architecture, biology, ecology and ethnography. Yet her work is full of recurring fascinations, among them astronomy, poetry (particularly Rumi), erotic desire, non-Western cultures and different forms of human and more-than-human knowledge. In the chapters that follow, I not only discuss each work on its own autonomous terms but also try to keep illuminated the shape-shifting, mycelial web of connections out of which the music emerges. It is a testament to the coherence of Lim's artistic vision – forged at an early stage in her career – that each addition serves to expand or refine that web, rather than tear or obscure it. In her music, the world possesses a limitless variety and is infinitely interconnected, manifested in an aesthetic of intense, highly differentiated polyphony whose individual voices are always audible, never neglected beneath the sheer number of simultaneous layers. Rather like the creatures of a rainforest, every voice has its own ecological niche. Together they contribute to Lim's unique style: lyrical and dramatic, contemplative and vigorous, intimate and wild.

Acknowledgements

I received the original commission for this book from Wildbird and Brian Howard a few weeks into COVID-19 pandemic, when it was very welcome indeed. I want to thank Brian for that initial invitation and for his steady editorial oversight ever since. Pete Readman and Peggy Polias both set a huge number of musical examples, many of them involving novel notational designs; thank you so much. Haotian Yu allowed me to reference an unpublished essay on Lim's *Invisibility*. In fortnightly classes my student Tyler Bouque provided ever-stimulating conversations about Liza and her music – and more than once introduced me to a new and refreshing perspective. Couldn't have finished it without you. More generally I owe a huge debt to Daryl Buckley and the incredible musicians of ELISION, for their work as new musical ambassadors, and for the warmth and generosity over the fifteen or more years in which they have folded me into Liza's musical world. I hope this book repays some of that faith.

All the composer's works are published by G. Ricordi & Co. Buehnen- und Musikverlag GmbH (a company of Universal Music Publishing Group) and examples used throughout this book are reproduced by kind permission of Hal Leonard Europe BV (Italy). The cover image is a reproduction of bars 1 and 2 of *Invisibility*, which is also published by G. Ricordi & Co. Buehnen- und Musikverlag GmbH and reproduced by kind permission of Hal Leonard Europe BV. I am very grateful to Andrea Natale at Hal Leonard and Verena Berger at Universal Music for helping secure these permissions.

Finally, I thank Liza herself. Throughout this project – and long before it – she has been unfailingly generous with resources, conversation and encouragement. But more than this, the chance to take such a deep dive into a composer's music is a rare privilege; to be able to do so with music that keeps on giving all the way down is very special indeed. For every thread that I have encountered and followed along the way I shall always be grateful.

References

Clarke, Eric, Mark Doffman and Liza Lim (2013). 'Distributed Creativity and Ecological Dynamics: A Case Study of Liza Lim's *Tongue of the Invisible*', *Music and Letters* v94, n4, 628–63.

Gruchy, Jane (2007). 'Alchemical Journeys – Part Two: Liza Lim', *Resonate Magazine*, 17 December, https://www.australianmusiccentre.com.au/article/alchemical-journeys-part-two-liza-lim.

Ingold, Tim (2010). 'The Textility of Making', *Cambridge Journal of Economics*, v34, 91–102.

Kohn, Eduardo (2013). *How Forests Think*. Berkeley and Los Angeles: University of California Press.

Leonard, Doug (2008). 'Fugue of the Senses, Geometry of Desire', *realtime*, n85, http://realtimearts.net/article/85/9017.

Lim, Liza (2004). *In the Shadow's Light*, 2004 [programme note], https://limprogrammenotes.wordpress.com/2011/07/31/in-the-shadows-light-2004/.

Lim, Liza (2009). 'Staging an Aesthetics of Presence', *Search: Journal for New Music* and Culture n6, http://www.searchnewmusic.org/index6.html.

Lim, Liza (2013). 'A Mycelial Model for Understanding Distributed Creativity: Collaborative Partnership in the Making of "Axis Mundi" (2013) for Solo Bassoon', CMPCP Performance Studies Network Conference, Cambridge, 4 April 2013. Available at http://eprints.hud.ac.uk/id/eprint/17973/.

Lim, Liza (2018). Untitled page, ELISION Ensemble website, http://www.elision.org.au/soundhouse/liza-lim/.

Speak Percussion (2016). 'Online Masterclass 11: Liza Lim on A Continuum of Sound' [video], http://soundsunheard.com/online-masterclass-11/.

Endnotes

1 Lim's violin playing can be heard on Ron Nagorcka's *Dawn in the Wombat Forest*, recorded in 1985 and released on his album *Atom Bomb Becomes Folk Art* (Pogus, 2014). Even at this early stage she shows an interest in the harmonics, distortion and transitions between tone and noise, as well as ways of creating musical connections between disparate elements (in this case, rainforest sounds, clavichord and dideridoo) that would become key features of her music.

2 A gesture Lim repaid with *The Weaver's Knot* (2013–14), written for the Ardittis' fortieth birthday celebrations.

3 'I really felt my creative power go somewhere else. The tide really went out a long way' (quoted in Gruchy 2007).

Chapter 1

Music for solo instrument

Solo instrumental works make up about one quarter of Lim's published output. They range from very short occasional pieces like *Dianna* (2020), commissioned by the Canberra Symphony Orchestra for its hornist Dianna Gaetjens, and the 'postcard piece' *Love Letter* (2011) for solo hand drum, to major artistic statements such as *The Four Seasons (after Cy Twombly)* (2008) and *Invisibility* (2009) for cello.

Like the others in this book, this chapter moves chronologically through a selection of works that span Lim's career. These have been chosen to present as wide a picture of her work as possible in the space available, while also allowing for some deeper analysis and investigation of individual works. In this chapter those works are: *Amulet*, weaver-of-fictions, *The Four Seasons (after Cy Twombly)*, *Invisibility*, *Axis Mundi*, *An Elemental Thing*, *The Su Song Star Map* and *bioluminescence*.

Amulet (1992)

Composed in the middle of the two-year period in which she was working on *The Oresteia*, *Amulet* for viola is the first solo instrumental work in Lim's official catalogue. It was written for ELISION's violist Jennifer Curl, one of the group's founder members. All of Lim's solo works have been written with specific players in mind, so they offer an opportunity to see in detail some of the ways in which Lim collaborates with her performers, and how she creates a kind of portraiture in her music. *Amulet* is a close relation to the string quartet *hell* (also 1992), written for the Arditti Quartet (the solo uses many of the same materials and gestures as the quartet, but it is not a transcription of or an extraction from it) and one of the first concrete productions to come out of Lim's visit to the ISCM's 1988 World Music Days in Hong Kong.

Although – like almost all of Lim's music – *Amulet* is written on a conventional five-line staff, with fully notated pitches and rhythms, its principal focus is neither melody nor rhythm but timbre and physical gesture. The first two bars show Lim providing as much detail for the performing manner as she does for the notes themselves: they contain instructions for playing *sul ponticello* (on the bridge), *col legno* (with the wood of the bow), arco, left-hand pizzicato, glissando, and near the bridge using different bow positions and pressure to create a range of harmonics (a non-standard technique that Lim marks *h. sul pont.*). Later techniques used include distorted tones, produced by applying a lot of bow pressure and a slow bow speed; sweeping the bow along (rather than across) the string; scraping the bow along the string to create a noisy attack followed by a discernible pitch; and a circular movement of the bow between the bridge and the fingerboard, giving rise to a range of harmonics and noise. As shown in bars 40 and 41, these actions may cut across the music's pitch structures as much as they may support them (note the spiral notation, indicating the bow's circular movement, quite independent of the underlying rhythms).

Example 1.1 *Amulet*, bars 1–2

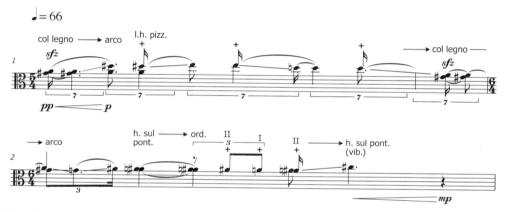

Example 1.2 *Amulet*, bars 40–41

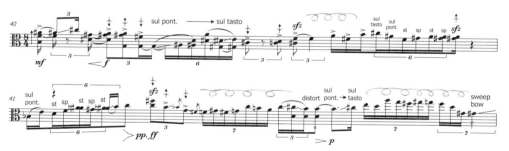

Amulet is a work almost entirely without melody or rhythm: it contains both, but performance directions such as those described make them hard to distinguish by ear alone. What are clearer are changes in attack and timbre. In this respect – and in its frequent focus on narrow bands of pitch – *Amulet* recalls Scelsi's monotonal works for solo violin, such as *Xnoybis* (1965). Two sonic elements in particular are characteristic: a woozy, whooping glissando that connects almost every pair of notes in the work; and left-hand pizzicati made while bowing simultaneously, a technique that creates a sharp, almost hiccupping sound, similar to the grace notes of the Scottish highland bagpipes. These two elements create a contrast between an extended horizontal line and a short vertical attack, opening out a musical space on the basis of timbre and physical gestures (wide movements of the bow versus tight precision of the plucking fingers) even as the pitches themselves remain very restricted.

In a note for the ELISION recording of *Amulet* (*After the Fire*, Vox Australis VAST019-2), ELISION clarinettist Carl Rosman quotes Curl saying that in learning the work 'I became confused as to whether it was the viola player balancing on the viola or the other way around'. This image speaks clearly to the symbiotic co-creative relationship between a performer and their instrument that we will see become a feature of Lim's practice. By enclosing *Amulet* within such a narrow musical space, Lim turns the listener's (and the performer's) attention to subtle changes in sound and articulation that might usually be (deliberately) obscured in a more conventional musical work. Our focus is turned away from notes – pitches, rhythms, harmonic relationships – and towards the physical actions and processes that lie behind them: muscular tension, force, pressure and arcs of movement. This radical reconception of music – as an art of doing, rather than of sounding – was one that attracted several composers in the 1980s and 1990s, among them Richard Barrett (b. 1959) and Klaus K. Hübler (b. 1956). It is fundamental to Lim's aesthetics and has informed all the music of her career.

weaver-of-fictions (2007)

After *Amulet*, Lim's focus to a large extent turned away from solo compositions. Her output in the 1990s includes *Burning House* (1995) for *koto* and voice (one performer; discussed in Chapter 3), *Philtre* (1997) for Hardanger fiddle or retuned violin, and *Sixteen touches of the zither* (1999) for *koto*, composed as part of the installation *Sonorous Bodies* with the artist Judith Wright. But it wasn't until 2007 that she began to write regularly for solo instruments, and the large majority of her works of this type date from this year onwards.

Like *Amulet*, many of these solo works relate to larger ones for ensemble, orchestra or the stage – some of which will be discussed later in this book. Lim's re-engagement with solo instrumental music was spurred by the composition of her third opera, *The Navigator*, out of which she extracted three solos: *Wild Winged One* for trumpet, *The Long Forgetting* for tenor Ganassi recorder and *weaver-of-fictions* for alto Ganassi recorder (she also extracted *Sensorium*, a version of the opera's second scene for soprano, countertenor, tenor Ganassi and contrabass recorders, harp and *viola d'amore*; all four works date from 2007). *weaver-of-fictions* serves as the opera's prelude.

The Ganassi recorder is named after the sixteenth-century Venetian musician Sylvestro Ganassi (1492–1565), author of an important treatise on recorder playing, *La Fontegara* (1535). Ganassi's treatise lists a number of fingerings that expand the recorder's range to more than two octaves; this was a novelty for the time and in fact very few Renaissance instruments that survive today can play more than one or two notes in Ganassi's system.

Nevertheless, modern instrument makers – spearheaded by the great Australian recorder maker Fred Morgan (1940–99) – have designed instruments that can play the full Ganassi system. Since Morgan introduced his instrument in the 1970s, it has become popular in performances of medieval and Renaissance music and has also had several contemporary works written for it.

In her programme note for *weaver-of-fictions*, Lim explains how, in Renaissance usage, the recorder – with its unstable, quivering sound, so precisely entwined with the breath and the body – was often associated with 'erotic, pastoral and supernatural themes'. The use of this instrument at the start of *The Navigator* serves to musically activate some of the themes that will be explored in the opera; *weaver-of-fictions*' title comes from a line in Patricia Sykes's libretto and refers to a descriptive name given to Eros by the poet Sappho. But the work exists in its own right, too, and is popular among contemporary recorder players. It was originally written as a study for Genevieve Lacey, a member of ELISION, who gave the first performance of an early version of the work at the fiftieth birthday celebrations for Daryl Buckley.

In *La Fontegara*, Ganassi also describes a number of elaborate ornamentations to be used in recorder playing, and in *weaver-of-fictions* Lim combines the instrument Ganassi inspired with the style of playing he encouraged. The work begins with a sensuously weaving melody written in the Aeolian mode on B – a B major scale with flattened third, sixth and seventh (NB: the alto Ganassi recorder sounds a major 2nd higher than written; for clarity I refer to the pitches *as written*). Although melody, as we will see, is a recurring feature of Lim's music, this is one of her most affecting, characterised by downward-stepping triplet motifs, single whole-tone steps up or down, and long notes at the end of phrases with a wide finger vibrato, characteristic of Renaissance recorder style.

Example 1.3 *weaver-of-fictions*, bars 1–4

Already, Lim has introduced a little ornamentation to her melody, in the form of grace notes and mordents. It might be argued, too, that the subtle variations she applies to the rhythm of the descending triplet figure also constitute a form of ornamentation (or perhaps a written-out rubato). From bar 5, however, the ornaments – really now foreground elements in their own right – start to take centre stage. In bars 5 and 6, parts of the original melody (especially the B to C♯ step) can be made out, but they are obscured by a range of melodic and timbral distortions, ornamentations and effects: trills, multiphonics, scattershot runs, overblowing and flutter-tonguing. When the melody does return, as it does between bars 12 and 16, it is now draped around these elements, like a heavy, velvet gown.

Example 1.4 *weaver-of-fictions*, bars 11–16

An acceleration of trills and runs brings the first section to an end. The second returns to the original tempo of crotchet = 50 but introduces completely new melodic material. Where the original melody was based upon the notes of the Aeolian mode on B, this section concentrates on the notes outside of that scale – in particular E♭, C and B♭, but later also F and G♯.

After several bars exploring this new tonal territory (while employing several of the ornamental gestures that were introduced in the first section of the work, such as multiphonics and flutter-tonguing), the melody returns at bar 32 and continues until a rising glissando across an augmented octave onto F♯ and a long 'window vibrato' (a vibrato made by vibrating the palm of the hand over the 'window' of the recorder mouthpiece) bring the work to an end.

The Four Seasons (after Cy Twombly) (2008)

Before the completion of Lim's piano concerto *World as Lover, World as Self* (2021), the piano had featured infrequently in her output. It is used in a handful of ensemble and orchestral works, and there is an important part for improvising pianist in *Tongue of the Invisible* (2010–11), but she has written little else for the instrument besides this. *The Four Seasons (after Cy Twombly)* is her only work for solo piano.

This fact offers a clue to Lim's instrumental style. We have already seen the importance of timbre and extended techniques to her music. Many such techniques are also open to the piano, of course. Works by Karlheinz Stockhausen (*Klavierstücke VII*, 1955) and Helmut Lachenmann (*Guero*, 1969) illustrate some of the sounds available at the keyboard of the instrument, and the possibilities expand dramatically if one explores inside the body, plucking, striking and scraping strings, frame, soundboard and so on (Henry Cowell's *Aeolian Har*p, 1923, offers an early example, and there have been numerous others since). And this is to say nothing of adding preparations to the strings, an idea pioneered by John Cage in his *Bacchanale* (1938). Yet there is an important difference between all these techniques and those we see in *Amulet* and *weaver-of-fictions*. The main techniques available on the piano – plucking or bowing a string, inserting a coin between strings, creating a halo of resonances by depressing keys silently – are like switches: they work either on or off. In contrast, many of the techniques used in Lim's other instrumental works – adding distortion by overblowing or increasing bow pressure, or adding vibrato or multiphonics – act like dials: they can be activated to greater or lesser degrees. What's more, it is possible to fade many of them in or out of a 'standard' pitched note. Lim suggests this herself in her performance notes to the string quartet *hell*, to which *Amulet* is related: 'The actions described below will often result in extraneous sounds such as harmonics, distorted noise occurring in an unpredictable manner. The "transitional" nature of the performing techniques creates a fragility of tone whose instability should not be minimized.' Unlike the viola or recorder, say, transitional states between greater or lesser degrees of noise or distortion are not easily achieved on the piano.

The Four Seasons is thus an unusual work in Lim's output, but that unusual quality offers insights into the core features of her aesthetic. All of it is played at the keyboard; there are no extended techniques inside or on the body of the instrument, and no preparations are used. This is not to say, however, that Lim does not find ways to expand and explore the palette of timbres available to her. All four movements explore types of resonance, both through different densities of harmony at the keyboard and through a range of pedalling techniques. As we will see, resonance and harmonic texture provide ways of creating 'continuous' sounds whose timbre can be changed gradually over time, despite the piano's naturally pointillistic percussiveness.

The Four Seasons is named after a series of four paintings painted between 1993 and 1994 by the American artist Cy Twombly (1928–2011), held at the Museum of Modern Art in New York. (A series of similar paintings with the same name, painted at the same time, is owned by the Tate Modern gallery in London.) Lim visited MoMA in January 2007 and was deeply inspired by Twombly's four paintings. In the programme note to her work she writes:

> The combination of ecstatic saturated colour, linear calligraphic dynamism and paint washes veiling poetic commentaries scrawled on canvas, gave me many ideas for a piano cycle in four parts. These "seasons" are seasons of an inner life – they are made up of "climates of feeling" – weather patterns that are sometimes extravagantly baroque in expression or shot through with an elegiac sense of the passage of time opening out to a ceremonial dance. (Lim 2009)

Just as Twombly's paintings only conjure the seasons in intangible, non-pictorial ways – certain colours, types of energy and movement – so do Lim's movements only loosely conjure Twombly's paintings and their themes. The work was commissioned by and is dedicated to the brilliant new music specialist Marilyn Nonken, whose daughter Goldie Celeste was born while the work was being composed and is the dedicatee of its last movement, 'Summer (Sema)'. It received its premiere at the Musica Nova festival, Helsinki. Like Twombly, Lim begins her cycle with 'Autumn', a decision that gives a vaguely symphonic shape to the cycle, placing her slow movement – 'Winter' – second in the sequence and reserving the celebratory, dancing 'Summer (Sema)' for the conclusion.

'Autumn' is in two large sections of approximately equal size, from bar 1 to bar 34 and from bar 35 to bar 64, with a shorter section from bar 65 to the end at bar 77 serving as a resolution of those two opposing blocks. The interval A to F♯ with which it begins, followed by an F♮ in the second bar, serves as the movement's principal motif. It can be picked out in three different versions in the first three bars alone and recurs in different forms throughout the first section and in the work's conclusion.

Example 1.5 *The Four Seasons*, 'Autumn', bars 1–3

When this motif recurs, its notes may be in a different order, but they are always the same pitches and almost always at the same register, meaning that all three of them act as pedals or drones that fade in or out of the foreground through this first section. In spite of whatever activity takes place around them, they are a constant presence, and a base against which relative degrees of density, activity, stasis or difference might be measured.

At bar 10, a high D is introduced as an important addition to this group of four recurring pitches, enlarging and slightly destabilising the group. Such destabilisations ripple through the harmonic language of the rest of this section, as new short-lived pitch centres are tried (among them a D♯ at bar 23 and an A♯ at bar 24) until any sense of centredness evaporates entirely for a slow, three-bar chorale-like texture at the end of the section which, nevertheless, temporarily resolves onto an F–F♯ dyad.

Example 1.6 The *Four Seasons*, 'Autumn', bars 32–4

The second section begins at bar 35, just after this 'suspended' moment. Unlike the first, this section does not focus on a small number of pedal notes or pitch centres, but instead moves rapidly through a series of different centres, never settling on one for longer than two or three bars. This gives the section a comparatively restless feeling as the music continually seeks a place on which to land.

Like the introduction of the D in the first section, the introduction of a high D♯ at the top of a broken chord in bar 53 seems to mark the beginning of the end of the section, as the D♯ becomes a new centre. In this case, however, it seems to arrest the rapidly diversifying shape of the music, precipitating a return to almost complete stillness by bar 63.

Example 1.7 The *Four Seasons*, 'Autumn', bars 58–64

The upward gesture, D♯–E–F in bar 63 reinstates for the first time one of the original three pedal notes, and this is quickly followed by an A, in its original register one leger line above the staff. This provides the framework for the F/F♯ dyad to re-emerge and draw the movement to a conclusion that resolves the tensions created by the second section. The movement ends with a long series of tremolos and rapidly repeated notes that eventually narrow down to a single F♮.

Following the frenetic dénouement of 'Autumn', the opening of 'Winter' presents a stark contrast. It begins with a slow, chorale-like melody, played in widely spaced (but not always parallel octaves). The sense of stillness and sparseness is unmistakable: one thinks of bare branches and frost-covered fields. This is perhaps the movement in which the connection with the season may be most immediately felt. Although the music does get faster following from this glacial opening, the octaves dominate the work's harmonic language.

Example 1.8 *The Four Seasons*, 'Winter', bars 1–3

In bars 8 and 9 Lim adds layers to the texture, with a middle voice of accented A♯s across three octaves, and then a held pianissimo F♯–G–G♯ cluster. Here we see Lim playing with some of the forms of resonance that are available to her, using harmony not in any functional, structural sense, but as a way to create timbres and musical spaces of differing degrees of closeness or openness. The low bass notes against the sustain pedal create a thick wash of harmonics, which are picked out by the two upper voices. These in turn, and in contrast, buzz dissonantly against each other. In bar 10 the high cluster is clarified as a single F♯, but now the A♯ in the middle voice is extended into an A♯–G–G♯ gesture which, against the sustain pedal, becomes effectively a cluster of its own. A third variation of this buzzing dissonance is created in bar 12 by the alternating of A♯ in the right hand and B natural in the left.

Example 1.9 *The Four Seasons*, 'Winter', bars 8–12

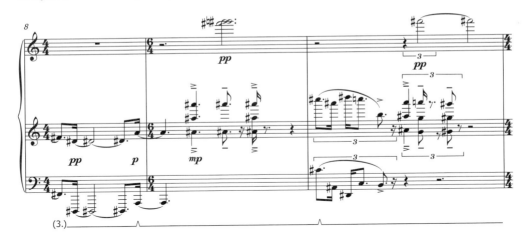

In the next few bars, these semitone dissonances develop gradually into descending chromatic scales in octaves, reaching a climax in bar 16. After this, the first section's energy quickly dissipates, ending at bar 24 with a low A, whose resonance is 'caught' by the middle, *sostenuto* pedal and held over into the second section. This section, beginning at bar 25, continues the use of octaves, but the two-part homorhythmic texture of the previous section is more loosely applied: in the first half of bar 25 the very low D♯ in the left hand and the repeated treble As in the right occur in isolation, while the D♯s that follow are staggered between the two hands. This breakdown in rhythmic synchronisation is followed by a harmonic breakdown hinted at by the accumulated cluster effect (A♯–B–C♮) in the left hand and the C–B trill in the right and then confirmed the rogue C♮ that is the left hand's final note of bar 26. This note – a decisive departure from the omnipresent octave texture – has what I will call a 'cleaving' effect: squeezing the the harmony to a single semitone also opens up and reveals the grain of the music, like splitting a log, or an atom.

Example 1.10 *The Four Seasons*, 'Winter', bars 25–6

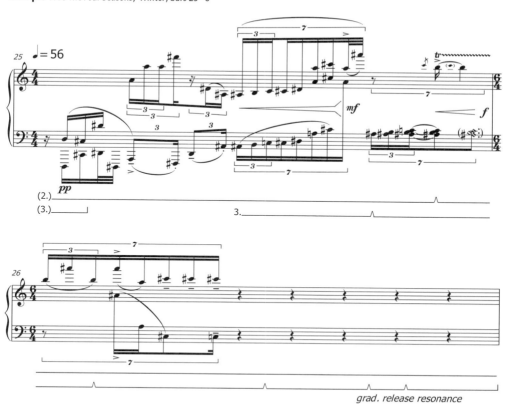

As in the first section, semitone dissonances like this develop once again into chromatic scales, but now the sense of splitting is emphasised by movements in contrary motion, culminating in the sweeping gestures of bars 41 and 42. The energy that is released in this section is massive and culminates in a series of fortissimo chromatic runs and granite-like snatches of melody in accented, quadruple octaves. When that energy is finally dissipated, the movement draws rapidly to a quiet close.

Example 1.11 *The Four Seasons*, 'Winter', bars 41–2

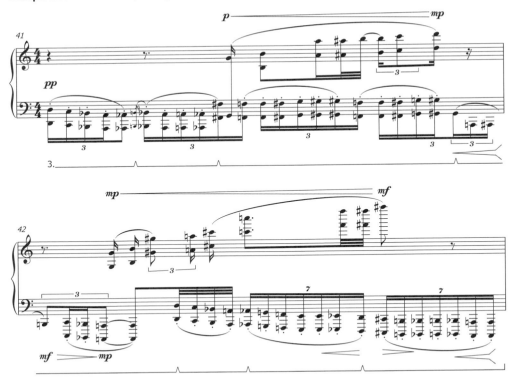

In contrast to the long, sustained passages of 'Winter', 'Spring' begins fragmentarily. The first bar is played almost exclusively in isolated notes and the music unfolds in short gestures almost throughout the movement. The rests become just as important as the notes. Before the movement begins, five keys – B, E♭, F, F♯ and G, all at the bottom of the bass clef – are depressed silently and held by the *sostenuto* pedal (this technique was often used by George Crumb, and can also be found in Berio's *Sequenza IV*, 1966). The sustained resonance creates a shifting, unstable bed that can be heard in these rests, activated by the frequent use of staccatissimo notes played forte and fortissimo, often at the ends of phrases.

Example 1.12 *The Four Seasons*, 'Spring', bars 1–3

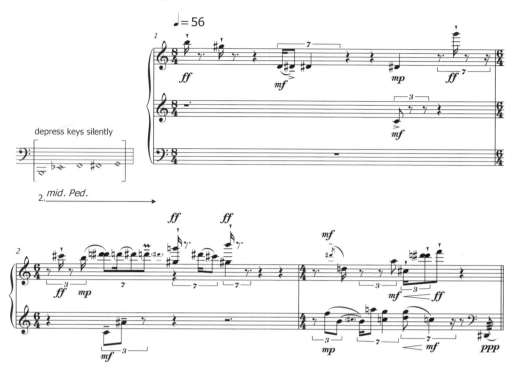

The leaping gestures, grace notes and mordents of the movement's opening gestures appropriately evoke birdsong. And the manner in which the music gradually builds from fragments of melody also recalls the waking of the earth at the beginning of Stravinsky's *The Rite of Spring*. After its first few bars, trills and tremolos are almost continually present throughout Lim's 'Spring'. Their presence may owe something to the Aboriginal 'shimmer' aesthetic that had recently become a feature of her music (see *Invisibility*, below), but they are also an extension of the movement's birdsong-like opening gestures and the use of rapidly repeating notes elsewhere in the work. (See, e.g., Examples 1.5 and 1.7.) Their use in 'Spring' and elsewhere in *The Four Seasons* reveals something of the fluid way in which Lim uses simple elements to create larger fields of interconnected materials. The first examples of tremolo or trill-like figures are the mordents found in bars 2 and 3, followed by a long D♯ tremolo that begins on the last quaver of bar 3 and continues to the end of bar 5. A precursor to both gestures might be found in the D–D♯ motif found in bar 1, which might be read as very slow, two-note trill; and in bar 6 all three of these types are heard together.

The trill/tremolo idea is developed in several ways. The repeated D♯s and G♯s of bars 12 and 13 might be read as slow tremolos, written out at different speeds. In bar 15 a whole-note trill between B♭ and C thickened with the right hand's interpolation of three B♮s. And in bars 16 and 17 this idea of adding notes to thicken or widen a trill/tremolo is developed in two ways: in bar 16 the B♭–C mordent becomes a B♭–B♮ trill, which then expands into a short flurry around those pitches (Ab–Bb–C–B♮). And at the end of bar 16 and into bar 17 a C–C♯ dyad switches between tremolos and written-out repeats before fanning outwards to include the D♯ above it. This three-note collection becomes the basis of flurry of triplet semiquavers in the next bar. Finally, in bar 23 trills and runs are used alongside each other as functional equivalents.

Example 1.13 *The Four Seasons*, 'Spring', bars 12–13

Example 1.14 *The Four Seasons*, 'Spring', bars 15–18

CHAPTER 1: Music for solo instrument   23

Example 1.15 *The Four Seasons*, 'Spring', bar 23

In this way, very different materials that appear much later in the movement, such as the slow repeated chords of bar 59 and the rapid scalar runs of bar 67, might be seen to stem from the same trill/tremolo idea.

Unlike the other three movements, 'Spring' has not asserted a strong pitch centre until now, which partly accounts for its more improvisatory, quicksilver feel. At bar 59, however, E♭ takes up this role. At first appearing within the slow chords just mentioned, it drifts between foreground and background over the next few bars, emerging in full isolation at bar 66 before fading out of sight in the movement's last few bars. While trills and tremolos have been the focus of this movement, its final few bars offer a good example of Lim's use of harmony as a means of controlling timbre and texture, and thus musical direction and form.

The subtitle of 'Summer (Sema)' refers to a Sufi ceremony involving singing, recitation and other rituals, but most particularly a whirling form of dance performed by Sufi initiates (known as dervishes) as a form of worship and ecstatic meditation. The origin of Sema (also spelled Sama) is credited to the thirteenth-century poet and Sufi master Rumi (Jalāl ad-Dīn Muhammad Rūmī, 1207–73), who is said to have become so entranced by the sound of gold being hammered as he walked through a town marketplace – and hearing in that beating sound the invocation 'There is no god but Allah' – that he stretched out his arms and began dancing in a circle. Rumi's words are not directly connected to 'Summer (Sema)', but he is nevertheless a background presence through the inspiration of the Sema dance.

'Summer (Sema)' begins with a sixteen-bar introduction centred around two main pitches. The first, F, is heard as a long monotone, rhythmicised as triplets in the first four bars and recurring throughout this introduction in either this register or the octave above. As we have seen elsewhere, Lim uses resonance and harmony to create a number of timbral variations on this F, adding a low F♯ to its decaying resonance in bar 4, placing it beneath a C♯–E dyad in bar 11, or situating it at the top of a three-note cluster in bars 14–15.

Example 1.16 *The Four Seasons*, 'Summer (Sema)', bars 14–15

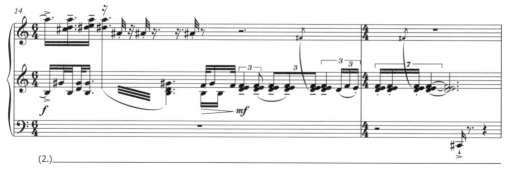

The second main pitch of this opening is more hidden: a silently depressed E, activated before the start of the movement and held throughout this introduction by the *sostenuto* pedal – rather like the effect used at the beginning of 'Spring'. As elsewhere in this work, the clash of adjacent semitones is a way for Lim to recreate on the piano the vibrant, distorted tone colours that she achieves in her other instrumental works through more physical means. The effect here is a subtle one, but it is enough to destabilise the expected piano sound.

The first main section of the movement (bars 17–50) begins with two bars of chromatic melody, ornamented with grace notes and mordents in a manner that recalls *weaver-of-fictions*. The melody begins and ends on F, with ornamentations on E (recasting the shadowy presence of the sostenuto E of the introduction). The rest of the section occasionally alludes to this opening melody (bar 19) or to pitches that were emphasised in the introduction, such as F, C and E♭/D♯ (bars 25–8), but for the most part it proceeds in a somewhat improvisatory fashion. Ornamental flourishes (both written out and otherwise) are frequent, and the section ends with a series of written-out tremolos that end on the same low F♯ that was first heard in bar 4.

Example 1.17 *The Four Seasons*, 'Summer (Sema)', bars 17–18

Example 1.18 *The Four Seasons*, 'Summer (Sema)', bar 19

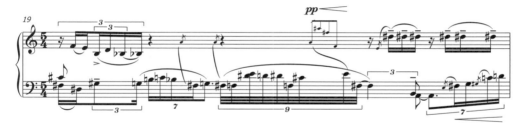

CHAPTER 1: Music for solo instrument

Example 1.19 *The Four Seasons*, 'Summer (Sema)', bars 25–8

At bar 51, the original melody returns, in a yet more ornamented guise. Like the section before it, this section also proceeds in a free manner, but this time for only fifteen bars.

Example 1.20 *The Four Seasons*, 'Summer (Sema)', bars 50–54

The movement's final section begins with the double barline at bar 65 and an increasingly frequent use of repeated pedal notes. If there is any representation of the dervish's whirling dance suggested by the movement's subtitle, it is surely in this last section, whose interlocking, repeating figurations (elaborations of the repeated pedal notes that occur throughout this movement, and of the trill/tremolo idea of 'Spring') recall the early piano music of John Adams (*Phrygian Gates*, 1977–8) or the harpsichord works of György Ligeti (*Continuum*, 1968): a series of *moto perpetuo* loops that gradually intensify and ultimately clarify into repeating quavers on a pair of major sevenths – D–C♯ in the left hand and A–G♯ in the right – that hammer out *The Four Seasons*' final semitone clashes.

Example 1.21 *The Four Seasons*, 'Summer (Sema)', bars 87–90

Invisibility (2009)

By Lim's own admission, *Invisibility* is a key work in her output. It consolidates several ideas to do with aesthetics, technique, collaboration and instrumental preparation that she had been exploring up to this point. These will recur several times throughout this book, and for this reason, I will treat this remarkable work for solo cello at some length. Following its premiere at the Huddersfield Contemporary Music Festival, UK, in

November 2009 (and a second performance in London three months later) *Invisibility* attracted international attention from performers, audiences and musicologists. It has been recorded twice by its dedicatee, Séverine Ballon (for Huddersfield Contemporary Records, 2010, and Aeon, 2015), and forms the focus of texts by the present author (Rutherford-Johnson 2011) and Lim herself (2009c).

The physical properties of instruments frequently inform the material, structure and aesthetic of Lim's works: in those we have already discussed, consider the pizzicato and glissando combinations of *Amulet*, the possibilities of vibrato and extended range in *weaver-of-fictions* and the use of resonance and pedalling effects in *The Four Seasons*. Instruments, Lim has said, bring their own 'forcefields' of energies and possibilities to her work.[1] This is especially evident in *Invisibility*. Two changes to normal cello technique are particularly important. The first is the use of two bows. One of these is a normal bow. The other is an invention of the Australian composer and violinist John Rodgers (b. 1962), in which the bow hairs are detached from the peg holding the bow hair and coiled around the stick before being reattached. When this 'guiro' bow is drawn across the string, it creates an uneven, perforated sound with many unpredictable layers of grit and noise (but still a recognisable pitch) as, in turn, wood and loosely coiled hairs come into contact with the string.

The second technical change is a radical *scordatura*. Lim asks for the bottom string (C) of the cello to be lowered by a semitone to B and the next string (G) by a whole tone to F; the third (D) string is untouched and the highest string (A) is flattened drastically by a tritone to D♯. There are several consequences to this. The first is that the open string harmony of the instrument is no longer constructed out of perfect fifths but is now a much more dissonant mix of a tritone, major sixth and semitone. This particular harmonic landscape has consequences for the overall sound of the cello and the sympathetic reverberation of its strings but is brought to the fore in the last of the work's three sections, which is played entirely on open strings. The second consequence is that the instrument's tessitura is split into two distinct regions: the lower half, represented by the two lowest strings, in something close to their usual spacing, and the upper half, represented by two strings that are very close together in pitch. This inevitably has an effect on how the player interacts with their instrument. The third consequeunce is that the relatively even spread of string tension in the usual C–G–D–A tuning is destabilized. The greatly detuned A string in particular will feel considerably looser under the cellist's fingers.

Lim's preface to the score highlights how physical performance parameters are part of the material of the work:

> The work is a study in flickering modulations between states of relative opacity/ dullness and transparency/brightness, between resistance (noise, multiphonics and other distorted sounds) and ease of flow (harmonics, clear sonorities). Striated, shimmer effects are created in the iteration between the competing planes of tension held in the retuned strings as they are affected by fingers and the varied playing surfaces of the two bows travelling at changing speeds, pressure and position.

While the *scordatura* has an obvious impact on the work's sound, the use of two bows is reflected in its structure. The first of *Invisibility's* three sections (bars 1–30) is played with the guiro bow. The second (bars 31–53) is played with the normal bow. And the third (bars 54–61) is played with two bows, the normal bow in the right hand, the guiro bow in the left (the fact that both hands are used to bow the cello is why this section is played all on open strings). As Lim's preface notes, the two bows not only sound different, but they also feel different to the player, providing different sensory feedback as they are drawn across the strings. These differences are not obstacles that the performer must negotiate and somehow flatten out (in pursuit of, let us say, an idealised 'classical' sound), but are written into the music's emphasis on sweeping movements and changes in bow speed and pressure. This difference in feeling – something that can only be truly known privately, by the player – is an important element in the work's themes and aesthetic.

Invisibility is one of several works Lim has composed in response to Australian Aboriginal culture. The first of them, *In the Shadow's Light*, is also the first time Lim uses the guiro bow, and Lim writes of this work that 'the tactile awareness that the musicians of the string quartet bring to the sounding of their instruments is of key importance in interpreting the music' (2005). The last, *Pearl, Ochre, Hair String* for orchestra (2009–10), may be interpreted as Lim's culminating statement on the cluster of ideas she explores in these works; it also features a prominent solo part for cello playing guiro bow. *Invisibility* (which to some extent is a study for *Pearl, Ochre, Hair String*) is thus of pivotal importance.

As described in this book's Introduction, Lim's direct encounter with Aboriginal culture in 2006 – and particularly the Yolngu people of northeastern Australia – precipitated a change in her work. Yet that change was an evolution that emerged from within her practice, rather than a radical shift in direction. In an article written at the same time as *Invisibility* and standing in part as an artistic statement of her work up to this point, Lim identifies in her music

> a recurring interest in cultural patterns that are in some way about the controlled revelation and also concealment of spiritual power, of the numinous. Revelation goes hand in hand with concealment – the potential of one state is held within the other so that there is an intimate relationship between the visible and the invisible. (Lim 2009c)

In Yolngu art, 'shimmer' is the visual effect created by the use of closely space dots or cross-hatching on a painting. The shimmer effect is regarded as emanating from the ancestral figures of Yolngu mythology: a painting's shimmer is not only a representation of ancestral power, but a direct manifestation of it. It is considered dangerous and thus knowledge of it is highly restricted and concealed behind layers of cultural process and privilege.[2]

The most obvious manifestation in *Invisibility* of these ideas of shimmer, revelation and concealment is the guiro bow itself. As Lim's programme note describes, 'Like the cross-hatched designs or dotting effects of Aboriginal art, the bow creates a highly mobile sonic surface through which one can hear the outlines of other kinds of movements and shapes'. When *Invisibility* is experienced live, the connection is even more apparent: not only the bow's sound suggests cross-hatching, but also its striped appearance. The levels of private knowledge within the work include not only the unusual feel of the guiro bow (and the difference in feeling between it and the normal bow) but also the feel of the retuned strings under the cellist's fingers. They extend, too, to the collaboration between Lim and Ballon out of which the work emerged, experimenting with and incorporating particular playing techniques (especially a range of harmonics) that Ballon developed in the course of rehearsing the work. The energetic properties of these techniques, and the means of transforming them into each other, form the basic grammar of the work. On each of these levels, *Invisibility* is a work whose meaning emerges through processes of doing, rather than passively observing.

The composer Haotian Yu (n.d.) notes the importance of 'Kadenzklangen' or cadence-sounds in *Invisibility*. The term comes from the 1966 essay 'Klangtypen der Neuen Musik' (Sound-types for New Music) by the German composer Helmut Lachenmann (b. 1935), in which it refers to sounds with a discernible two-part structure comprising an impulse or attack and a resonance or decay – like the striking of a gong or a piano key. Although the cello itself is not an especially resonant instrument, Yu identifies composed-out versions of such cadence-sounds at both surface and structural levels of Lim's work.

The first comprises the first bar. The cellist plays a series of notes on the open fourth string, dampened by the left hand (to make their pitch unclear), each executed with a single bow stroke. The notes change progressively across three parameters: they accelerate, they grow louder (from piano to mezzo-forte) and they become increasingly dry, from playing *ordinario* to using a circular movement of the bow on the string – a technique that in the context of the guiro bow produces only a thin scratching sound. These processes reach a climax on the triplet, mezzo-forte quavers midway through the bar. This is the 'impulse' part of the sound cadence; the 'decay' is the three slow, fingered harmonics that appear to emerge from out of this point, a point of relative stability in pitch, tone/noise content and rhythm. The crescendo to forte is the opposite of a typical decay shape, but what is of interest in this work is the way in which sonic and performance energies are balanced against one another.

Example 1.22 *Invisibility*, bar 1

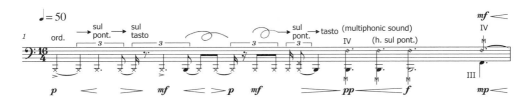

A different cadence-sound is articulated in bar 2, from the rapid flurry of mezzo-forte notes (an energetic action of a new kind) to the gradual collapse into pitchless, sibilant bow sweeps (which themselves taper off in energy) at the end of the bar.

Example 1.23 *Invisibility*, bar 2

These two bars not only present a pair of cadence-sounds, but also comprise a larger one together: a complete musical phrase that is articulated not through melodic or harmonic form, but through changes in sound, intensity and performance action. *Invisibility* is structured as a series of phrases like these, separated by relatively long silences.

The first two bars also act as an introduction; like the beginning of 'Summer' from *The Four Seasons* and as we will see to a much larger extent in some of Lim's ensemble works, it is focused – almost drone-like – on a small number of pitches (in this case the cello's low B open string). In bar 3 the first of a group of recurring ideas is introduced, in the form of a *jeté* up-down glissando from B quarter-sharp to F to E♭, preceded by a grace note. (This in itself is a cadence-sound in miniature, from the grace note attack to the decaying energy of the *jeté*, but it also serves as the impulse for a larger cadence-sound that encompasses the whole of bar 3 and ends – again – with the sweeping bow.) This gesture appears at least twice more, at bars 12 and 34, in slightly varied forms; in all three instances the gesture initiates a much longer musical phrase.

Example 1.24 *Invisibility*, bars 3–6

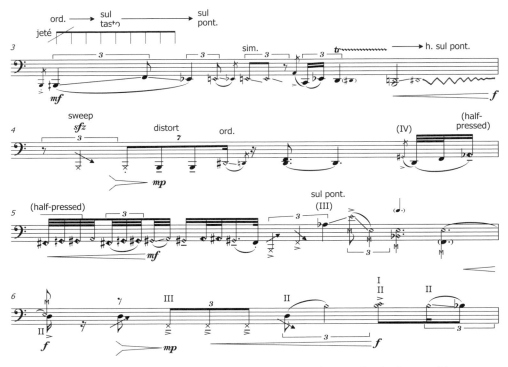

A second recurring gesture is introduced at bar 10. This is a dyad of natural harmonics on B and middle C, played on the first and second strings. In terms of its compressed sound and physical gesture (because of the retuning of the strings the cellist's two fingers are practically touching one another) this is another example of the 'cleaving' idea mentioned before. It also represents a marked contrast from the more sonorous, sweeping, noise-rich gestures that have so far dominated: its precise, narrow, high-pitched morphology is an opposing pole to the *jeté* gestures of bars 3 and 12, between which it acts like a refrain or a response.

Example 1.25 *Invisibility*, bars 10, 14, 18, 23 and 39

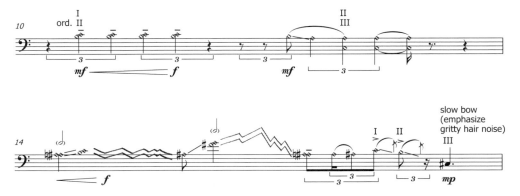

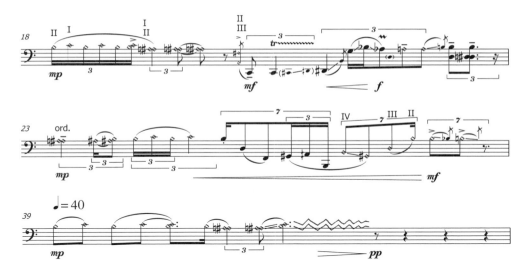

In the manner of a refrain, this dyad is heard several times in the work (it is in fact anticipated at bar 6; see Example 1.23). As Example 1.25 shows, each recurrence is different from the others in terms of its rhythmic profile (more or less even in pulse); its degree of ornamentation or elaboration; and the synchronicity or not of the two notes. The example at bar 10 represents what we might call a 'zero case', of the gesture in its simplest form – even rhythm, no ornamentation, simultaneous pitches – while the example that follows, at bar 14, represents the opposite extreme: complex rhythm, highly elaborate ornamentation, non-synchronous pitches. The other four instances (including the fleeting example at bar 6) articulate different degrees of variation in these three parameters. It is also possible to interpret across the group as a whole a long-range cadence-sound, with the compressed, rhythmically regulated triplet minims of bar 10 loosening into the smeared alternations (fading into rough tremolo-glissandi) of the last example at bar 39.

The appearance of these motif-like gestures in both the first (guiro bow) and second (normal bow) sections suggests a degree of musical continuity between them. However, the second section also offers a development of those materials and the introduction of new ideas; where the first section gravitated to the upper strings, the second dwells on the lower. The most substantial addition, however, is a *moto perpetuo* section constructed around loops of triplet quavers or regular semiquavers, separated by brief, quasi-melodic flourishes. This climactic passage use of *moto perpetuo* recalls similar examples in other works by Lim (compare the ending of 'Summer (Sema)'), but it also acts as a culmination of the musical expression of shimmer: a perforation of the sound continuum into a series of grains or stripes, emphasised by the addition of bow sweeps to each note that almost literally cut lines across the sound.

Example 1.26 *Invisibility*, bar 43

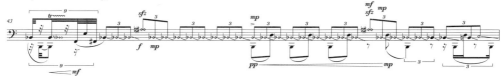

The conclusion to the long cadence-sound of this section is a slow subsidence, passing down the open strings onto the low B♮ with which the work begins, and that defines the bottom of the cello's range. The arrival on this note heralds the start of the final section. Playing the open third and fourth strings with the normal bow in their right hand, the cellist takes up the guiro bow with their left and uses it to play the open first and second strings. The remainder of the work is played on the four pitches thus available – B, F, D and D♯. Over the resonant low B float the more fragile notes of the upper strings, a sonic form whose timbre and voicing resembles the 'spectral' gestures found in works by Gérard Grisey or even Horatiu Radulescu, although without their precise relation to the harmonic series. (We will encounter more harmonic formations like this.) Where the work's first two sections gravitated towards different areas of the cello's register, the third section brings them together in balance.

Example 1.27 *Invisibility*, bars 51–4

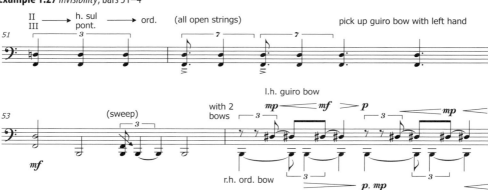

Nevertheless, this apparent balance conceals the ongoing instabilities of the work. While the right hand passes the predictable friction of the standard bow across the relatively familiar tensions of the bottom two strings, the left hand must negotiate both unpredictable bow friction and highly divergent string tensions. Stable ground and shimmering haze are thus dramatically combined through forms of private knowledges, known only to the cellist. In the moment of its performance, *Invisibility* realises the systems of restriction, obscuring and revelation of Yolngu art.

Axis Mundi (2012–13)

In 2010 Lim began a creative association, lasting until 2016, with the Cologne-based ensemble Musikfabrik. During this period, she explored further the collaborative practices that she had developed in her work with ELISION and its soloists, a peak of which was represented by her work with Ballon on *Invisibility*. Out of these explorations Lim developed what she calls a 'mycelial model' of creativity (inspired by the metaphor used by the British anthropologist Tim Ingold [2011] of fungal mycelia – the vast networks of underground threads by which fungi transmit nutrients and other elements between themselves and plants), in which both participants within a collaboration are drawn into an intertwining practice that extends beyond the score itself (Lim 2013b). As is often the case, this development did not mark a radical break in Lim's style or approach but was rather an articulation or clarification of ideas that had been latent or undescribed for some time. The metaphor of a 'mycelial' way of working grew out of the seven-year collaboration with Musikfabrik, but as we will see in later chapters its origins go back further than this.

One of the chief musical creations of Lim's association with Musikfabrik was *Tongue of the Invisible*, written for the group's twentieth birthday in 2011 (see Chapter 3). After the composition of Tongue, however, Lim was invited to write two solo works: *The Green Lion Eats the Sun* (2014) for double-bell euphonium player Melvyn Poore, and *Axis Mundi* (2013) for bassoonist Alban Wesly. As is often the case, both are effectively studies for a larger composition; in this instance, the opera *Tree of Codes* (see Chapter 6).

As usual, the creation of *Axis Mundi* began with the practicalities of the instrument. In essence, a bassoon is a long wooden tube, drilled with air holes and covered with an extensive key system that barely manages to control the instrument's inherent 'out-of-tuneness'. These irregularities of tuning and colour became a source of fascination and exploration for both Lim and Wesly, with the player not only offering the composer a pool of sounds and techniques for use (the more typical new music transaction between performer and composer, such as between Ballon and Lim in the creation of *Invisibility*), but also entering into a collaborative spirit that extended into creating an entirely new way of conceiving of and notating timbre and multiphonics on the bassoon.

Recognising both the impracticality and unreliability of fingering charts for multiphonics and other colour effects on the bassoon (impractical because of the density of information that must be read by the player, often at speed; unreliable because small variations between instruments, crooks, reeds, and environmental conditions render a precise match between fingering and resultant sound impossible), Lim and Wesly sought an alternative approach. Their solution was to make two small alterations to the standard notation. First, notes whose sound is to be altered are inscribed with diamond noteheads. Second, these altered notes are to be played with an additional hole on the instrument either open (vented) or closed. Which hole is simply marked above the staff with a + or - symbol, and the note name of the respective hole. The note is otherwise fingered (and notated) as normal, and the extra hole remains open or closed until it is replaced with another letter, or until a non-diamond notehead is reached. This notation has the great practical advantage of removing the dense information of fingering charts. It also creates a new form of compositional material in the form of 'scales' of timbre that are manifestations of 'knots' of sound at different nodal points along the length of the bassoon. In Example 1.28, after the initial D (played as normal), the notes of the first bar are all played as written, but with bassoon's C-hole vented (the –C notation above the first B and continuing throughout the bar). At the start of bar 2, the A-hole is vented instead, and then the C once more (briefly returning to standard fingering with the D and C♯ at the centre of the bar).

Example 1.28 *Axis Mundi*, bars 1–2

The sonic landscape of these different timbres and multiphonics – some of which may be explored further by changes in air pressure and embouchure – is inherently unstable and unpredictable, and can change between instruments, players or environmental conditions. Like the bow and fingers moving across the altered landscape of *Invisibility's* cello, it is a form of knowledge that can only be realised by doing, by navigating it and realising its sounds and energies in the moment of performance.

Axis Mundi's title alludes to *Yggdrasil*, the cosmic tree of Norse mythology, which connects heaven and earth; and to the 'world tree' in Siberian shamanism, which acts as a ladder between lower, middle and upper worlds. The image of the tree is a potent one, resonating with the wooden 'trunk' of the bassoon itself, as well as the mycelial networks that connect trees around the world. For Lim, 'The breath of the musician travelling the hidden pathways across and through [the knots of sound within the bassoon's tubing] activates the many voices of a "singing tree"' (Lim 2013a).

An Elemental Thing (2017)

An Elemental Thing is one of a small group of works written for the Australian ensemble Speak Percussion, another important collaborator in Lim's recent music, who also worked with her on the music theatre work *Atlas of the Sky* (2017–18). Lim's first composition for the group was the 'postcard piece' *Love Letter* for solo hand drum, written for Speak's tenth anniversary in 2011. Composed on a flight between Manchester (UK) and Melbourne, *Love Letter* follows the tradition of James Tenney's *Postal Pieces* (1967–71), eleven almost conceptual works Tenney wrote for friends on postcards, in lieu of sending actual letters. Lim's *Love Letter* comprises just four instructions[3]:

1) write a letter to your Beloved

2) transpose the letters of each word into rhythmic information including silences

3) assign rhythmic layers for performance by left and right hands

4) perform the work exploring subtle gradations of timbre at different locations on the drum surface using fingers, palms, fingernails, brushes, superball.

Even within this concise, almost bureaucratic format many elements of Lim's style and aesthetic can be detected: an emphasis on the physicality of instrumental performance; the instrument as a terrain for exploration and play; music made as a complex of interacting elements; the idea of translation and forms of hidden or veiled knowledge; and the principle of intimacy – the concealed text is a love letter, after all, written by the performer. All these elements, as well as the musical idea of *Love Letter* itself, are carried forward into *An Elemental Thing*, written for and made in collaboration with Speak's founding artistic director Eugene Ughetti.

Like *Invisibility*, Lim describes *An Elemental Thing* as a significant work in her development, and it is among her longest solo works. It is surprising, then, that it is written for the seemingly limited possibilities of a solo woodblock. But the implements used to play the woodblock are just as important as the block itself. In turn these are: double bass bow, two contrasting 'rasp sticks' (doweling rods with either notches cut into them, or threaded with small metal rings), three thin rattan sticks (one slightly thicker than the others), medium-soft mallet, bullet vibrator, hard mallet, superball mallet and rute or ruthe (multi-rod; a drumstick made from a bunch of thin canes), as well as the percussionist's hand, arm and fingers; the whole set-up is also amplified. These different means are chosen to generate as much timbral variation as possible, and to seek ways of turning a dry percussion instrument into something that can 'sing'; they were devised by the composer in collaboration with Ughetti, who gave the work its premiere at Queensland Conservatorium of Music in September 2017. Every sound can be further altered or modulated by the percussionist moving their free hand or arm across the mouth of the woodblock, somewhat like a trumpet's wah-wah mute; lines drawn above or below the staff indicate the degree of relative openness or closedness. In these ways, the woodblock is invested with something like a 'voice' that can range from whispers to croaks, moans and other expressive sounds.

Example 1.29 *An Elemental Thing*, bars 1–3

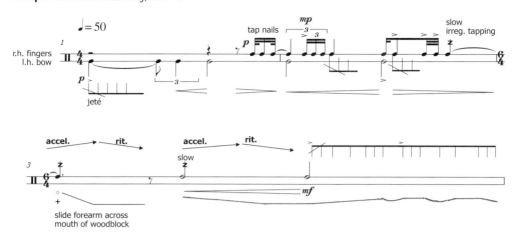

An Elemental Thing can be divided into six main sections, with the first four and the last two grouped loosely together. Each is defined by the implements used to play the woodblock, moving through the sequence above. Some sections or transitions feature more than one of these implements, but once a section is over its implement is not reused, with the exception of the percussionist's modulating arm. The work as a whole has a playful, even improvisatory quality, which emerges from its creation: once Lim and Ughetti began exploring what sounds were possible the work was written very quickly, in just a week. Part of its spirit derives from those acts of experimentation and discovery. Nevertheless, there is an underlying logic to the overall form.

Like the dyad refrains in *Invisibility*, the six sections are all related in one aspect (in this case, the combination of sustained and percussive sounds, and their possibility of modulation using the hand or arm) but differentiated in terms of others: here, primarily the implements used to produce the sound. In the fifth and longest section, the percussionist uses a small vibrator against the block to create a constant buzzing noise, modulating the sound with their free arm. This is the section most directly connected to the *Love Letter* concept, as the woodblock is given a text to 'speak' (excerpted from the essay 'The Stars' by Eliot Weinberger [2007]) that is indicated in the score as a guide to shaping its sound (and is in fact silently spoken by the percussionist).

Example 1.30 *An Elemental Thing*, bar 48

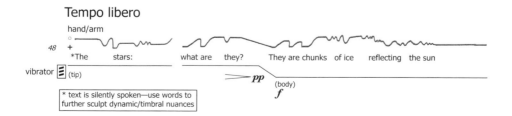

Of course, the text cannot be heard, even in the hands of a virtuoso like Ughetti. As with *Love Letter*, what is achieved, however, is a way of giving expressive shape and intent to the sounds, as well as a task for the performer of realising a private form of knowledge (encoded within actions) as a public utterance. With its long duration, the use of the text and, even, its unexpected introduction of a vibrator as a sound-producing implement, this is the most striking of the work's six sections and may be read as a goal for the overall structure. Yet its underlying principles can be found in every section, and the contrasts and transitions between them govern the work's form.

The *jeté* bow that begins the work establishes the fundamental two-part dynamic between striking and stroking. The tapping fingers add to the striking element before fingertips, palm and fingernails are rubbed across the block to create different sustained sounds. With the fingers now producing both sustained and percussive sounds the bow is no longer needed. After a few more bars, once the fingers have demonstrated, as it were, all they can, two rasp sticks are introduced. These are also bowed across the mouth of the block, but with their notched edges they produce a perforated stream of tiny percussive strikes that recalls *Invisibility*'s guiro bow, rather as though the double bass bow and tapping fingers are brought together in a single implement. The polyrhythm between the two sticks produces a familiar shimmering/looping/*moto perpetuo* pattern (Example 1.31), given greater depth by the microrhythms within the sounds of the sticks themselves.

Example 1.31 *An Elemental Thing*, bar 16

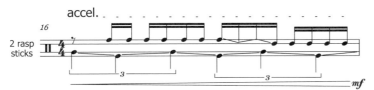

The work proceeds with each section exploring a different balance of sustained and percussive: thin rattan sticks produce rapidly buzzing tremolos; a vibraphone mallet emphasises the striking element (perhaps the sound furthest away from the sustained hiss of the bow at the start of the work), although using accelerating and decelerating rhythms, as though the preceding tremolos have been very slowed down; the vibrator also serves as a means of creating a continuous sound out of rapid individual pulses; a superball mallet stroked across the block creates a broken sound continuum as its rubber head grips and bounces against the wood; and finally the canes of the rute create another kind of broken, scratchy sound as they are rubbed and rolled across the woodblock's mouth. The work does not end with a double barline but fades into silence and one more text, serving as an epigraph, from Virginia Woolf's *The Waves*:

> There was a star riding through clouds one night and I said to the star, 'Consume me'.[4]

The Su Song Star Map (2017)

The Su Song Star Map for solo violin was written for the Armenian player Ashot Sarkissjan (second violinist of the Arditti Quartet), who gave its premiere in February 2018 at CFA Concert Hall in Boston, Massachusetts. (Lim has also produced a version of this piece for viola [2019] for the Spanish violist Alfonso Noriega.) The composition is named after a celestial map produced by the Song Dynasty scientist and engineer Su Song (1020–1101), one of five published in his *Xinyi Xiangfayao* ('Essentials of a New Method for Mechanizing the Rotation of an Armillary Sphere and a Celestial Globe') of 1092; Su's five maps are the earliest to have survived in printed form.[5]

Like many of Lim's other solo works, *The Su Song Star Map* contains thematic ideas that run across her output. Most obvious of these is an interest in astronomy and astrology (in relation to both scientific and mystical forms of thought) that is a feature of many recent works. *The Su Song Star Map* is also incorporated into the violin part of *Extinction Events and Dawn Chorus*, where it forms part of that work's collection of 'anthropogenic debris'. As another example of Lim's writing for solo strings, there are features of the work that can be traced back to *Invisibility* and *Amulet* (including the use of a scordatura that slackens the violin's G string by a minor third, giving the instrument a looser, grungier lower range); and it is one of a group of works from the mid-2010s, including *Extinction Events* and the violin concerto *Speak, Be Silent* (2015), that prominently feature Lim's own instrument. Finally, as with *An Elemental Thing*, *The Su Song Star Map* is an example of Lim investing instruments with the qualities of a human, speaking voice. There is no attempt to represent a particular text, but the score is marked throughout with vocal expressive markings covering a range of sound distortions: poco distort, husky, throaty, distort. 'In general', writes Lim in the score's preface, 'all distortions are of a vocal, emotional type, like a singer's catch in the throat or a veil of whisky and cigars over the sound'.

All of these aspects are discussed elsewhere in this book. Here, we will focus on one technical aspect of the work: the use of loops and repeat marks. This is connected to several of the ideas mentioned above, and it is a feature of many of Lim's works of the 2010s (Lim first used repeat marks in this way in the cello solo *an ocean beyond earth*, 2016). An example can be seen in the first bar.

Example 1.32 *The Su Song Star Map*, bar 1

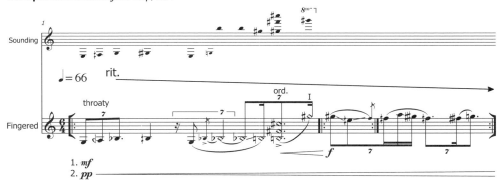

While the whole of this bar is repeated, within it is a smaller repeat of the G♯, E quarter-sharp, F♮ grace note figure in the bar's middle. 'Nested' repeats like these are used frequently throughout the piece. Sometimes they appear wholly within a larger repeat, as in this instance; at others they may overlap one another, meaning that small patches of music are repeated multiple times, as in Example 1.33, creating swirls and eddies within the music that seem to glitch time or fold it in on itself.

Example 1.33 *The Su Song Star Map*, bars 30–34

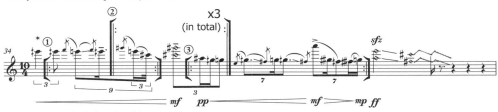

* numbers clarify the order of the repeated sections

Outside of overtly repetitive musical practices such as minimalism, repeat marks are rare in late twentieth- and early twenty-first-century composition; Helmut Lachenmann's use of them in one passage of his *Kontrakadenz* (1970–71) is an exception made more famous for its scarcity. In her article 'An Ecology of Time Traces in *Extinction Events and Dawn Chorus*' (2020), Lim traces the origins of her own usage to the written-out almost-repeats found in the music of Morton Feldman (what that composer called 'crippled symmetries'), and the self-generating micro-canons of Aldo Clementi (a composer ELISION performed many times in their early history). Lachenmann is surely there too, as are the *moto perpetuo* loops that are a recurring feature of Lim's music. A more important influence comes from two of Lim's former colleagues at the University of Huddersfield, the British composer Bryn Harrison and the Canadian Cassandra Miller, who both make innovative use of repeat marks:

> Building on Feldman's aesthetic world of timeless suspension and Aldo Clementi's mobile constellations of sound, Harrison, in pieces such as *Repetitions in Extended Time* (2008), composes with large cycles of repetitions irregularly dispersed across

multiple lines in which an ensemble only comes into alignment at longer-range structural points. Even more influential for me has been Miller's work for solo violin work entitled *for mira* (2012), in which the music is heard in three repetitions at decreasing tempi, within which there are variations created by sampling and repeating different subsets of the score at each iteration. (Lim 2020)

In Lim's approach, interlaced repeats create an effect rather different from that of exact repetition (although *The Su Song Star Map* also contains examples of the latter). While these, Lim writes, have the effect of suspending time and halting forward momentum, interlaced repetitions like those in Example 1.33 allow for a more complex mixture of past, present and future, in which 'a segment of what one has just passed gets caught up in a whirlpool (a loop or a glitch) before going on but then perhaps tracks further back into the past before passing through the same points again'.

Repeats aside, the opening bar offers a shape through which to interpret many subsequent phrases in the work's first few pages (and possibly aspects of its overall form): a rising scale, grinding up from the depths of the instrument, answered by faster chromatic or microtonal descending scales and figurations in a higher register, often employing harmonics and other effects, before returning to the lower register again. This shape is less precisely defined than some of the motif-like gestures we have seen in other works – the melodic spirit of *The Su Song Star Map* exemplifies the free fantasia style of *weaver-of-fictions* or the beginning of 'Autumn' from *The Four Seasons* rather than the more constrained gestures of *Amulet, Invisibility* or *Axis Mundi* – but it nevertheless offers a general morphology.

The first thirty bars of the work can be heard as an expansion of the rising scale part of this shape, as phrases begin on successively higher notes until reaching a series of 'bright, brassy', fortissimo F♮s at bar 30, played ordinario and with no other ornamentation. This moment is shown in Example 1.43: after another bar of figuration that acts as a counterweight, the music inverts its centre of gravity from a low to a very high register, as though hanging downwards rather than growing upwards.

This second section of the piece places a greater focus on straight repetitions, as in the passage from bars 41 to 52, in which there are many more loops – either written out or enclosed in repeat marks – some of them repeating six or eight times, as though the whole piece has become temporarily trapped in one large whirlpool.

Example 1.34 *The Su Song Star Map*, bars 41–4

After the whirlpool, the music becomes temporarily fragmented: as it tries to piece itself together again it is at times unable to articulate much more than a howl of non-harmonic multiphonics (indicated, as in *Invisibility*, by an M over the notehead). Eventually, at approximately bar 61, it returns to the fantasia-like melodic style of the beginning and a greater emphasis on the instrument's lower range. Like the phrase of bar 1 the work ends in similar registral territory to which it began, but this time sounding as husky harmonics shrouded, we must assume by now, in plenty of whisky aromas and cigar smoke.

CHAPTER 1: Music for solo instrument

Example 1.35 *The Su Song Star Map*, bars 86–8

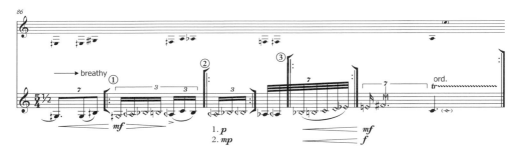

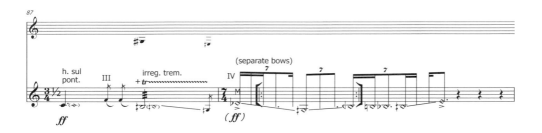

bioluminescence (2019)

From Debussy's *Syrinx* and Varèse's *Density 21.5* to Brian Ferneyhough's *Unity Capsule* (1975–6), flute repertory through the twentieth century transformed the instrument from a meek signifier of pastoralism and calm melody into a highly mobile site of innovation in technique and timbre. Using every element involved in playing the flute, composers developed a large reservoir of sounds – from percusssive key slaps and tongue rams to vocalisations, breath tones and harmonics – that extended the instrument's timbral range far beyond its melodic origins. One of the chief innovators in this area is the Italian composer Salvatore Sciarrino (b. 1947), who worked with the Italian flautists Robert Fabbriciani and Giancarlo Graverini to develop a large number of novel sounds, many of which can be heard in his seven pieces for solo flute collected under the title *L'opera per flauto* (1977–89).

A second aspect of the flute's modern tradition is its close association with the mystical or spiritual, a fact presumably related to its own ancient history (Paleolithic flutes more than 40,000 years old are among the oldest known instruments, and flutes feature prominently in early Chinese, Sumerian, Indian and European cultures). That extensive history is possible in part due to the simplicity of the flute's construction (essentially just an open tube that is blown into), which also accounts for its flexibility of sound, especially with regard to changes in air pressure or embouchure. These associations are drawn out in Debussy's music for flute, for example (not only Syrinx, but also the solos in *Prélude d'après-midi d'un faune*), as well as Ferneyhough's, particularly *Cassandra's Dream*

Song (1970) and *Mnemosyne* for bass flute and tape (1986); the work titles in Sciarrino's *L'opera per flauto* refer to magical spells as well as Hermes, Venus and the Egyptian god Aton.

Both technical innovation and mystical associations are apparent in Lim's work. As well as other effects, *bioluminescence* makes use of one of Sciarrino's inventions, the 'Re-Re♯' trill, introduced in his *Come vengono produtti gli incantesima?* ('How are spells produced?') and featured extensively in *Canzona di ringraziamento* ('Thanksgiving song'; both 1985). This technique involves trilling the flute's D and D♯ trill keys with the right hand while fingering chromatic runs with the left; the effect is to create microtonal glissandi between the pitches C♯ and D♯ that seem to sound independently of the actual fingerings, as though a hidden layer of the music has been peeled away. Exactly how Sciarrino intends the trill keys to be used is open to speculation (he does not provide any details in his scores), but Lim makes use of two variants. The first alternates the trill keys, producing a relatively smooth glissando effect, while the second trills both keys together to produce a more distinct outline of individual pitches. By creating this distinction, she strengthens the integrity of the sound as malleable musical material rather than just a passing effect. Example 1.36 shows the two variants, marked by unboxed (keys alternating) and boxed (keys together) indications above the staff. The first bar of this example also illustrates some of the wide range of other trill and multiphonic effects used in this work.

Example 1.36 *bioluminescence*, bars 3–4

CHAPTER 1: Music for solo instrument

The title of *bioluminescence*, meanwhile, refers to the ability of certain animals to emit light using bacteria in their bodies. The example Lim gives is the much-studied Hawaiian bobtail squid (*Euprymna scolopes*). The bioluminescent bacterium *Vibrio fischeri* colonizes a special light organ in the squid, entering into a symbiotic relationship in which it draws nutrients from its host, while providing camouflage at night (giving the squid the appearance of moonlight to deceive predators).[6] The creation of an 'invisibility cloak' from shimmering patterns of light, especially as the product of a collaborative partnership between two species, is an irresistible intersection of themes for Lim, and further parallels can be drawn between this and the way the Sciarrino trill conceals one sound behind the fluttering surface of another.

Like several other examples in this chapter, *bioluminescence* is also a study or generative work for a much larger composition: *Sappho/Bioluminescence* (2019), part I of the orchestral triptych *Annunciation*. Similarly to Lim's reuse of *The Su Song Star Map* in *Extinction Events and Dawn Chorus*, the flute solo *bioluminescence* is woven through the orchestral work. The solo score's preface features a fragment by the ancient Greek poet Sappho (in the translation by Mario Petrucci [2008]), and there is clearly a sense here that Lim is drawing not only on the modern scientific observations of squid and other marine creatures (the preface also includes a quotation from Darwin's journals), but also mystical, even erotic associations that have accumulated over the long, long history of the flute itself:

Pick any path of concrete or
crock to this spirited place
whose orchard-body belongingly
offers that flickering, altered aroma
– groves on fire

bioluminescence was written for the Australian flautist Paula Rae, who, as one of the original members of ELISION, has played Lim's music for more than thirty years (the multiphonic fingerings used in the score of *bioluminescence* were devised by her). The work thus shows the extent to which that relationship with the group and its members continues to nourish Lim's music into the third decade of the twenty-first century.

References

Haraway, Donna (2016). *Staying with the Trouble: Making Kin in the Chthulucene*. Durham, NC: Duke University Press.

Ingold, Tim (2011). *Being Alive: Essays on Movement, Knowledge and Description*. London: Routledge.

Lim, Liza (2005). *In the Shadow's Light (2004)* [programme note], https://limprogrammenotes.wordpress.com/2011/07/31/in-the-shadows-light-2004/.

Lim, Liza (2009a). *The Four Seasons (after Cy Twombly), 2009* [programme note], https://limprogrammenotes.wordpress.com/2011/08/01/the-four-seasons-after-cy-twombly-2009/.

Lim, Liza (2009b). *Invisibility (2009)* [programme note], https://limprogrammenotes.wordpress.com/2011/08/02/invisibility-2009/.

Lim, Liza (2009c). 'Staging an Aesthetics of Presence'. *Search Journal for New Music* 6, http://www.searchnewmusic.org/lim.pdf.

Lim, Liza (2013a). *Axis Mundi (2012–13)* [programme note], https://limprogrammenotes.wordpress.com/2014/06/09/axis-mundi-2012-13/.

Lim, Liza (2013b). 'A Mycelial Model for Understanding Distributed Creativity: Collaborative Partnership in the Making of "Axis Mundi" (2013) for Solo Bassoon', CMPCP Performance Studies Network Conference, Cambridge, 4 April 2013. Available at http://eprints.hud.ac.uk/id/eprint/17973/.

Lim, Liza (2020). 'An Ecology of Time Traces in *Extinction Events and Dawn Chorus*'. *Contemporary Music Review* 39, no. 5: 544–63.

Lim, Liza (2021). 'How to Make a Woodblock Sing: Artistic Research as an Art of Attentiveness'. In *Creative Research in Music: Informed Practice, Innovation and Transcendence*, edited by Anna Reid, Neal Peres Da Costa and Jeanell Carrigan. New York: Routledge.

Morphy, Howard (1991). *Ancestral Connections: Art and an Aboriginal System of Knowledge*. Chicago and London: University of Chicago Press.

Petrucci, Mario (2008). *Sappho*. London: Perdika Press.

Rutherford-Johnson, Tim (2011). 'Patterns of Shimmer: Liza Lim's Compositional Ethnography'. *Tempo* 65, no. 258: 2–9.

Weinberger, Eliot (2007). 'The Stars'. I*n An Elemental Thing*. New York: New Directions. Ch. 31.

Yu, Haotian (n.d.). 'A Phenomenology of "Shimmer": *Klangtypen* and *Arpeggio* in Liza Lim's *Invisibility* (2009)' [unpublished].

Endnotes

1 Conversation with the author. Cf Ingold 2013, passim.

2 For an extended explanation of the role of shimmer in Yolngu culture, and the ontological system it structures, see Morphy 1991.

3 The full score is available at https://limprogrammenotes.wordpress.com/2011/08/02/love-song-2011/.

4 Lim also quotes this line in her programme note to an ocean beyond earth (2016), a work inspired by NASA's Cassini mission to Saturn. It seems to capture for her something of the complex mixture of observation and desire that infuses her own musical star gazing.

5 The map is reproduced in the preface to Lim's score, and may be viewed at https://limprogrammenotes.wordpress.com/2018/01/01/the-su-song-star-map-2017/.

6 A striking feature of the squid–bacterium relationship, which has profound implications for our understanding of inter-species evolution, is the fact that the bacteria 'are fully part of the squid's developmental biology' (Haraway 2016, 66). Not only do the squid require the bacteria to make their light organ work, but infection by *Vibrio fischeri* is necessary for juvenile squid to make the organ *in the first place*. That is, the bacterium has shaped the evolutionary development of the bobtail squid as a species. The emergence of species as mutually creative encounters between creatures, not as the product of isolated creatures adapting to their environment, as in classical Darwinian theory, has parallels with the way in which Lim shapes interactions between instruments, as we will see in the next chapter.

Chapter 2

Music for chamber ensemble

Thanks to her association with ELISION, many of Lim's earliest compositions are for chamber ensembles, often including unusual instruments. The first work in her official catalogue is one such piece, *Garden of Earthly Desire* (1988–9) for an ensemble of eleven instruments that includes mandolin, harp and electric guitar. She has written around twenty more since then. They range in scale from duos such as the short *Ming Qi (Bright Vessel)* for oboe and percussion (2000) and the longer *Ehwaz (journeying)* for trumpet and percussion (2010), to the thirty-minute string quartet *In the Shadow's Light* (2004) and the chamber concerto for *sheng* and nine instruments, *How Forests Think* (2016). Unlike the solo works, many of these compositions are independent of others in Lim's catalogue, but, as we shall see, they are still created within a rich network of thematic and personal connections.

The chapter begins with four works that established and defined Lim's early voice – *Garden of Earthly Desire, Koto, Inguz (fertility)* and *The Heart's Ear* – and continues with three that introduce and enlarge upon important themes and concepts in her later music: *Songs Found in Dream, Ronda – The Spinning World* and *How Forests Think*.

Garden of Earthly Desire (1988–9)

Garden of Earthly Desire was commissioned by ELISION as one half of an evening-length double bill created with the Australian puppetry group Handspan Theatre (founded in Melbourne in 1977 and active until 2002). Lim's work involved the puppeteers being conducted as though they were part of the music, somewhat like an opera; the other work on the programme, by Lim's former teacher Richard David Hames, drew the musicians into the visual aspects of the performance through masks and costumes. Both were developed in workshops between Handspan and ELISION, during which the paintings of Hieronymus Bosch (particularly his famous triptych *The Garden of Earthly Delights*) and the figures of the tarot deck (used as a storytelling device in Italo Calvino's 1973 novel *The Castle of Crossed Destinies*) were explored as possible inspirations. Since

48   The Music of Liza Lim

its two performances with Handspan in October 1989, *Garden of Earthly Desire* has been performed as a standalone musical work.

As Lim's first work for ELISION, and the first work of her post-student career, *Garden of Earthly Desire* represents a foundational moment. It is remarkable, then, to hear how fully formed her voice was at this early stage. She was just twenty-three years old, and although many additional sides to her music have been added in the three decades since, *Garden of Earthly Desire* sowed the seeds of many of the ongoing features of her music. On ELISION's website, Lim writes of the role the sound of that group and its individual members played in its creation:

> An aesthetic world was also established in that first commission in which the timbral richness of the 'cello as played by Rosanne Hunt, matched by Daryl Buckley's sumptuous electric guitar, and a complex polyphonic language of struck and plucked sounds (Peter Neville [percussion], Stephen Morey [mandolin] and Marshall McGuire! [harp]) against sustained fluttering sliding tones (Paula Rae on flute, Stephen Robinson on oboe, Jane Robertson on clarinet) continue to be a reference point. (Lim n.d.)

This factor is immediately apparent in the music: *Garden of Earthly Desire* is like a 'concerto for ensemble', in which every player from flute to double bass has their moment as a soloist. (This generous sharing of responsibilities and attention is an enduring quality of Lim's artistic outlook.) The work is played continuously but can be divided into several subsections, marked by changes in instrumentation and character. The music was already substantially written before Lim made the connection with Bosch's painting, but she notes the correspondence between the tripartite structure of his picture and the 3 x 3 x 3 structure of her composition, reflected most strongly in the ritornello effect of the 'bloody traceries' music, which marks out the three main divisions of the music.

Figure 2.1 Subsections of *Garden of Earthly Desire*

bar	expressive marking	instrumentation	section
1	knife edge, bloody traceries	solo oboe and piccolo, plucked trio; ensemble	A1
40	pregnant, fecund	ensemble (cello and electric guitar solos)	B1
81	deliberate and violent	piccolo and percussion; ensemble	C1
114	bloody traceries	plucked trio; ensemble (partial recap of A1)	A2
147	diabolical	cello, guitar, percussion trio; ensemble	B2a
181	incendiary, convulsive	strings	B2b
201	insects	ensemble; piccolo and tambourine	C2
213	ecstatically	ensemble	B2c
224	knife edge, bloody traceries	oboe solo, plucked trio; ensemble (partial recap of A1)	A3
233	fecund	ensemble	B3
266	insects	ensemble; oboe and percussion	C3a
282	T. S. Eliot: 'prayer of the bone on the beach'	flute, percussion	C3b

The ELISION sound that attracted Lim can be heard from the start. The oboe is the first soloist, its sinuous melody supported by plucked/percussive group of mandolin, electric guitar, harp and percussion (ceramic bowl and two Japanese temple bells tuned to F and F♯). Initially, the roles in this accompanying group are evenly balanced, creating what we might call a 'compound' timbre in which the different but related sounds of each instrument combine to create a sound that is diverse and ever-changing in its details but unified on a more generalised level. In fact, despite the apparent distinction between solo and accompaniment, the guitar – the most sustaining instrument of the accompaniment group, and capable of matching the oboe's glissandi and pitch bends – serves as a bridge between the two. At bar 2, the oboe's G is anticipated by the guitar's high G, *laissez vibrer* harmonic; at bars 5 to 7 the melodic shapes of the two instruments appear to be in dialogue with one another, with the guitar's G♯–C glissando paralleling, and extending in time the oboe's leap from B♭ to A; at the end of bar 6 the guitar's figure foreshadows the oboe's grace notes in the next bar, before a series of sustained notes and pitch bends in bar 6 that sound almost as though they are in canon with each other; and finally a final, quasi-homorhythmic gesture at the start of bar 8 ends the phrase.

Example 2.1 *Garden of Earthly Desire*, bars 1–8

If we consider the instruments of the accompaniment group as a spectrum, with the guitar as the most melodic/sustaining instrument at one end, the percussion at the other and the mandolin and harp in between, we can trace similar patterns of echoing, foreshadowing and quasi-connection through Example 2.1. (Interestingly, Lim has described the work she composed before *Garden*, the now-withdrawn *Blaze*, as Boulezian in style, and it was Boulez who pioneered such a conception of the ensemble as a continuum of related timbres in, for example, *Le marteau sans maître*, 1955 [see Boulez 1986, 340].) Thus, although the opening bars of the work suggest a strong melody-plus-accompaniment arrangement, in fact the ensemble texture is highly fluid: throughout the work no instrument is ever truly prominent, or not for more than a few bars. Even then, any solo instrument is almost always placed in a relationship that reveals an unexpected part of its character. Such pairings recur throughout: flute, triangles and bell tree from bar 81; cello, distorted guitar and congas from bar 147; piccolo and tambourine from bar 207; and oboe and drums from bar 272, among many less prominent examples. Each of these exotic combinations emerges in a manner that is both organic and unexpected; as in Example 2.1, they follow logical steps to apparently illogical outcomes. The overall effect clearly recalls the surrealistic human-animal hybrids of Bosch's painting, whose bizarre arrangements of limbs and other organs are unnaturalistic even as they extrapolate from nature itself. Example 2.2 illustrates on a larger scale how the piccolo and tambourine duo from bars 207 to 212 bridges two sections of tutti ensemble music.

Example 2.2 *Garden of Earthly Desire*, bars 203–13

CHAPTER 2: Music for chamber ensemble

The music at bar 203 ends a short section headed 'Insects' (the first of two so named) and is dominated by insect-like scratching and fluttering sounds such as the *jeté* markings in the strings, the runs of harmonics in the flute and the tremolos of the mandolin. The tambourine thumb roll at the end of this section introduces a new sound, but one that is clearly related to the others, particularly the mandolin's tremolos. The seven-bar tambourine and piccolo duo that follows builds upon this tambourine sound with a melodic piccolo fantasia that peels away from the tambourine's percussive rhythmic foundation: in bar 207, for example, the tambourine's two rolls reinforce (with some rhythmic slippage) the piccolo's sustained E and F; in bar 208 the two instruments are aligned rhythmically, with the piccolo drawing apart its own flourish at the end of the bar; and so on. Like the oboe and guitar at the beginning of the work, the two instruments follow rather than imitate one another. The two contrasting elements of this section are rhythmically undifferentiated rolls and trills, and precisely defined percussive or melodic rhythms. In varying degrees and combinations these may be aligned with one another, like the rhythms in bar 208, or juxtaposed, as in bars 209–10. The section that follows extrapolates these two elements for full ensemble in a manner that supports its expressive marking of 'Ecstatically': the trills are taken up by the wind, strings, mandolin and harp, in such a way that any rhythmic coordination is blurred still further, while the percussion, and then harp and violin, takes up the role of rhythmic articulation within this exuberantly shimmering mass.

As well as Bosch, *Garden of Earthly Desire* is inspired by Calvino's novel *The Castle of Crossed Destinies*. In that book, a group of travellers spends the night in a castle. Each of them has been robbed of the power of speech, and to pass the time they use a deck of tarot cards to tell their stories to one another. The book is narrated from the point of view of one of those travellers, who is trying to interpret the cards and how they fit together into a narrative. Often they have to speculate wildly on the intended meaning, or focus on incidental details in order to construct a satisfying narrative. Central to the novel is the question of interpretation and the ease with which meanings can be inscribed and reinscribed depending on context or presentation. Each storyteller invests the cards with different meanings (through their juxtaposition with other cards, their arrangement on the table, or the addition of facial expressions such as anguish or surprise), and each new story uses part of the arrangement of cards from the previous one as its beginning. This open-ended, improvised chain of interpretation and reinterpretation clearly resembles the shape-shifting ensemble combinations of Lim's composition. Her programme note describes how some figures from the tarot itself are given musical analogues: 'There is the Juggler – the alchemical, mercurial figure engaging in a dialectic of extremes; the High Priestess – totem of initiation and the gathering of energizing forces; the Empress – fecund, pagan, teeming with life' (Lim 1989). These all describe musical sections rather than individual instruments and some (surely by design) are easier to interpret in this way than others – two sections marked 'Fecund', for example, at bars 41 and 233, presumably refer to the Empress; the Juggler may be evoked in sections with such markings as 'Deliberate and violent' (bar 81) or 'With the utmost delicacy' (bar 272), sections which also feature the most 'extreme' duo combinations of wind and percussion.

Example 2.3 *Garden of Earthly Desire*, bars 272–5

The work's last pages introduce a third influence, a line from 'The Dry Salvage', the third of T. S. Eliot's *Four Quartets*. Lim has said[1] that there is no conscious link between this poem and her more recent music, but, as we will see, Eliot's image of drifting wreckage is echoed in her later work – most notably *Extinction Events and Dawn Chorus*. Perhaps it is possible to say that the image of forms created from the debris of modernism and progress is one that resonates deeply with Lim, as it did for Eliot himself, particularly in *The Wasteland*. In another foreshadowing of later music, *Garden of Earthly Desire* ends in a form of white noise distributed across the ensemble, as the players (apart from flautist and percussionist) take up soft, unpitched rattles for the final three bars. As we will see, this 'fade into noise' idea recurs frequently in Lim's music, a malleable symbol to which she is able to return again and again.

Example 2.4 *Garden of Earthly Desire*, bars 296–9

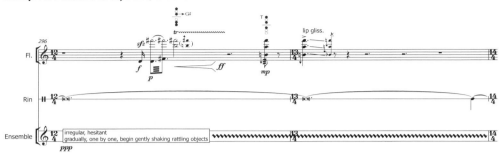

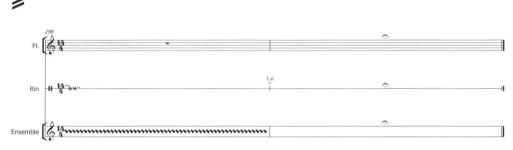

Yet perhaps the most characteristic and enduring feature of Lim's chamber music is the 'complex polyphonic language', influenced by the interlocking, hybrid characters and narratives of Bosch and Calvino. As we have seen – in the combination of percussive and sustained sounds in *Amulet* or *An Elemental Thing*, for example – many of her solo works make use of contrasting sonic elements to create novel compound instruments. Within a solo, though, these elements are contained within the self-contained universe of a single player on a single instrument within a unified region of space and time (the performance itself). Once more than one instrument or player is on stage, those strikingly self-possessed materials (and people!) are urged into collaborative or complementary partnerships – even symbioses – characterised by more social dynamics such as growth, transformation, accommodation or cooperation.

Koto (1994)

We have seen already the inspiration Lim takes from instrumental performance practices and their histories. This first stage generally arises from either a direct commission or a personal relationship with the player(s) concerned. The next step is to create a baseline of musical material that emerges from that instrument and that person. For every work in the previous chapter, Lim identified something about its respective instrument – whether a novel technique, as in the pizzicato/glissando combinations of *Amulet* or the quasi-vocalisations of *The Su Song Star Map*; something deeply embedded in the instrument's history, as in the ornaments of *weaver-of-fictions* or the Sciarrino trills of *bioluminescence*; a unique property of that instrument's sound, as in the layered resonances of *The Four Seasons* or the strange harmonics of *Axis Mundi*; or a study of one facet that has otherwise been taken for granted, as in the string tensions of *Invisibility* or the woodblock's 'mouth' in *An Elemental Thing*. Identifying this particular element or collection of elements – the instrument's forcefield – has a double effect. First, it reduces the musical possibilities available, acting as a focal point to which all other compositional decisions will be related. Second, and contrarily, it provides a foundation from which exploration can take place: as any artist knows, limiting one's options is a spur to greater, not lesser creativity. This second effect is most vividly demonstrated in *An Elemental Thing*, which transforms an unpromising starting place into one of Lim's most unusual works.

This fascination with instruments in themselves (encouraged by her collaborators' unusual playing resources and similar taste for adventure) has led Lim to compose for instruments from many different cultural and historical contexts. Besides the Ganassi recorder of *weaver-of-fictions* these include Baroque cello in *Street of Crocodiles* (1995), Indonesian *angklung* and Chinese *erhu* in *The Alchemical Wedding* (1996), Norwegian Hardanger fiddle in *Philtre* (1997) and *Winding Knots: 3 Knots* (2014), Australian didgeridoo in *The Compass* (2005–6), and Chinese *sheng* in *How Forests Think* (2016). Lim's first work to include a non-Western instrument was *The Oresteia*, which makes use of the Turkish *bağlama saz* (a long-necked lute), but *Koto* was her first to directly address music from outside the Western tradition. Her programme note introduces her approach:

> As a composer, the meta-language of a musical culture is what always attracts my ear – so for instance, in Korean classical court music and various Korean folk instrumental traditions, what I find fascinating is the way an ensemble plays in a heterogenous unison – ie: together but apart – each line more or less following the same contour but slightly apart and with different accentuations and ornamentation, resulting in a shimmering, buzzing effect.
>
> In various Japanese traditions, what I notice is the asymmetry of phrases, the role of silence to create tension, the way sound fluctuates between noise and pure tone. (Lim 1994)

Elsewhere, Lim has said that what first attracts her attention when engaging with non-Western or historical cultural forms are 'qualities of a certain kind of vibrancy or a sense that the culture has found a way of expressing life force'. Her process of composition begins by drawing a technical language from such qualities: 'I am looking for those moments of heightened intensity which are key points in the work, and then seeing what are the components that are coming together in that, how are they functioning' (Rutherford-Johnson 2011, 5–6). In *Koto*, aspects of the centuries-long performance history of the *koto* – a Japanese plucked zither, featuring thirteen strings with bridges that can be moved quickly to create different tunings – are extrapolated across the whole ensemble, including to instruments sonically and culturally a very long way away from the *koto* itself, such as flügelhorn and steel drums. As well as asymmetrical phrases and combinations of tone, noise and silence which are deeply embedded in Japanese cultural practices, Lim makes use of what she calls the particularly 'calligraphic' quality of the *koto*'s sound, a combination of its plucked, percussive attack and song-like resonance (to which effects like vibrato may be applied). Her composition both amplifies and elaborates the expressive and sonic potential of the *koto* itself and offers an accumulation of historical and cultural signifiers from both East and West that act in a productive friction with one another.

Although much of Lim's method is intuitive, she often refers to theories and frameworks from outside music as a way of enabling the sorts of cultural translations that she is seeking. A recurring example is the theory of pattern languages developed by the architect Christopher Alexander (1977). A 'pattern' in Alexander's theory is an abstraction of a design problem into a balanced collection of forces and desires. A waiting place, for example, requires an entrance, room for those waiting to congregate, some form of comfort and so on. That pattern may be applicable to several situations – such as a waiting room or a bus stop – but its form is fixed. A 'pattern language' is the collection of interlinked patterns that make up a more complex structure, such as a hospital or a public transport system. The key step is the abstraction of specific objects into transferable sets of functions and forces. A pattern language is used to establish a central principle or concept for the composition; this in turn is used to generate a vocabulary of gestures, materials and sounds that may be applied at any level of the work. In this way, Lim is able to engage with another cultural object, such as a *koto* (or an Aboriginal knowledge system, or a bioluminescent squid), and give it a new expression within the vocabulary of the Western concert hall without resorting to an orientalist appropriation of mere surface features. As she puts it, the pattern language theory 'is a way of approaching a knowledge system which utterly fascinates me but of which I am clearly not a part' (Rutherford-Johnson 2011, 6).

In *Koto*, the basic pattern is something like the combination of plucking and reverberating actions (the *koto*'s distinctive 'Kadenzklang', to recall a term from the previous chapter), as well as a sense of line and curve generated from swiftly executed, self-contained gestures. The piece falls into three main sections. The first takes up approximately two-thirds of the piece, from bar 1 to bar 103. Here the pattern and its implications are most clearly heard. The *koto* is constantly present throughout this section (save for the last dozen bars), and while it is not a solo instrument in any concerto-like sense, it clearly leads the ensemble, providing the general shape of its gestures and the different energetic forces that it must resolve. This relationship is apparent from the beginning, where the viola closely shadows the *koto* in terms of both pitch and rhythm, while also extrapolating some movement of its own out of the *koto*'s sound: its resonant low D is given a glissando flourish to E by the viola; the vibrato of the long-held C three-quarter-sharp is developed into double-stopping and a written-out viola vibrato; and the *laissez vibrer* of the *koto*'s final note is developed and extended into a transition to noisy *sul ponticello*. In all three parts of this gesture, Lim uses the 'pattern' of a particular moment in the *koto*'s music (the fading of energy represented by the laissez vibrer, or its intensification represented by the vibrato) to guide the viola.

Example 2.5 *Koto*, bars 1–3 (koto and viola only)

A more complex example immediately follows, with the introduction of the two cellos. With the viola still shadowing the *koto*, the cellos progressively abstract its lines still further, creating a spectrum of related qualities between the instruments that recalls the start of *Garden of Earthly Desire*.

In her programme note Lim makes a significant reference to the heterophonic style of traditional Korean music (which has its own version of a *koto*, the *gayageum* or *kayagum*): 'what I find fascinating is the way an ensemble plays in a heterogenous unison – ie: together but apart – each line more or less following the same contour but slightly apart and with different accentuations and ornamentation, resulting in a shimmering, buzzing effect' (Lim 1994). We might call her technical response to this phenomenon 'dynamic heterophony'. Dynamic heterophony is a mode of writing frequently used by Lim in which the contour of a melodic line is applied in a loose, fluctuating way across several instrumental parts at once. The musical braids that result are made up of similar threads, but in relationships to each other that can be variously displaced, reinforced, blurred, extended or anticipated. In such a manner of composing there is no 'central' or principal line (to which the others are subordinate). Rather, there is something like a 'cubist' or pluralist perspective, in which each viewpoint, each 'take' on the melodic line, is equally valid and contributes to a collaborative whole. Moreover, this community of voices is constantly changing in its inter-relationships (hence 'dynamic') like a living – that is, realistic – society. In this way, Lim's musically original, vibrant and fascinating approach acquires political and ethical dimensions.

Dynamic heterophony can be applied across any musical parameter, but it works particularly well for pitch, rhythm and timbre. We have seen early examples in *Garden of Earthly Desire* – the piccolo and tambourine duo, for example (Example 2.2) – but in *Koto* it becomes a central compositional device. At some points the music may crystallize into rhythmic or pitch alignment (as it briefly does in bar 1); at others it may be a diffuse cloud. Dynamic heterophony occupies the space between these two extremes, but it contains the potential to become either. The *koto* is a good starting place because its distinctive *Kadenzklang* can be magnified and developed by other instruments – even somewhat extravagantly, as in Example 2.6 (note the passing of ideas upward from the *koto* to flügelhorn, oboe d'amore and piccolo, continuing long after the *koto* has finished playing).

Example 2.6 *Koto*, bars 36–8 (strings omitted)

After the long first section the *koto* falls silent for several pages with the beginning, at bar 104, of a substantial duo for the two cellos. This continues the style of dynamic heterophony, but this time (unusually!) for a pair of instruments of the same timbre, and without the *koto* at all to lead.

Example 2.7 *Koto*, bars 107–9

As the other instruments return, beginning with the flügelhorn at bar 121, the strings and oboe d'amore at bar 129 and the *koto* at bar 133, the style of dynamic heterophony continues, with the *koto* now fitting into, rather than leading, the music's form. At bar 142 a new texture is dramatically instigated with the introduction of a death poem by the nineteenth-century Japanese poet Bokukei.

The use of poetry as a way of bringing a composition to an end (or, paradoxically, greatly opening up its resonances and meanings) recalls the reference to Eliot's *Four*

Quartets at the end of *Garden of Earthly Desire*, as well as the longer example that would come twenty years later in *An Elemental Thing*. In the final pages of Koto, Lim brings the flautist and percussionist into a vocalising duet, the former speaking syllables of the Japanese poem into her instrument in various distorted manners, the latter declaiming them (on inhaled breaths) over the sound of his. With the sound of the koto now behind us, the work ends with an invocation of another Japanese music, the highly stylised speech-song of Noh theatre.

Example 2.8 *Koto*, bars 158–end

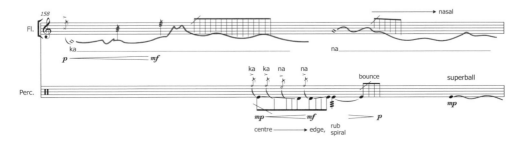

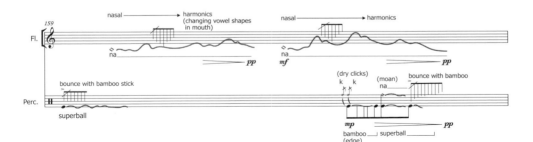

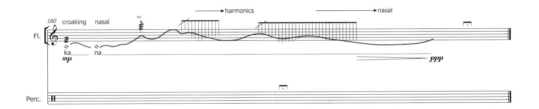

CHAPTER 2: Music for chamber ensemble 65

Koto was commissioned by ELISION and first performed by them on 29 July 1994, with Satsuki Odamura, *koto*, and conducted by Sandro Gorli. It is dedicated to the artist Domenico de Clario.

Inguz (fertility) (1996)

Inguz (fertility), for clarinet and cello, is one of a small group of Lim's works whose titles refer to Viking runes; the others to date are *Ehwaz (journeying)* (2010) for trumpet and percussion and *Gyfu (gift)* (2011) for solo oboe. (A fourth, *Perth (initiation)* for flute and percussion, was written around the same time as *Inguz* but withdrawn after a few performances. Another work with the name *Ehwaz* was also envisaged for violin and cimbalom, but this was never realised; the later work is unrelated to this.) The rune inguz – which takes the shape of two intersecting, mirrored zigzags, or a pair of Xs resting on top of each other, a form of line-based calligraphy stylistically remote from the curving Japanese penmanship that inspired *Koto* – has a collection of meanings associated with fertility, creativity and new beginnings, and Lim's composition was written for the clarinettist Catherine McCorkill and cellist Chris Lockhart Smith on the occasion of the birth of their daughter. It was first performed on 25 November 1996 by ELISION's Carl Rosman and Rosanne Hunt.

The duo format of *Inguz* allows us to look a little more closely at Lim's use of dynamic heterophony. The closeness between the two instruments is more loosely applied than it is in *Koto*. While there are moments when the clarinet and cello play almost in unison there are equally places where they act in more or less complete independence (most notably in the six-and-a-half-bar cello solo from bars 37 to 43). Between these extremes are several degrees of greater or lesser synchronicity.

Figure 2.2 shows a five-part division of this spectrum. It should be noted that this division is an analytical convenience and the placement of any given passage of music into one of these categories is somewhat subjective: the divisions are not strictly measurable and there is a certain amount of overlap or fluidity between them. It should also be noted that while terms like 'unison' or 'homorhythm' have strict musical definitions, in the case of Lim's music it is rare for either to occur without some embellishment, whether in the form of the harmonic addition of other pitches, a blurring of rhythmic synchronisation or the addition of ornamentation or timbral variation. Nevertheless, a blunt tool can still be useful, and in the case of *Inguz* it helps us see the different kinds of interaction Lim composes between her two instruments, and the way in which she moves freely between them.

Type	Name	Description
(1)	Unison	Synchronicity across both pitch and rhythm
(2)	Homotone/homorhythm	Synchronicity across either pitch or rhythm
(3)	Dynamic heterophony	Broad following of the same pitch and rhythmic contour, flexibly applied but with some coincidence of one or the other
(4)	Independent counterpoint	Two or more parts in a complementary but otherwise independent relationship
(5)	Solo/fragmentation	complete independence of parts, either as extended solos or interlocking solo fragments

Figure 2.2 Degrees of instrumental synchronicity in Lim's music

Any point in the work may be described according to one of these five degrees of synchronicity. The work begins with a one-bar cello solo, type (5). With the clarinet's entry this becomes independent counterpoint (4) for two bars before a synchronised C (with added cello E♭) on the second beat of bar 4 initiates a bar of dynamic heterophony (3) and then another short cello solo (5).

Example 2.9 *Inguz*, bars 1–5

CHAPTER 2: Music for chamber ensemble   67

Although I have presented these degrees as a progression from 1 to 5, Lim is able to move freely between them in any sequence. What for convenience is shown here as a linear spectrum is in fact more like a circular network, in which each point is only one step away from every other. Example 2.10 shows the clarinet and cello in independent counterpoint (4) before suddenly coming together as unison, type (1), for three beats in bar 15. This is the most clearly defined moment of type (1) in the work so far, although there is still a slight degree of asynchronicity in the clarinet's anticipation of the cello before beats 3 and 5 of the bar. This unison is followed by two beats of dynamic heterophony (3) (bordering on independent counterpoint, (4)) at the start of bar 16, and then a clarinet solo (5) to the end of bar 17.

Example 2.10 *Inguz*, bars 13–17

There are other ways in which Lim establishes degrees of connection between the two instruments. In bar 2, for example, although I have described this as independent counterpoint by virtue of the different shapes of the two instrumental lines, the instruments are also closely connected by their shared D♭. Paired with a transfer of activity and dynamic level from one to the other across the duration of the bar, this makes it appear as though the clarinet's line is emerging out of the cello's. Between bars 3 and 4 the favour is returned, as the cello's low C sounds as a resonant undertone beneath the clarinet's high C, providing an overhanging scaffolding under and out of which the cello can develop its own solo line in bar 5.

Much later, the intersecting solos (5) of bars 46 and 47 pass a high G♯ between them (played as a harmonic by the cello in the last two beats of bar 46), using pitch-centricity as a way of creating continuity between different moments.

Example 2.11 *Inguz*, bars 46–7

More long-range instances of pitch continuity run throughout the work. Key pitches, already visible in the examples given, include C, E♭, G and G♯. In addition to these, the cello's circling around D/D♯/E in bar 1 is a recurring motif; so too is a sliding, sustained E♭–G/G♯ harmonic in the clarinet – both of which are brought together in the work's final bars.

Example 2.12 *Inguz*, bars 53–4

Inguz's overall dialogue between flaring independence and intersecting contact – two elements circling around and interacting with one another – is a reflection of the inguz rune's shape of swerving, intersecting diagonals, and entwines together Lim's music, the image and meaning of the rune, and the work's dedication to the birth of a child.

The Heart's Ear (1997)

The score to *Inguz* is headed with lines of poetry by the poet Rumi:

Someone asks, How does love have hands and feet?

Love is the sprouting-bed for hands and feet!

Your father and mother were playing love-games.

They came together, and you appeared!

This inscription, which is obviously relevant to *Inguz*'s concept (particularly the interdependence of union and independent creation), is notable for being one of the first occasions Lim cites Rumi's poetry in her music; with *Inguz* and *The Alchemical Wedding* for chamber orchestra (1996), *The Heart's Ear*, for flute/piccolo, clarinet in A and string quartet (both viola and cello play with their lowest strings tuned down by a semitone), is among her most significant early engagements with this influence. It was commissioned and first performed by the Australia Ensemble, whose members included *Inguz*'s co-dedicatee, clarinettist Catherine McCorkill.

Rumi was an important Sufi master whose followers founded the Mevlevi (Mawlawiyya) order of dervishes – the famous 'whirling dervishes' – in early fourteenth-century Turkey;

his poetry is some of the world's most treasured literature. (For another example of Mevlevi influence, see the earlier discussion of 'Summer (Sema)', from *The Four Seasons*.) Lim engages with Sufi heritage in *The Heart's Ear* principally through the quotation of a melody played by the master Turkish musicians Kudsi and Süleyman Erguner. Example 2.13 shows Lim's arrangement as it appears at the start of her composition. Another, even simpler version, appears at bars 63–7: this placement of an unadorned, 'original' statement of the melodic material in the middle rather than at the start of the work anticipates the 'zero case' form of the recurring B–C dyad of *Invisibility*; see Example 1.25. (The original melody quoted in *The Heart's Ear* can be heard as 'Makam Bayati' on the Erguner brothers' 1988 album *The Mystic Flutes of the Sufis: Preludes to Ceremonies of the Whirling Dervishes*.)

Example 2.13 *The Heart's Ear*, bars 1–2

Where the focus of *Koto* was a particular sound and/or performing gesture, in *The Heart's Ear* the attention is on melody: melody, that is, in the sense not of an agreeable tune (although this is arguably also a feature), but in the sense of long, monophonic lines, organised around pitch relations and often divided into quasi-singable phrases. In this respect *The Heart's Ear* is one of the most melodic works of Lim's early career. As a consequence, it features a much greater emphasis on synchronicity types (1) and (2) (unison and homotone/homorhythm), as well as (3) (dynamic heterophony) and (5) (solo writing). Indeed, while I noted above that strict unison is rare in Lim's music, *The Heart's Ear* offers something of an exception. There is also very little independent counterpoint in the piece and what there is, is often brief. Where there is dynamic heterophony this, too, is closely aligned rhythmically and does not exhibit the same degree of slippage between voices as we have seen in, for example, *Inguz* or *Garden of Earthly Desire*; see Example 2.14. Often, dynamic heterophony is used in this work in a sense closer to that found in many traditional musics, as a way of embellishing a central melodic line; Example 2.15 gives one example of a heterophonic texture flowing in and out of strict unison.

Example 2.14 *The Heart's Ear*, bars 21–2

Example 2.15 *The Heart's Ear*, bars 48–9 (cello omitted)

If there is a pattern to the Sufi melody that Lim quotes, it is related to the dialogue between stillness and spontaneity, or meditation through movement, that also informs the whirling of the sema dance. In the original melody this is manifest in a combination of sustained focal pitches and flickers of spontaneous ornamentation, an articulation of the idea of alertness and attentiveness that is captured by the term 'sema', and that Rumi described as listening with the heart rather than the body. In her elaboration of this pattern in *The Heart's Ear*, Lim stretches the dichotomy between stillness and spontaneity. Focal pitches or pitch centres are used frequently, but change throughout the piece: in Example 2.13, for example, the focal pitch is middle D, but by bar 14 F♯ is beginning to become established as a focus, and in bars 20–22 (Example 2.14) both D and F♯ might be described as focal. At other points, B is also used, as well as G. (If these four pitches suggest an overall tonality of G major this can only be claimed as, at most, very deeply concealed. On the contrary, the use of focal pitches spaced in thirds removes any sense of tonal direction that stepwise pitches, or intervals of a fourth or fifth, might create.)

In addition to its melodic character, *The Heart's Ear* is also unusual among Lim's chamber works for its relatively limited use of unusual timbres or extended instrumental techniques. Aside from a few moments of flutter-tonguing for the flute, the only deviations from standard playing practice for the two wind instruments are entirely pitch-based: trills, glissandi and quartertones. Techniques for the strings extend a little further, adding harmonics on the bridge (*h. sul pont.*; see Chapter 1), *jeté* and some use of harmonics, as well as some left-hand pizzicati in the first violin solo with which the work concludes.

The ornamentations often act as ways of 'bending' or colouring the focal pitches of the melody, not only in the sense of simple pitch bends (like those on a guitar), but also with respect to rhythm, timbre and wider melodic contour. When these ornamental 'bends' occur in the middle of sustained pitches they give the sound a restless quality more closely matched to the principle of *sema*; at the ends of phrases they serve to delay or enrich their conclusion. If we look again at Example 2.13, we can see finely worked examples of dynamic heterophony that enact these forms of bending. In bar 1: the slight rhythmic uncoordination of the three voices, the microtonal variations between parts, and the subtle timbral difference between the flute's descending staccato semiquavers in the last beat of the bar and the clarinet and viola's glissando across the same interval. In bar 2: a slightly wider 'bend' with the greater difference in rhythmic and pitch activity between cello and the wind instruments, the semitonal clash between flute and clarinet, and the cello's swoop down and up on beats four and five. Across the next few bars this opening up is developed further: there is a brief moment of polyphony in bar 4, and then a fragmentation of the quasi-homophonic texture into short solos and duets on the following pages.

In comparison to these relatively subtle examples (which nevertheless have a big impact on the sound of the piece), Example 2.16 shows a more extreme interpretation, with the cello adding variations in pitch, rhythm and timbre all at once.

Example 2.16 *The Heart's Ear*, bars 126–7

In all such instances, Lim is exploring the sorts of energetic impulses that motivate a great deal of her music. 'Bending' is related to the concept of 'cleaving' already discussed; both ideas have to do with the use of degrees of closeness or separation to control and shape musical energies. Where cleaving is associated with harmony, bending can act across multiple parameters and is a more dynamic gesture, like a guitar pitch bend, or the fall of a rope, or the curve of a pen. Despite the unusual characteristics of *The Heart's Ear*, Lim has returned to many of its features in her subsequent works.

Songs Found in Dream (2005)

In contrast to the first eight years of Lim's professional career, the eight years between *The Heart's Ear* and *Songs Found in Dream* produced only a small number of chamber works – notably *Veil* (1999) for flute and bass flute, bass clarinet, trumpet, percussion, piano violin and cello; *Ming Qi (Bright Vessel)* (2000) for oboe and percussion; and *In the Shadow's Light* (2004) for string quartet. Much of her creative energy over this period was taken up instead with the composition of her second opera *Yuè Lìng Jié* between 1997 and 1999; and then between late 2001 and 2004 the birth and early years of her son, during which time she took almost a complete break from composing. *Songs Found in Dream* is thus one of the first creations of what we might consider the second period in Lim's career. Like *Invisibility*, it belongs to the group of works that Lim composed in the mid-2000s that are inspired by Australian Aboriginal culture and thought. Indeed, *Songs* is the first work still in Lim's catalogue that she lists as part of this group (Lim 2009, 5 n10), although both *In the Shadow's Light* and *The Quickening* (2004–5) refer to the Aboriginal concept of shimmer, and *Mother Tongue* (2005) was inspired by the language of the Yorta Yorta people. Written for oboe, clarinet and bass clarinet, alto saxophone, trumpet, two percussion, cello and double bass it was commissioned by the Salzburg Festival for Klangforum Wien, who gave its first performance at the Salzburg Summer Festival in August 2005, conducted by Stefan Asbury.

The concept of 'song' is essential to many Aboriginal peoples. In her programme note, Lim writes that 'The dreamscape of "song" and "singing" in Aboriginal culture is intimately connected to the land. When one walks through country with a custodian of the land, one begins to see that every stone, every plant, every inch of earth is named . . . and contains within it whole histories and liturgies of people and ancestors' (Lim 2005). A song can carry several simultaneous meanings, and, as explored in *Invisibility*, access to these layers of knowledge depends upon a person's status within the community. On a practical level, the songs provide a form of map – 'songlines' – as their words relate to the location of natural landmarks that can be used to navigate over long distances. On another level, however, those landmarks also relate to the activities of mythical beings. In this way the knowledgeable singer can interpret a mythology and a cosmology as well as songlines from just one song: a single line, therefore, can trace a path through and between many dimensions simultaneously.

Although played as a single movement, *Songs Found in Dream* falls into five sections, which we might think of as five songs. Each features a recurring group of musical materials, in particular rhythmic pulses and other forms of sonic pointillism. Pulsing patterns are used in Aboriginal music as an analogue to the visual shimmer of dots and lines found in, for instance, Yolngu bark paintings, and there are echoes in Lim's use of rainsticks, log drums and woodblocks to the actual sounds and instruments of Aboriginal percussion music. But Lim extends the principle beyond mere imitation, creating forms of musical shimmer in trills, split tones, harmonics, breath tones and other means to break up, striate and perforate the sound.

The point of shimmer, in both Lim's music and Yolngu painting, is the creation of an unsteady, flickering surface over a solid ground. A close reading of the first two bars of *Songs Found in Dream* will show one example of this, and the way in which Lim's 'shimmer' language is an extension and development of the dynamic heterophony of her pre-2001 music.

Example 2.17 *Songs Found in Dream*, bars 1–2

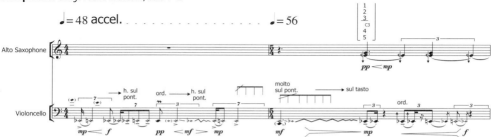

The four crotchets of bar 1 are clearly demarcated: only the first two are linked by a tie. On the level of the solid ground, then, the rhythm is a simple minim-crotchet-crotchet. On the middleground, however, those crotchet beats are subdivided into groups of septuplet semiquavers and triplet quavers. Furthermore, the septuplet semiquavers are generally written as syncopated quavers. Thus, the articulations of beat 1 fall on semiquavers 1 and 6 (of seven); of beat 2 on semiquavers 2, 4 and 6 (of seven); of beat 3 on quavers 1 and quaver 2 (of three) and of beat 4 on semiquavers 2 and 4 (of seven). Leaving aside the triplet of quavers of beat 3 for now, the predominant pulse in the bar might be rewritten in terms of 14 quavers, revealing two micro-phrases that move from rhythmically uncertain stasis (crotchets 1 and 3) to assertive quaver pulses (crotchets 2 and 4, leading into crotchet 1 of bar 2). The specified dynamics and articulation marks would seem to reinforce this phrase structure: mobile dynamics (crescendo/diminuendo) in the first half of each micro-phrase, steady accents or tenuto marks in the second.

Or, to put it another way, we have a relatively straightforward rhythmic ground and a fluid and highly ornamented surface. The insertion of a quaver triplet rather than the dominant semiquaver septuplets on crotchet 3 further emphasises this point: as soon as a second ground (of 14 quavers to the bar) is suggested, the parameters are tweaked and the surface rises clear of its ground once more: we might interpret this as a form of the 'bending' (here applied to rhythm) that we have seen in *The Heart's Ear*. On top of all this, Lim adds a further layer of activity through the use of brittle harmonics and *jeté*. These add further spirals of turbulence that break up the middleground of pitch and rhythm.

The harmonic-drenched drone of Example 2.17, initiated by the cello and taken up and extended by the alto saxophone in bar 2, resembles the openings of two other works of this period, *Invisibility* and *Pearl, Ochre, Hair String*. It clearly resonates with Lim's concept of musical shimmer, but precursors can be found in her earlier writing for cello too, particularly in *Koto* and *Inguz*; (see, eg, Examples 2.7 and 2.9). Variations of this idea may be found at the start of the second song (Example 2.18), in the middle of the third song (Example 2.19) and at the start of the fifth (Example 2.20).

Example 2.18 *Songs Found in Dream* bars 20–21

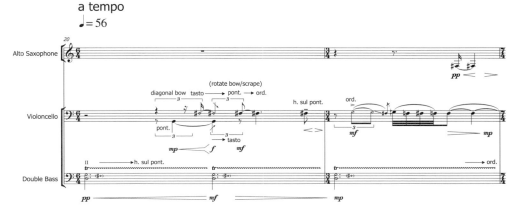

Example 2.19 *Songs Found in Dream* bars 54–7

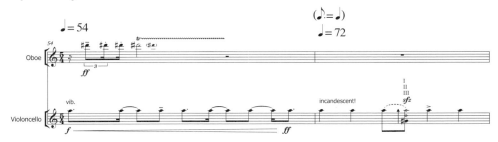

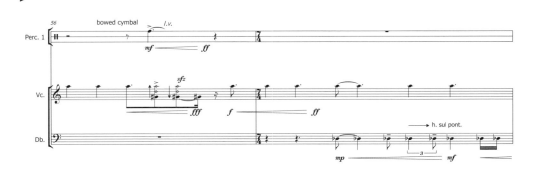

CHAPTER 2: Music for chamber ensemble

Example 2.20 *Songs Found in Dream* bars 98–9 (cello only)

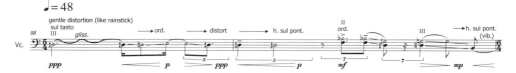

Other recurring elements include harmonic trills, played in particular by oboe, clarinet or saxophone (although an example is also incorporated into the cello's harmonics/drone idea in Example 2.18), accented or staccato semiquavers, and different forms of pulsation, either on individual instruments or as a form of ensemble homophony. Pulses may also occur on pitched tones or with varying degrees of noise. The short fourth song is comprised almost entirely of homorhythmic breath noise pulses played across the full ensemble (Example 2.21).

Example 2.21 *Songs Found in Dream* bars 91–3

These differing elements represent a spectrum of variations on the shimmer idea, somewhat similar to the spectrum of kinds of polyphonic synchronicity I described in relation to *Koto*. As in that piece, Lim not only draws freely from the spectrum but also makes sure to articulate its widest boundaries. At one end of the spectrum, we might put unpitched pulsation, such as that of Example 2.21, or of the sound of a woodblock tremolo or granular sound of a rainstick. This is 'shimmer' in its baldest form, in which sonic ground and surface are equivalent. Towards the other end, we might place the flickering, unstable surface of the opening harmonic/drone motif, in which the shimmer idea is articulated across several parameters. Somewhere in between are the wind instruments' harmonic trills (a relatively stable rhythmic shimmer paired with a more unstable pitch configuration) and the staccato semiquavers (a form of pulsation but with an added pitch component). At the very extreme are the passages of ensemble polyphony, which extend the multi-parametrical shimmer of the harmonic-drone idea across the full instrumental ensemble.

Ronda — The Spinning World (2016)

In 2016 Lim was one of four composers commissioned by Ensemble Modern and the German Academic Exchange Service (DAAD) as part of 'Re-inventing Smetak', a project working with the instruments and legacy of the composer and instrument builder Walter Smetak (1913–84).[2] At the invitation of the Goethe Institut, she spent two weeks in the city of Salvador, Bahia, Brazil, where she spent time at the Museum Solar Ferrão, which houses the more than 150 instruments Smetak invented and built, and met members of his family and the musicians who worked with him.

Born in Zurich, Smetak migrated to Brazil in 1937 and settled in Salvador. An esotoric thinker and inveterate instrument builder, he might be thought of as something like a Brazilian Harry Partch. In the 1960s and 70s he influenced the artistic movement known as Tropicália, a characteristically Brazilian mix of the popular and avant garde that was based in Salvador. His brightly painted instruments are constructed of gourds, wire, wood, polystyrene and other materials. Sometimes resembling familiar instruments (drums, violins and so on), sometimes resembling nothing ever seen before they are as sculptural as they are musical; some are designed to produce resonances that can only be felt, not heard.

In *Ronda – The Spinning World*, Lim uses three of Smetak's instruments: the Ronda itself, an hourglass-shaped cylinder made of two gourds, strung with horizontal strings, that produces a metallic scratching by rotating a handle while bowing the strings (it is a little like a hurdy gurdy, although in that case it is the circular 'bow' that rotates while the strings remain still); Trés Sois, a set of three large discs strung with wire spokes that are plucked by pegs on the instrument's frame when they are spun, producing accelerating and decelerating streams of approximately pitched pizzicati; and Piston Cretino, a brass-like instrument comprising a mouthpiece, a length of garden hose and a plastic funnel that uses the musician's belly as a crude wah-wah mute.[3] Developing the spectrum of

CHAPTER 2: Music for chamber ensemble   77

instrumental relations introduced in *Garden of Earthly Desire*, Lim uses all three as extensions of her nine-instrument ensemble: two Rondas are played by the violinist and violist; the Trés Sois is played by the harpist; and two Pistons Cretino are played by the horn player and trombonist. The percussion set-up, meanwhile, includes several instruments of Afro-diasporic and Brazilian origin, among them drums, a guiro and a reco-reco (another type of scraper).

While Lim treats the sounds of the Ronda and Trés Sois as extensions of the Western strings and harp, the Piston Cretino reverses Smetak's influence back into the ensemble, its unpredictable and obviously comic nature giving Lim permission to write unapologetically wild, unfettered music for the two lower brass. Notable is the instruction to play on several occasions with a contrabassoon reed inserted into the mouthpiece, a preparation that produces an especially outlandish, unstable sound that is among the most (deliberately) vulgar in Lim's output.

The three brass instruments add a theatrical dimension, with instructions to play at different places in and around the audience. The trumpet player begins on a podium in the centre of the audience but moves to the back of the hall in the last quarter of the work. The horn player and trombonist begin at audience level either side of the stage, facing each other. With their first use of the contrabassoon reeds they slowly walk down the two sides of the hall until they are behind the audience. Then, playing Piston Cretino, they walk in opposite circles (one clockwise, one counter-clockwise) to the front of the hall again before arriving in front of the middle of the stage (Example 2.22). From here they make one last walk, continuing the two circles to arrive once again at the back of the hall, where they are joined by the trumpet.

Example 2.22 *Ronda – The Spinning World*, bars 155–8

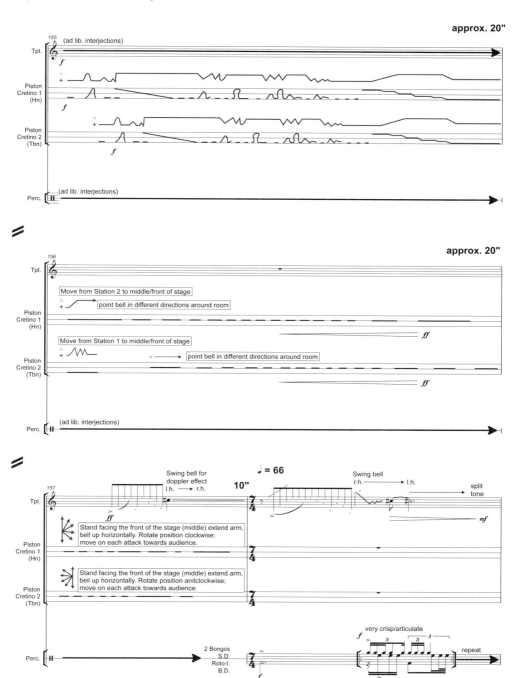

In her writings around *Ronda*, Lim notes the importance of circles and spinning to the pattern language of Afro-Brazilian culture: pertinent examples include the energetic circles of the martial art capoeira and the ritual song and dance circles of the Candomblé religion. Circular movements are thus composition's guiding concept. The Ronda and Trés Sois provide examples of how that movement may be realised in sound. The circular movements of the horn player and trombonist are clearly another manifestation: where the string players and harpist express rotation through their Smetak instruments, the brass players do so with their movements through space. Finally, Lim makes use of repeats to create small rotations and whirls within the music. These are predominantly given to the percussionist (as in Example 2.22), who thus articulates their own form of circularity.

Example 2.22 is a particularly striking page of the score. Although unusual for this piece, it is notable for several features, in particular: the use of time brackets as a structuring device (rather in the manner of John Cage's late number pieces), the graphical notation of the Piston Cretino music, instructions for staging and movement, and the use of repetition marks (see percussion part) within a semi-improvisatory context. All these features have become more prominent in Lim's most recent music. In this way, *Ronda – The Spinning World* begins lines of investigation that will be followed in later works.

In 2017, Lim extracted and adapted the virtuoso trumpet part of Ronda as a standalone work, *Roda – The Living Circle*, extending further the references to spinning and capoeira (a *roda* is the 'living circle' of participants within which capoeira takes place). *Roda* was written for ELISION's trumpet player Tristram Williams, and first performed by him in Melbourne in August 2017.

How Forests Think (2015–16)

At the start of his book *How Forests Think* (2013), the ethnographer Eduardo Kohn writes of a lesson he learnt while conducting research in the Runa village of Ávila, in Ecuador's Upper Amazon:

> Settling down to sleep under our hunting camp's thatch lean-to in the foothills of Sumaco Volcano, Juanica warned me, 'Sleep faceup! If a jaguar comes he'll see you can look back at him and he won't bother you. If you sleep facedown he'll think you're *aicha* [prey; lit., 'meat' in Quichua] and he'll attack.' If, Juanica was saying, a jaguar sees you as a being capable of looking back – a self like himself, a *you* – he'll leave you alone. But if he should come to see you as prey – an *it* – you may well become dead meat.

Such encounters, Kohn continues, 'force us to recognise that seeing, representing, and perhaps knowing, even thinking, are not exclusively human affairs. How would coming to terms with this realisation change our understandings of society, culture, and indeed the sort of world that we inhabit?' (Kohn 2013, 1).

Although Lim was inspired to compose her work soon after Kohn's book was published, she didn't correspond with Kohn himself until she happened to meet his parents at a performance of *How Forests Think* at New York's Lincoln Center in 2017; and then two years later when she and Kohn taught at the summer programme of the Banff Centre for Arts and Creativity in Alberta, Canada, where *How Forests Think* was performed and where Lim gave a lecture on the work. (Kohn himself has described the existence of Lim's composition as 'really exciting'; Kondo 2021.) Reading Kohn's book, it is striking how much its themes overlap with those of Lim's music – as well as the examination of extra- and non-human systems of knowledge that are its principal subject, it touches on shamanism, language systems and even, at one point, the symbolic power of whirlpools. Yet these were topics in Lim's music long before Kohn's book was written. When asked about the connections between her work and Kohn's she says that the way such correspondences like this happen in her career is often 'serendipitous – a kind of synchronicity that brings things into proximity that can then interact and then lead to other things'.[4]

The musical work *How Forests Think* is a chamber concerto for *sheng* and nine instruments, written for the *sheng* virtuoso Wu Wei and members of the ELISION Ensemble, and is dedicated to John Davis, CEO of the Australian Music Centre (retired 2021). It was composed for ELISION's thirtieth birthday and was first performed by them at the Bendigo International Festival of Exploratory Music in September 2016. It is in four movements: I. Tendril & Rainfall; II. Mycelia; III. Pollen; IV. The Trees.

A *sheng* is a Chinese mouth organ. One of the world's oldest instruments to have a continuous performance tradition, examples survive from the time of the Han dynasty (206 BC to 220 AD), and pictures of shengs exist from as long ago as 1100 BC. An ancestor of the Japanese *shō*, it is constructed of vertical bamboo pipes that rise upwards from a wooden or metal bowl (traditional instruments typically have seventeen pipes, but modern chromatic examples may have thirty-two or more; Wu Wei uses an instrument with thirty-seven). Each pipe contains a reed and is made to sound by covering a fingerhole near its base; to the bowl at the base of the bundle of pipes is attached a mouthpiece. The *sheng* may be played on both the inhale and the exhale; glissando effects (on single notes, chords and parts of chords) may be achieved by partially covering the fingerholes, and a wide range of pulsing effects are possible using traditional breathing and tonguing techniques.

In her programme note, Lim writes of the *sheng* that 'There is something intensely organic in how the interactions between breath and bamboo pipe create a flowering of sound that may not be completely predictable – one hears a trace of the wind in the forest.' As well as the *sheng*, there is a forest-like nature to several other instruments in her chosen ensemble. Oboe/cor anglais, clarinet, cello and double bass are all made of wood, and this 'woodiness' is emphasised in the case of the last two with the use of guiro bows in the second and last movements. In the last movement in particular, cor anglais and cello are utilised as the principal instruments. The percussion part also prominently features organic materials: temple block, rainstick, hand drum (inverted with pebbles placed inside), dried peas, wooden tray, and a violin, also played with guiro bow. Alongside these wooden instruments are those made of manmade, or inorganic materials: drums, cymbal, *rin* gongs, Chinese opera gong and Tibetan singing bowl, to say nothing of the flute, alto saxophone, trumpet and trombone that make up the ensemble.

While around half of Lim's ensemble is clearly 'forest-like', more interesting, perhaps, and more relevant to her aesthetic is how the less obviously forest-like instruments are incorporated into this world. In these cases, the forest is less important as a source of sounds or materials (wind, wood, rain on leaves) and more as a spatial and organisational metaphor like that explored in Kohn's book. Once again, it is a matter of finding common ground between unusual instrumental combinations through processes of cooperation and mutual transformation.

The first movement begins with the alternation of a melodic alto saxophone line and the granular ssshhh of a rainstick, clearly intended to symbolise the complementary natural elements of the movement's title. A tendril and a shower of rain are different in form – one is a continuous, single line; the other a discontinuous mass of points – but they are also complementary: the pattering sound of leaves means that rain is falling; the presence of rain means that tendrils will grow. Each is an indication of the other, and so it is that the forest 'thinks'.

Although it is used in all four movements, the *sheng* is most prominent in this first one, and with its glissandi and pulsing effects Lim uses it as a bridge between both 'tendril' and 'rainfall', or saxophone and rainstick. (The saxophone itself forms another instrumental bridge, of course, between woodwind and brass, or natural and manmade.) The duality of line and pulse is familiar from other works by Lim – *Songs Found in Dream*, for example – but here it is applied at length for the first time to an ecological metaphor.

Example 2.23 *How Forests Think*, movt I, bars 5–6

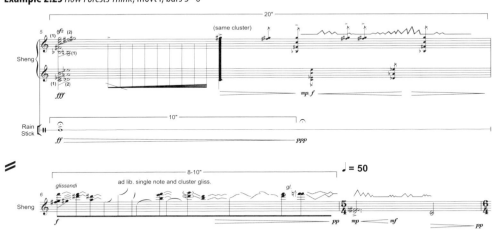

Among the different instrumental combinations in this movement, the most unusual is that between cello and cymbal found between bars 74 and 84 (overlapping slightly with the entry of the full ensemble at bar 82). By employing the familiar Lim device of transitioning between *ordinario* and *sul ponticello* bow positions, the cello is able to activate a number of noisy harmonics that draw its sound towards that of the cymbal. The cymbal, meanwhile, placed on the skin of a timpani, acquires a resonating soundbox like the cello's, as well as a means of creating glissando-like effects.

Example 2.24 *How Forests Think*, movt I, bars 78–81

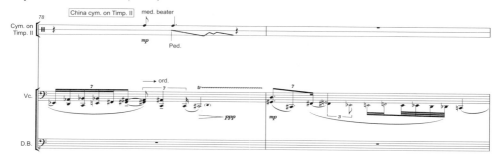

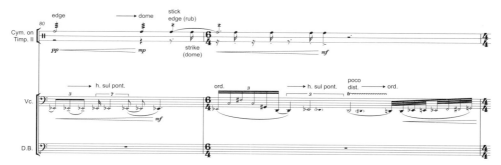

However, it is also important that no instrument is just doing one thing, or one type of thing: trumpets can be melodic, and thus close to flute, oboes, clarinet and saxophone; or, using mutes, drones and other effects, closer to strings or even percussion. By using breath tones, key slaps or pulsing effects, wind instruments can bridge between *sheng* and percussion. And so on. The apotheosis of this sort of instrumental bridging is the duo of *sheng* and cymbal at the end of the movement, which becomes a cymbal solo in which the percussionist – in a mirror of the work's beginning – plays the role of both rainfall and tendril in the accentuation of sizzle and harmonic effects using different beaters and striking or rubbing different parts of the instrument.

Movements two and three further explore forms of forest-based connection. Although on other occasions Lim has referred to a 'mycelial' way of working (eg Lim 2013), in the second movement of *How Forests Think*, 'Mycelia', she is referring directly to mycelium itself as a living entity, as well as the pattern it suggests for modes of connection and interaction. Several features of the movement are particularly notable. It begins with cello and double bass playing with guiro bows. They are joined by the *sheng* and by a violin (played by the percussionist) that is laid across a kettledrum – a gesture that inverts the 'celloisation' of the cymbal in the first movement; here a string instrument is treated as though it were a percussion instrument. Much of the music for this movement is very unstable in sound, even by Lim's standards: as well as the guiro bows for the strings, there are split tones in the brass and extremely breathy wind sounds. Towards the end of the movement the *sheng* player recites in Chinese a line by the poet Jimu Langge (b. 1963): 'In a forest far from poetry, love emerged'. After this, the flautist is asked to 'Tell a love story' by vocalising into her flute – a gesture that recalls the instrumental vocalisations of *Koto* and, more recently, *Love Letter*, and unravels the flute's sound into a jumble of pre-vocal flutters, clicks and hisses.

'Pollen' takes another form of organic connection as its inspiration, this time the minute particles of pollen, each precisely shaped (and, viewed under a microscope, in an astonishing variety of forms) to fit only the pistil of its own species. In contrast to the fragile, noisy sounds of the first two movements of the work, 'Pollen' is relatively pitch-based, indicated most clearly by the use of vibraphone for the percussion. There are still some noisy sounds, notably the use of *sul ponticello* in the strings, but otherwise this movement features some of the most pitch-oriented music of this period in Lim's career. The glittering soundworld, led by the vibraphone, is suggestive of clouds of pollen grains.

The fourth and final movement is something different again. In its use of time brackets and a form of controlled indeterminacy (at times reminiscent of the mobile techniques of the Polish composer Witold Lutosławski), it connects to a thread of improvisation and quasi-improvisation that emerges periodically in Lim's music, and that we will discuss further with respect to *Tongue of the Invisible* and the installations she made with Domenico de Clario. The movement is in two halves. In the first, sounds are played within time brackets (of between four and thirty seconds) like those seen in Example 2.22. The percussionist drops dried peas into a Tibetan singing bowl and Chinese cymbal – a return to the 'rainfall' sounds of the first movement. The *sheng* player vocalises harmonics in the style of Mongolian throat singing. After around two minutes the saxophone, trumpet and strings add groups of pulsed breath or pedal notes and the winds and trombone play isolated, static chords held for several seconds at a time. Out of the fifth of these chords a bass flute solo emerges, followed by thirty seconds of Mongolian-style chant and then a return of the strings' breathy noises. These continue now as a bed beneath the second half of the movement. This takes the form of a series of melodic 'islands', freely placed in time by cor anglais and cello, to which the *sheng* improvises short responses.

Example 2.25 *How Forests Think*, movt IV, bar 20

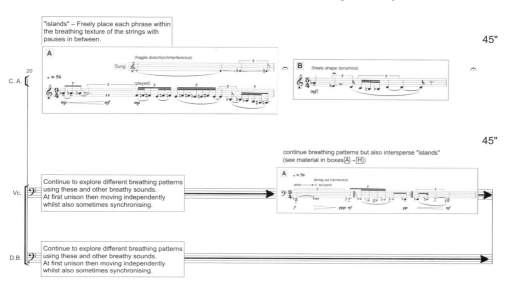

The texture here is deliberately sparse; apart from a few percussion touches and the addition of quiet whistling notes from the rest of the players (and the conductor!) this is all there is for the work's final three and a half minutes. The creaking of bark in response to changes in temperature; the fall of acorns or dead twigs to the ground; the patter of rain on leaves: trees don't make sound themselves, but sound occurs as the result of things acting upon them (wind, sun, rain, gravity). The sounds Lim asks for in this movement, and particularly the things she asks her performers to do, seem designed to evoke a similar sense of passivity. It is not unusual for her to write a work that concludes in such an open-ended way (see the endings of *Garden of Earthly Desire*, *Koto*, even *Invisibility*), but whereas those endings serve as dissipations of the work's energies, the final movement of *How Forests Think* is more like a settling; a sinking or grounding into a world beyond the human, like the forests of the Upper Amazon.

References

Alexander, Christopher et al. (1977). *A Pattern Language.* Oxford: Oxford University Press.

Boulez, Pierre (1986). *Orientations*, ed. Jean-Jacques Nattiez, trans. Martin Cooper. London: Faber.

Kohn, Eduardo (2013). *How Forests Think.* Berkeley and Los Angeles: University of California Press.

Kondo, Hiroshi (2021). 'Toward a New Way of Making Allies with Forest: How Forests Think and Afterward'. *More-Than-Human* n9. https://ekrits.jp/en/2021/01/4098/.

Lim, Liza (n.d.). 'Liza Lim', ELISION Ensemble website, https://elision.org.au/soundhouse/liza-lim/.

Lim, Liza (1989). *Garden of Earthly Desire* (1988–89) [programme note], https://limprogrammenotes.files.wordpress.com/2011/07/garden-of-earthly-desire.pdf.

Lim, Liza (1994). *Koto (1994)* [programme note], https://limprogrammenotes.wordpress.com/2011/07/31/koto-1994/.

Lim, Liza (2005). *Songs Found in Dream (2005)* [programme note], https://limprogrammenotes.wordpress.com/2011/08/01/songs-found-in-dream-2005/.

Lim, Liza (2009). 'Staging an Aesthetics of Presence'. Search *Journal for New Music* 6, http://www.searchnewmusic.org/lim.pdf.

Lim, Liza (2013). 'A Mycelial Model for Understanding Distributed Creativity: Collaborative Partnership in the Making of "Axis Mundi" (2013) for Solo Bassoon'.

Rutherford-Johnson, Tim (2011). 'Patterns of Shimmer: Liza Lim's Compositional Ethnography'. *Tempo* v65 n258: 2–9.

Endnotes

1 Correspondence with the author, March 2021.

2 The other composers were Arthur Kampela, Daniel Moreira and Paulo Rios Filho.

3 Pictures of all three instruments may be seen at https://limprogrammenotes.wordpress.com/2016/12/26/ronda-the-spinning-world-2017/.

4 Conversation with the author, July 2020.

Chapter 3

Music for voice

We will have more to say about the more-than-human world in due course. But for now, we turn to the most human instrument of all. In addition to her operas, Lim has written several times for voice, with or without instruments. Apart from one occasion, the now withdrawn *Sri Vidya* for choir and orchestra (1995), however, this has always been for single voices at a time. This chapter considers the following works: *Voodoo Child, The Quickening, Mother Tongue* and *Tongue of the Invisible*. As well as these, Lim's official catalogue includes Li Shang Yin for coloratura soprano and fifteen instruments (1993); *Burning House*, for singing *koto* player (1995); *3 Angels* for soprano, mezzo soprano and bass-baritone, in the form of one song for each voice (2011); and four shorter voice and instrument duos (three of them drawn from her operas) – *Athena's Trumpet* for high soprano and piccolo trumpet (1993/2020), from *The Oresteia*, which can be paired with another duo, *The Incandescent Tongue* for soprano and trumpet (2020); *Chang-O* for baritone and percussion (1998), from *Yuè Lìng Jié*; and *Boat Song* for baritone and bassoon (2013–16/2019), from *Tree of Codes*. Finally, there is a text piece, *tree song* (2021), for voice or voices, whose score simply reads: 'Make friends with a tree, sing into their ear'.

Voodoo Child (1989)

Lim's earliest vocal work was commissioned by Germany's Radio Bremen, which became aware of her music at the 1988 Hong Kong ISCM festival. It was first performed by Ensemble Avance and the soprano Ingrid Schmithusen, conducted by András Hamary. Like *The Oresteia, Voodoo Child* turns to the poetry of Sappho, whose words Lim also quotes in the score of the orchestral *Annunciation Triptych*. In this way, *Voodoo Child* initiates a preoccupation that has resonated through at least the first thirty years of Lim's career.

Lim's attraction to Sappho's poetry began in 1987 when she was studying with Ton de Leeuw and Brian Ferneyhough in the Netherlands. Living away from Australia for the first time, she used Sappho as a 'home base' to which she found comfort in returning.[1]

She has described the appeal of Sappho's poems, almost all of which survive only in fragments, as follows:

> I've always felt drawn to past and lost, i.e. no longer spoken languages, and discovered them as the source of my musical ideas … As for the ancient Greek of Sappho's poetry, we no longer hear how it sounded, its likely pronunciation is in the dark even to specialists. But it is precisely this vacuum created by the lost knowledge that keeps open a fertile psychic space for me, in which the necessity and function of music, the creation of a sound world for these lost words, becomes an aspect of the creative energy that triggers the compositions. (Quoted in Rosman 1999, 35–6; my translation)

The text Lim uses is one of Sappho's most famous. Known as 'Sappho 31', or 'Phainetai moi' after its opening line, it describes the intense sensations (perhaps love, perhaps jealousy) evoked by seeing from a distance one's lover talking to another person.[2]

To create a ten-minute musical form out of Sappho's momentary flash of sensation, Lim must give it a narrative shape of some kind. Like *Garden of Earthly Desire*, she divides *Voodoo Child* into three parts. The first and second are further divided by changes of tempi into three subsections (crotchet = 58, 66 and 80). Each part begins in a similar manner, as though the music is restarting itself. This pattern is repeated in the third part, but without the final crotchet = 80 subsection. In an early sign of the interest in Sufi music and mysticism that would become a feature of Lim's later music, the two crotchet = 80 subsections are marked 'dervish' and feature a predominance of trills and tremolo gestures, which rhyme with both the whirling dance of the Sufi dervish and the ecstatic trembling of Sappho's narrator. Lim does not attempt to make audible the sounds of Sappho's words. Instead, she fractures, elongates and elaborates them, sometimes to extreme lengths. For example, the word κακχέεται, 'pours down', begins at bar 102 near the end of part two but does not end until bar 124, at the start of part three and following nearly fifteen bars of rest for the singer.

Across the whole work, Lim uses intensification of expression as a way of extending the single moment of Sappho's poem. In the first section this takes place in particular on the parameters of pitch and register. Example 3.1 shows the very beginning. From an E♭, trombone, timpani and soprano (all instruments capable of reproducing microtones and glissandi) gradually expand outwards in small intervals. The entry of the flute at the end of bar 1 adds a D, then an E♮. Over the next few bars cello, clarinet and violin add more notes and expand the range into the upper and lower registers. Beginning with the percussive notes of the timpani and the buzzing flutter-tongue of the flute, the ensemble gradually moves away from sustained notes and smooth lines to staccato figures which, as Rosman (1999) observes, allow for a smooth integration of the piano (the only member of the ensemble not capable of playing sustained pitches) into the overall texture.

Example 3.1 *Voodoo Child*, bars 1–2

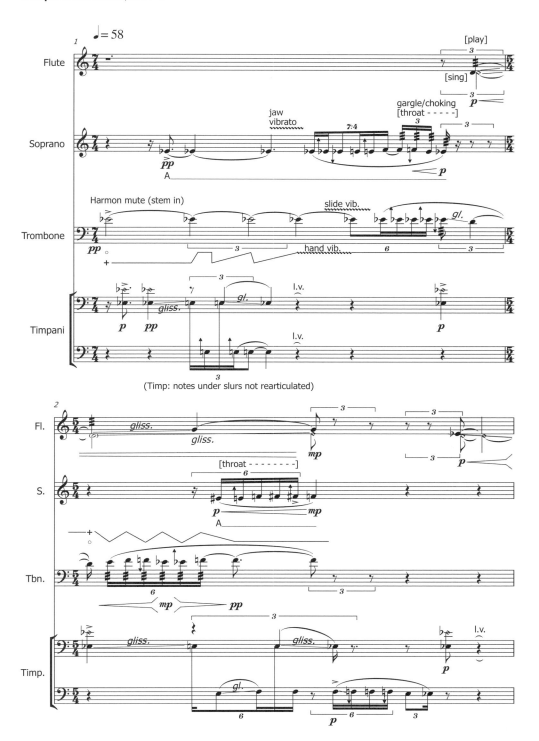

Example 3.2 *Voodoo Child*, bars 10–12

CHAPTER 3: Music for voice

The voice follows this trajectory, indicating that Lim treats it as a member of the ensemble rather than a soloist. In Example 3.1, the vibrato of its first few beats (both suggested and written-out) align it with the trombone's various hand and slide vibrati; with the gargling/choking effect made at the back of the throat on beat 6 it anticipates the flute's complex flutter-tongue-with-singing sound on beat 7. The timpani joins this sonic collection with its rolls and micro-glissandi. In Example 3.2, the soprano first acts in quasi-canon with the clarinet, while its trilled G♯ on beat 3 synchronizes with, and provides cover for, the piano's entry on a tremolo high G (further supported by the timpani's roll on a low C). As the ensemble moves towards a spiccato texture that is increasingly shaped by the piano, the soprano falls silent, and over the next few pages returns only intermittently (at points when the piano itself is mostly or completely silent).

Parts two and three further develop these ideas of intensification and expansion. In particular, Lim organises an expansion of timbre, from predominantly clean pitch to predominantly noise and unpitched sounds. In the third part the voice makes use of distorted and spoken sounds, the percussion is almost all unpitched, the winds, strings and trombone make use of various percussive sounds, and the piano – so dominant in the first part – is almost completely silent. The music ends with the last two notes of the voice gasped on indrawn breaths, a sonic analogue to the near-death at the end of the poem and perhaps the work's only moment of true word-painting. Rosman likens the desiccated, attenuated textures of this final part to the 'ghostly' conclusion to the second movement of Mahler's Fifth Symphony (1999, 33). We might also hear in it an example of Lim's favoured concluding shift towards noise.

Of all the instruments used in *Voodoo Child*, the piano is the one least like a voice – at least as Lim treats it here – and it is notable the piano is the instrument that is treated most like a special case. As we have seen, it is the last instrument to enter, and only does so when the timbral ground has been sufficiently prepared. After its entry it dominates the rest of the first section, shaping its texture and register in such a way that the voice struggles to insert itself. Most strikingly, at the end of the 'dervish' subsection of part one the piano takes a cadenza that dramatically expands the music's register to the extremes of treble and bass as only a piano can.

Example 3.3 *Voodoo Child*, bars 56–7

As the voice comes to the fore in the 'noisier' third part, however, the piano once more falls silent. Yet it would be a mistake to think of *Voodoo Child* in terms of a concertante opposition of voice and piano. Although one does seem to silence the other, this occurs not because the two instruments are in conflict but because they are distant points on the same spectrum. As in the works we saw in the previous chapter, the music of *Voodoo Child* adapts around the instruments that are playing at any moment. When the soprano is singing, the ensemble leans towards sustained or smooth sounds for which the piano is less well-equipped. When the piano is playing, however, the ensemble reorients towards more jagged, pointillistic sounds. And there are of course boundary sounds for each, such as the voice's gargling/choking effect mentioned above, or the piano's tremolo.

With this view in mind, then, we can see a general approach towards text-setting. By downplaying the intelligibility of Sappho's words (which is in any case obscure) Lim can concentrate on their broader expressive content. The piano (or any other instrument, for that matter) is not counterpointing or accompanying the voice but elaborating upon that expressive material. When the voice reaches its limit, another instrument takes over. Voice is not opposed to instrument; poetry is not opposed to music.

The Quickening (2002–5)

The Quickening is written for soprano and *qin*, a seven-string Chinese zither that is rather like the Japanese *koto* but with a single fixed bridge, rather than movable bridges for each string. It was commissioned by the Festival d'Automne à Paris and premiered by ELISION soprano Deborah Kayser, and the Chinese *qin* player Yang Chunwei. It is dedicated to Joséphine Markovits, co-artistic director of the Festival d'Automne.

Although *The Quickening* is typically performed as a standalone work, Lim considers it as half of a pair, together with the string quartet *In the Shadow's Light*, that she calls a 'ceremony of the seasons'. (The two works were played together for their premieres.) 'These "seasons"', she writes in her programme note (2005),

> are aligned to the turning points between autumn-winter and spring-summer, metaphors for journeys into death and into life. Both works inhabit a dream-world where things are not grasped directly, where sensations are filtered through different kinds of veils. These veils might be experienced as a tangle of submerged pathways through which one senses the movement of creatures on the surface above; perhaps as a trance of saturated light coming from a place beyond, or as oscillating interference patterns created by intersecting lines and arising from the coupling and uncoupling of sonic elements.

These lines contain the first reference in Lim's writings to a 'shimmer' effect like that of Aboriginal Australian art, and although Lim herself does not count *The Quickening* or *In the Shadow's Light* among her other 'shimmer' works, together they mark clearly the emergence of an idea that soon became a recurring subject of her music. (Indeed, her note for *The Quickening* refers to 'songs found in dreams'!) *In the Shadow's Light* also features Lim's first use of the 'guiro' bow that will become so prominent in *Invisibility* and *Pearl, Ochre Hair String*.

For now, though, Lim's models remain more Chinese than Australian. The *qin* (or *guqin*) is the oldest and most revered instrument in Chinese culture. Sometimes known as 'the instrument of the sages', its origins are believed to date back at least 3,000 years. Lim's chosen text is four fragments by the Chinese poet Yang Lian (b. 1955), published in his 1999 collection *Where the Sea Stands Still*, where they are translated by Brian Holton; Lim sets the Chinese originals. Her composition is in five movements: 'The Quickening', 'One lip, one tongue', 'Ceremony for Childbirth', 'Xīn (heart)' and 'Cicadas in the body endlessly cry'. All are for both players except the third, for soprano and reciting qin player (no instrument); and the fourth, for qin solo (no words spoken or sung). Although most of *The Quickening* was composed in 2004 and 2005, the fourth movement was composed in 2002.

Lim's treatment of the voice and its text in *The Quickening* is markedly different from that in *Voodoo Child*. Whereas in that work, the voice is treated as a special member of the instrumental ensemble, in *The Quickening* voice and qin shape their own distinct roles, complimenting rather than aligning with one another. Following the taxonomy introduced in Chapter 2 they are mostly in a relationship of type (4). (independent counterpoint) or type (5). (solo/fragmentation). Crucial to this relationship is a particular quality of Chinese music, and especially music for *qin*, in which the silences between notes are as important as the notes themselves, and equally charged with musical affect.

The relationship between the two musicians is in fact unusually loose – certainly more than for any work Lim wrote before 2004. This unusual character indicates a change in technique away from the continuities and variations of pitch and rhythm that characterise the dynamic heterophony of her earlier works towards less quantifiable unities of phrase, trajectory or even energy. While her note refers to a guiding principle of 'the coupling and uncoupling of sonic elements' – the building blocks of the dynamic heterophonic style, in fact – the extra weight given to the spaces and silences between notes shifts the emphasis of *The Quickening* towards the latter. This change in emphasis towards separation rather than union (in fact two aspects of the same idea) is appropriate to the work's theme of the creation and emergence of new life (the separate coming into being of mother and child); it also anticipates the looser structures of diverse elements found in later works.

This new emphasis is most apparent in the work's first movement, in which the two instruments are only rarely synchronised. Example 3.4 is representative. In bar 7, the only synchronisation (and then only in terms of rhythm) is the triplet quaver at the start of beat five. But even this short moment is disguised, first by the glissandi by which both parts approach this note, which obscures the synchronous attack, and second by the fuzziness of the voice's whisper tone and then its immediate fall into silence. In bar 8, the two parts do lock together rhythmically, as they do from time to time in the first movement – often doing so, as here, on slow monotones. But even here there is an uncoupling as the soprano articulates its second note as an inhaled gasp, a gesture that sets the flow of her sound in opposition to the *qin*'s, inward, rather than outward. (In the next bar the *qin* continues with two more slow chords, with the addition of a dissonant D♯, as though answering in its own way the soprano's uncoupling/distorting gesture.)

Example 3.4 *The Quickening*, movt I, bars 7–8

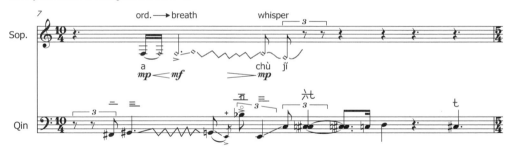

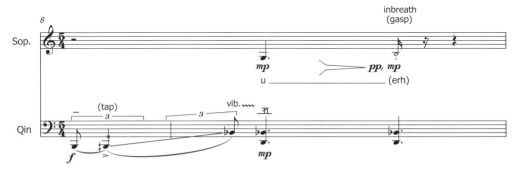

Unlike the *koto*, the *qin* is played without plectrums, making it capable of a much wider range of attack and timbre depending on which part of the finger (fleshy pad, nail etc) is used. There are three basic techniques to playing the instrument – open string (*san yin*), harmonics (*fan yin*) and stopped string (*an yin*) – but purportedly more than 1,000 variations and combinations of these exist, of which around fifty are used in modern practice; there may be as many as fifteen different forms of vibrato.[3] This vast catalogue of techniques – and several millennia of performance history – characterises the *qin* as an instrument of enormous variety and subtlety of sound. Probably sensibly, Lim does not attempt to engage in detail with historical techniques; her preface describes a few special notations, but these are all easily written in Western notation (mordent, left-hand plucks etc; the score itself includes further indications for strumming, vibrato and similar effects). Instead, she asks the *qin* player to shape the tonal qualities of each sound for themselves: 'Basic fingering and some technical information is given in the score but details of the subtle positioning of left hand fingers and the direction, speed and striking surface of the right hand are left to the performer's discretion.'

If there is a coupling between the two musicians, it would seem to take place on the levels of gesture, technique and energy. Lim's writing for soprano follows that of the *qin* in making use of the voice's own vast capacity for timbral variety. Even the two relatively sparse bars of Example 3.4 contain four different means of vocal production (ordinary singing, breath, whisper and inhaled gasp) as well as vibrato and glissando techniques, to say nothing of the different text syllables on top of these. Nevertheless, in comparison to *Voodoo Child* the words are relatively clearly articulated, language barriers notwithstanding.

The second movement extends the variety of timbres used, introducing more distorted sounds for both voice and *qin*. It begins with the soprano alone. In her first five bars she must successively mouth words silently, use inflected speech (adding a throaty quality), make sounds with her throat and breath, make choked sounds, sing with intermittent distortion, add tongue percussion, hiss, and finally sing. Only with this last does the qin enter, providing reinforcement and ornamentation to the vocal line with short, delicate gestures. Other vocal techniques in this first section of the movement include voiced whisper, singing with the mouth closed and stifled cry.

Example 3.5 *The Quickening*, movt II, bars 1–5

The longer second section of the movement follows a clear direction from this fragmentary, often quite jagged texture that is diverse in pitch, rhythm, timbre and articulation with every moment, to a sound that is essentially static in all parameters: it ends with four and half bars of the soprano sustaining an ululating tremolo on D♯.

This path is led by the *qin*, which moves progressively from repeated notes within the context of more varied gestures, to an irregularly pulsing pedal which becomes a regular strum, to percussive strumming across dampened strings, and then finally the circular strumming shown in Example 3.6. As Example 3.6 shows, the soprano broadly follows this direction, but retains a variety of musical elements for a little longer. In this way, while the two parts are 'uncoupled' with respect to pitch and rhythm, they are 'coupled' to a larger timbral structure that unfolds across the whole movement.

Example 3.6 *The Quickening*, movt II, bars 17–18, 34–5, 49–50

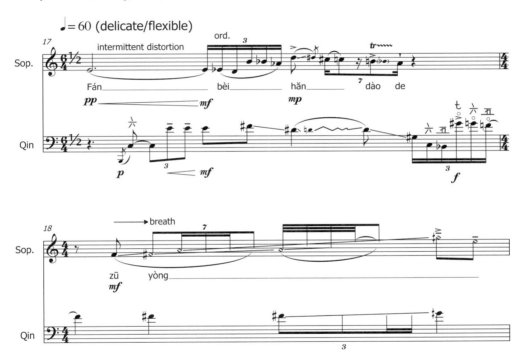

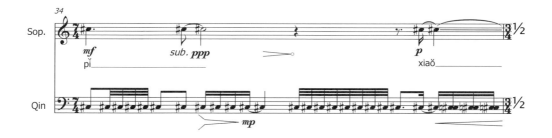

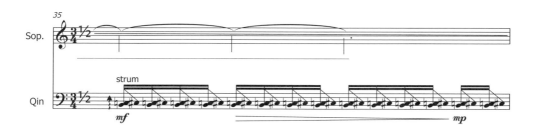

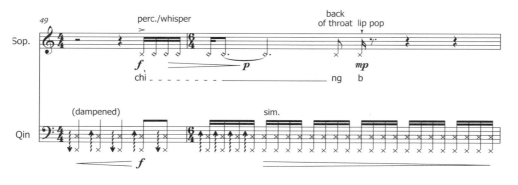

The *qin* is silent for the third movement: its player joins the soprano with murmured recitations. The dominant features of this movement are the soprano's (and later the *qin* player's) use of her hand as a mute, and the addition of sharp tongue clicks (resembling the percussive *qin* strumming of the previous movement), notated on a separate line above the main staff and articulating a different rhythmic line to the sung vocal. In this way the voice is split into three levels of abstraction: recited text, sung voice and percussive clicks. The movement is short; through its course first the sung voice recedes from view and then the recitation, leaving only a series of soft clicks to end. This is childbirth not as the pain and noise of popular representation, but as the emergence and separation of something small and fragile from within a larger body.

Example 3.7 *The Quickening*, movt III, bars 1–2

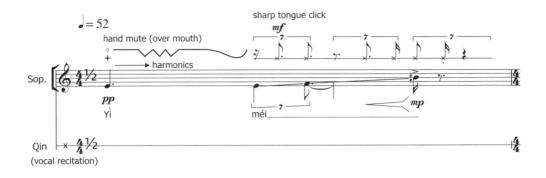

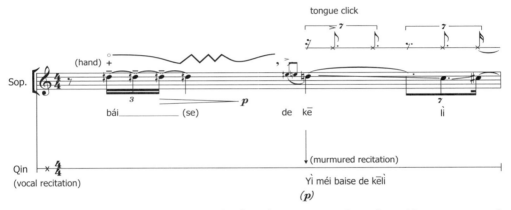

According to a note on the score, the fourth movement, 'Xīn (heart)' was composed on 10 May 2002, two years before the rest of the work and just five months after the birth of Lim's son, to whom it is dedicated. In contrast to the third movement, the fourth is pitch-oriented, with few noise effects: the special techniques employed are predominantly harmonics and vibrato/glissando effects, and thus connected to traditional *qin* performance. As Example 3.8 shows, these are used extensively, particularly the latter. (The Chinese characters beneath the staff indicate which string is to be plucked.)

Example 3.8 *The Quickening*, movt IV, bars 29–36

Of all the movements, this one is the most loosely structured. There are few recognisable repeated motifs, and although it ends with a centring/focusing on the two pitches of A♭ and B♭, this is not part of a discernible wider harmonic or gestural trajectory. Rather, the movement takes the form of a fantasy in phrases of varied length, often separated by rests of one or more beats but otherwise all different from one another. The movement has an improvisatory quality which, combined with the *qin*'s soft dynamic and subtlety of tone, give it an intimate and contemplative feel.

The fifth movement of *The Quickening* restores both musicians, although it is dominated by the voice; the movement is repeated three times, during which the *qin* is silent except for a series of chromatic sweeps and tremolos played with a dry, indistinct tone at the end of each repeat. The soprano sings with a 'wacky whistle' (a small plastic and felt semicircle that is placed against the roof of the mouth) to create a range of high-pitched, distorted and animal-like noises, notated as wavy lines indicating approximate pitch and duration. This is Lim's first use of this device, but she returns to it in later works, most notably *The Navigator*. In its shift from relatively clearly defined pitches and even melodies, to noisier, less clearly defined materials, this last movement completes a familiar sonic trajectory. It also completes, and adds a new dimension to, the narrative of emergent and separating identities that is the theme of this work, placing the two musicians in almost completely divergent roles and splitting the soprano's voice into its own diverging layers.

Example 3.9 *The Quickening*, movt V, bars 5–6

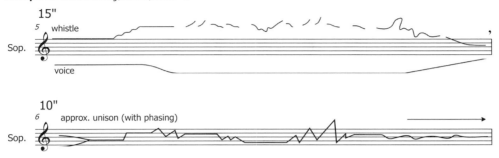

While I have drawn contrasts between *The Quickening* and *Voodoo Child*, one last comparison may be useful, with the other duet work discussed in this book: *Inguz (fertility)*, for clarinet and cello. Like T*he Quickening*, *Inguz* takes childbirth as its theme, dedicated as it is to two performer colleagues of Lim and their baby daughter. In comparison with *The Quickening*, *Inguz* features a much greater continuity of sound and phrasing: the music runs in an almost unbroken flow from beginning to end, with no rests and with the ending of each phrase overlapping with the beginning of the next. Partly as a consequence, and partly because of the more penetrating sound of clarinet and cello as opposed to soprano and *qin*, the music is more forceful than that of *The Quickening*. Extending the Chinese connection, we might describe the two as 'yang' (active, bright, male) and 'yin' (passive, shaded, female) expressions of the same experience.[4] Returning to the metaphor of pregnancy itself, the emphasis in Lim's later composition on difference and of rapid changes in energy and direction expresses the idea of two beings who are separate while contained within one body, and the flips and pivots of 'the quickening' by which this is expressed.

Mother Tongue (2005)

When Lim wrote *Mother Tongue* for soprano and fifteen instruments, it was her largest concert work for voice to date. Commissioned, like *The Quickening*, by the 2005 Festival d'Automne à Paris, together with Ensemble Intercontemporain and ELISION, it emerged out of a suggestion by Joséphine Markovits that Lim look more closely at Aboriginal Australian culture. It was first performed at the Cité de la Musique in Paris by Piia Komsi and Ensemble Intercontemporain, conducted by Jonathan Nott, the day after the premieres of *In the Shadow's Light* and *The Quickening*. *Mother Tongue* is a major work that reveals much about changes in Lim's musical thinking in the mid-2000s, as well as her increasingly sophisticated approach to language and text setting.

Lim's original inspiration was a list of ninety-two words compiled by Stephen Morey – a linguist and, as a mandolinist and sitar player, a founder member of ELISION – from the recollections of an elderly Yorta Yorta woman, then one of the last remaining native speakers of her people's language.[5] Endangered languages like Yorta Yorta recall Lim's interest in lost and no-longer spoken languages, like the Ancient Greek of Sappho. The list of words included fundamental terms of endearment and kinship: like the first ones learnt as a child and those that, seemingly, endure to the very end of a language's life. In an interview with Véronique Brindeau, Lim has noted that she found this list of words doubly moving, 'since these are words that I know from my own lost mother tongue of Hokkien Chinese dialect as well as the kinds of words that my young son was acquiring in his first speech' (Brindeau 2005). The concepts of familial and linguistic motherhood are closely bound together.

Although she initially experimented with the Yorta Yorta words as a possible text, Lim found them too 'raw' to work with; she was also mindful of cultural protocols surrounding the use of Indigenous knowledge. Instead, she commissioned the Australian poet Patricia Sykes to write a text that would mediate between these words and her response to them. Sykes's three poems extend their view to include references to and words from mother tongues from around the world and throughout history. These include *tik*, a root word in many languages that is thought to be one of the first words ever spoken, as well as words from the click language N|u of the San bushmen of the Southern Kalahari, one of the world's most endangered languages;[6] the secret women's language of Nüshu, from Hunan Province, China; Navajo; Finnish (one of Europe's most unusual languages, being unrelated to Greek, Latin or Slavic; it is also Komsi's mother tongue); and the Australian indigenous languages of Kukatja, Walpiri and Yorta Yorta itself. While Sykes's poems are to be read in a linear fashion, they therefore create around them a large space of cross-linguistic references.

Following Sykes's poems, Lim's composition is in three movements. While many features recur, the minor third dyad, F–Ab, with which the work begins most clearly delineates its overall form. It serves a sort of leitmotif for the mother tongue itself, as well as associated concepts like motherhood, birth and origin. Its importance is reflected in the work's instrumentation: the percussion set-up includes a Thai gong tuned to F, used to give a memorable colour to these moments. Furthermore, the soprano in movements 2 and 3 plays a cello tuned to a scordatura from lowest string to highest of F–F–F (unison with second string)–Ab. The first violinist also has a second instrument, retuned to F–Ab–F–Ab, which they use in movement 3. These general tonal shapes provide our first entry into understanding the overall form of the work:

> **Movement 1, 'Century, the Continuance'.** ABA form. Dyad is prominent at the beginning, and then again at bar 27, where a new section begins after what we might call the opening prelude, and where the text switches for the first time into English (from its Finnish first line, *'tämä kieli jota vaalin'*; 'this tongue I am cradling'). Disappears for the long central section before returning at bar 151 ('but love songs are breeding in the abdomens') and again at bar 177 (the final word of 'in every mother tongue'). The movement ends with a coda of words from Indigenous and extinct languages, with relatively little associated pitch content.

> **Movement 2, 'latitude of gain'.** 'Cadence' form. At the start of the movement Ab (written as G♯) is prominent, in a different minor-third dyad with B. At bar 60 F returns prominently in the soprano on the return of the word 'mother' (*'mother-of-*

the-evening, stem-mother'). At 'returning' (bars 93–4), the A♭ is also restated by the soprano, and then further emphasised at 'to a birthing ground'. Here the soprano begins playing her cello with two bows in a circular motion, establishing a pedal on F; with the words 'new rain' her voice concludes the cadential leap from A♭ down to F that shapes the movement's form.

Movement 3, 'longtitude of loss'. Rondo. A folk-like melody in F minor sung over a string drone on F and A♭ serves as the ritornello for this movement. It is heard at the beginning, where the drone is played by the open strings of the soprano's cello (using two bows in alternating motion – a foreshadow of the ending of *Invisibility*); then at bar 61, where the string drone (more ornamented this time) is played by the first violinist on retuned violin; and finally at bar 140 through to the end, again with the drone part played on retuned violin.

Sykes's poems play on the pun of mother tongue and motherhood. 'Century, the Continuance' describes the birth-like emergence – 'from the womb's rift valleys' – of individual mother tongues out of the primordial *ur*-language of vocal noises. By beginning her poem with one image of the tongue and ending it with another, Sykes provides a premise for the ABA tonal structure of Lim's music, which thus establishes the tongue not only as a point of arrival (the 'mother tongue' that is actually spoken) but also as a point of origin (the 'mother'). Meanwhile, the central section of the first movement (from Sykes's 'broken silence' to her 'ravage of voices') recreates the emergence of language from purely sonic material into song, beginning with *tik* ('were you the first?') – a sound that, incidentally, is intimately and fundamentally connected to the action of the tongue. The movement concludes with a series of words from endangered but existing mother tongues.

The second movement traces the creation of language from 'fragments of my beginning' to 'a birthing ground whose voices shimmer like new rain'. Beginning with sounds from bassoon and voice whose effortfulness recalls the strains of childbirth, it ends in a transitional state – like labour itself – between non-existence and existence, the moment of creation, ripe with potential.

By the start of the third movement the anticipated birth has taken place (off-stage, as it were). The music – a simple folk-like melody over drones on A♭ and F – reaches a state of calm that is rare in Lim's music, and clearly of special significance. The work's conclusion emphasises the centrality of its theme of motherhood with cadence-like repetitions (with variations) of the word 'mother' on the two drone pitches.

Mother Tongue's direct engagement with language and the voice provides an opportunity to examine in more detail Lim's approach to text-setting, and the relationships she composes between text and voice, and voice and instruments. Figure 3.1 illustrates the framework that informs the analysis that follows.

Figure 3.1 Analytical framework for the relationships between text, voice and instruments in *Mother Tongue*

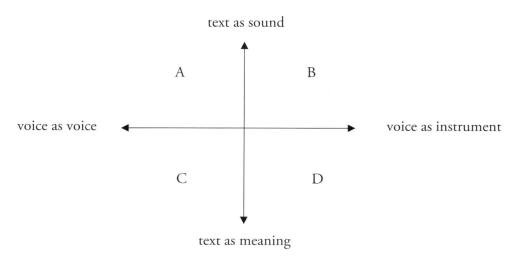

The horizontal axis on the diagram represents the continuum between vocal (voice-as-voice) and instrumental (voice-as-instrument) forms of singing that we have already outlined in this chapter. As with the spectrum of heterophony described in Chapter 2, at any given moment the music might be located at more than of these points, or it might move quickly between them. In all of Lim's vocal works, their realms bleed into one another: the blending of voice, trombone and flute in *Voodoo Child* (Example 3.1) or the detailed balancing of voice and *qin* in *The Quickening* (Example 3.4). Lim's setting of of the pre-linguistic *tik* in *Mother Tongue* (Example 3.10) exists on either one side or the other along the horizontal line. But whether it is led by the instruments (with rattle and viola as instigators) or by the voice (as the climactic centre of the overall gesture) is open to interpretation. For clarity I will make interpretive decisions throughout my analysis, although rarely can moments in Lim's music be precisely described as one thing or the other.

Example 3.10 *Mother Tongue*, movt I, bars 66–7

CHAPTER 3: Music for voice 107

The vertical axis on my diagram represents a second, intersecting continuum between text as sound, that is, non-semantic noise, and text as meaning, that is, language. Broadly speaking, words, sentences and other linguistic structures can be placed at or close to the text-as-meaning pole; phonemes and even smaller particles of speech such as tongue clicks or hisses can be placed at or close to the opposite one. Some text units in *Mother Tongue* may be placed in more than one location, however, or may move location depending on context and/or usage. As shown in Example 3.10, Lim gives the proto-linguistic *tik* the qualities of a non-linguistic percussive sound, which are anticipated and further expanded upon by the instrumental ensemble in a variety of related sounds – *col legno* tapping, pizzicato, reed squeaks, tongue rams, breath noises and rattles. Yet in Sykes's poem it retains meanings both semantic (as the root of words like the French *doigt* and the English *digit*) and symbolic (as a representation of primordial language). In Example 3.11, which shows the return of the F–A♭ dyad towards the end of the first movement, the soprano is clearly leading the music, yet even so its initial *jeté* effect derives from that of the violin. Although the meaning of the words is intelligible, effects such as the nasal quality added to 'songs' and the breathiness of 'are' emphasise these words' origins in non-linguistic sounds, and so they retain aspects of both.

Example 3.11 *Mother Tongue*, movt I, bars 152–4

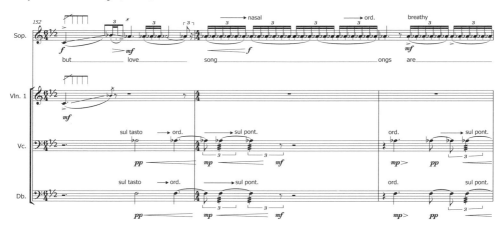

Out of the two-axis diagram we can derive four quadrants, A, B, C and D, which represent the four possible relationships between text and voice. Every moment in the piece may be interpreted in terms of these four regions or types of vocal writing. As we might expect (and as the two examples already given demonstrate), actual moments in *Mother Tongue* are rarely this schematically defined. Nevertheless, as with the five-part scale of heterophony, this diagram is a useful preliminary tool with which to approach the work's distinctive style and methods.

Examples from each quadrant may be found in the first movement. The simplest to identify is quadrant C. This is the one in which the voice is used as a voice and the text functions semantically, and the one into which almost all Western song may be placed. In this movement it appears relatively rarely, however. Example 3.12 is taken from shortly after the voice's first entrance (only soprano and steel drum are shown), yet even here a precise definition is not possible. The first half of bar 13 does indeed look like conventional song, with strings and trumpet (not shown) providing an accompaniment. The word *kieli* – Finnish notwithstanding – is intelligible, at least *as a word*, and the soprano's line is distinct from any instrumental part. By the end of bar 13 and going into bar 14, however, these two aspects are less clear. First, the soprano's long extension of *kieli's* vowels across a series of different timbres, concluding with a 'bright tone' that matches that of the steel drum, tilts the text into sound rather than meaning; second, the drums and soprano converge on a unison B♮ at the start of bar 14. As the voice becomes more sound-like, therefore, it also merges in pitch and timbre into the instrumental texture – type C becomes type B.

Example 3.12 *Mother Tongue*, movt I, bars 13–14 (soprano and steel drum only)

In quadrant D, the voice is also closely blended with the instruments, but the meaning of the text in this instance is retained. This may be the next most common type in Western music: a famous example might be the 'Death' section of Schubert's Lied 'Der Tod und das Mädchen', D 531, in which the sounds of voice and piano are almost inseparable (the faster 'Maiden' section is of type C). In *Mother Tongue*, a good example is found at the setting of 'words' in Example 3.13. Obviously, this is a semantically significant moment in Sykes's text, and the instrumental elaboration of the soprano's line is in part intended to draw attention to this. But it also creates a plural perspective, with each instrument a different, heterophonic realisation of the vocal line (or, conversely, the voice just another instrument).

Example 3.13 *Mother Tongue*, movt I, bar 44

In Example 3.14, the speech-like quality of the notation emphasises the sonic character of each word, and the manner in which 'every tongue bathes in every other tongue', as Sykes's poem puts it, as the sound of each word morphs into the next. Only the soprano part is given in the example (strings, flutes and percussion add other effects), but we might describe place this moment in quadrant A: text that is predominantly sonic in character and led by the voice.

Example 3.14 *Mother Tongue*, movt I, bars 179–87

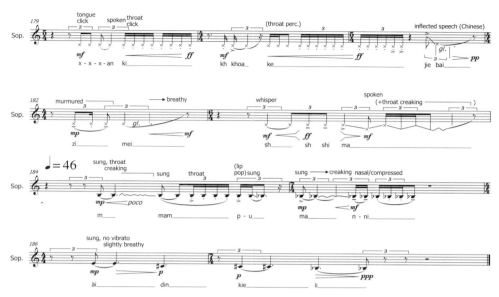

This type is the hardest to identify. First, Lim's frequent entwining of voice and instruments makes moments of voice-as-voice relatively rare; and second, since the vocal part is based in a poetic text, only occasionally can it be completely separated from linguistic meaning. An example of the latter might be the setting of the proto-linguistic *tik*, but as we have seen, even here a trace of semantic meaning is retained; furthermore, as Example 3.10 shows, the soprano in this passage functions as midway between voice and instrument.[7]

As it is, Example 3.14 retains elements of both voice-as-instrument and text-as-meaning. Another possible alternative is offered in Example 3.15, from slightly earlier in the movement. Here, the voice is heard with no instrumental accompaniment, so may be read as purely voice-as-voice (an impression strengthened by the operatic flourish – a fleeting reminiscence of Mozart's 'Queen of the Night' aria? – that is the soprano's rising staccato scale). Moreover, the extension of the vowel of 'my' into pure vocalese, including *jeté*-type effects, reinforces this moment as text-as-sound.

Example 3.15 *Mother Tongue*, movt I, bars 122–5

However, even such a seemingly clear instance is illusory. The soprano's brief solo triggers a rich instrumental passage (the voice continues; an example of type C), which culminates around a dozen bars later with a figure played by steel drum. As we saw in Example 3.12, Lim often connects the steel drum sonically with the voice, and here it picks up the voice's high B♭ (written A♯) from bars 124–5, as well as its rapid staccato articulation. What initially appeared to be an instance of voice alone (type A) is now revealed to be a discontinuous pairing of voice with instrument (type B).

Just as the first movement features relatively few passages in type C, the second and third movements also emphasise certain types. The changing profile in the relationship of voice to text across all three movements reflects the work's larger thematic argument. The second movement, 'latitude of gain', features predominantly types B and D, emphasising the voice-as-instrument half of the diagram. The movement begins with the soprano transforming the word 'in' into a series of sonic effects on the note G♯ (A♭) (type B). Later, Lim introduces a new technique which further emphasises the instrumental quality of the soprano's part in this movement: while continuing to speak or sing, she must beat her chest to a second rhythm, adding a visceral pulse to the sound. This percussive effect is echoed and elaborated by the timpani and double bass, who also make use of unusual techniques of their own.

Example 3.16 *Mother Tongue*, movt II, bars 35–7

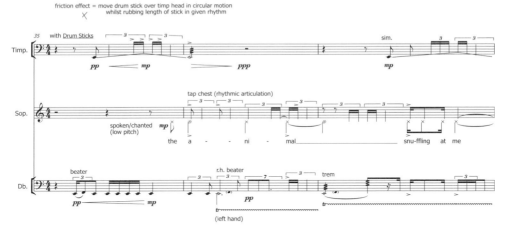

Finally, the movement's focus on the voice-as-instrument culminates in the soprano taking up her cello towards the end of the movement. As she does, and begins to bow the lower strings of her cello (all tuned to F), the work recentres itself on its main pitch. The soprano also sings an unmissable melodic cadence via A♭ onto F. But the arrival of this moment, dramatic as it is in so many respects, is left incomplete by the circular movement of those bows. This device can be traced back to *The Oresteia*, where a singer is also asked play cello (see Chapter 6).

Example 3.17 *Mother Tongue*, movt II, bars 109–11

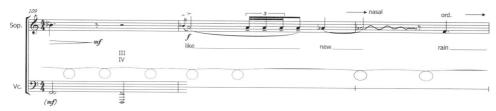

The soprano becoming an instrumentalist adds a new dimension to our analytical model. But it also reinforces its premise that the spectrum between 'voice' and 'instrument' is thematically important. As she so often does, having arrived at a binary position Lim sets out to show how one 'opposing' pole is actually contained within the other. As related examples we might recall the relations of voice and piano in *Voodoo Child*, or voice and *qin* in *The Quickening*. The binary axis, despite my own representation, is in the end more like a circle – note the movement of the soprano's bows! – one of Lim's favourite geometries. As a cycle of birth and regeneration motherhood is, of course, a resonant metaphor for this idea.

Becoming a mother is also a threshold moment in a person's life. And there is a similar sense of transition in how the noise, confusion and movement of the end of the second movement (for all that it is rooted in the F pitch centre) is reborn or reconstituted in the calm of the beginning of the third. Although the musical materials are rather different, the effect – an ending that opens out or exhales into a new or potentially new beginning – recalls the dissolutions into hushed noise that we have seen in the final pages of many earlier and later works and that we will see again. Here, however, we are shown more of what this new beginning is like, with consequences for the work's conclusion.

The differences between the end of the second movement and the beginning of the third (shown in Example 3.18) illustrate the need for novel analytical tools in order to understand Lim's music. A harmonic or pitch-oriented form of analysis, for example, would have recognised little difference between the two passages, both of them grounded as they are in the F–A♭ dyad. The quadrant diagram, however, registers a change from type D at the end of the second movement to type C at the start of the third. This represents a shift from the voice as an instrument to the voice as a voice, alongside a preservation of the semantic use of the text.

Example 3.18 *Mother Tongue*, movt III, bars 1–7

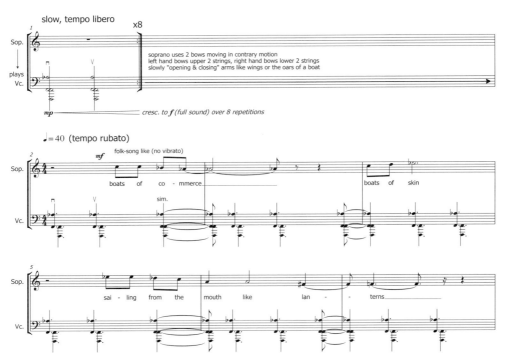

What is more, if the end of 'latitude of gain' represents an extreme case of the voice as an instrument (type D), the beginning of 'longtitude of loss' represents an idealised case of the song-like voice (type C): as Example 3.18 shows, Lim's music here is almost nursery rhyme-like in its simplicity, a pure song like we have not previously encountered.[8] Reflecting the 'birth' of language that took place at the end of the second movement, the music of the third is overwhelmingly of this type, as though the voice has emerged out of the sonic, instrumental and pre-linguistic stew of the first two movements. The striking texture of its opening bars thus sets a template for what follows.

Although it is never quite replicated, that first texture returns twice more, as the 'ritornello' of the movement's rondo-like form. For both returns, the soprano's cello is replaced with a violin whose strings have also been retuned, in a different voicing, to F and A♭ (played by the first violinist). This substitution retains the folk-like drone of the open strings, and the crucial minor third interval, but switches the deep resonance of the cello for the thinner, more fragile sound of the violin. On being born, language – or the child – becomes vulnerable.

At bar 76 and to the end of this section, Lim introduces a randomised metallic tinkling/scraping, a new sound created by the novel technique of swirling two marbles inside the steel drum. She notates this in the same way as she does circular bow movements, with a freehand spiral drawn over the stave; a very particular kind of *Kadenzklang*, the sound resembles the Trés Sois of *Ronda – The Spinning World*, although it was composed ten years before she knew the Smetak instruments. As in that work, the circular motion becomes a way of creating points of sound (the text's 'footprints in the mouth' and 'pinpoints [of] a galaxy'), but it is also an action (the circling marbles) that is inseparable from the sound it makes, an intertwining of the physical and the sonic.

Example 3.19: *Mother Tongue*, movt III, bars 76–81

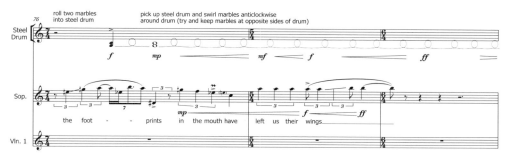

The swirling marbles return a few pages later, now illustrating 'punctuating light / endlessly / at play / with memory and precision' – an image related to the earlier one of the galaxy's pinpoints, but with an aspect of play (childhood) that marbles neatly capture. As so often, Lim is able to realise within a single sonic idea (marbles rolling around inside a steel drum) a complex web of intersecting images and concepts.

By now it is apparent that the F–A♭ minor third that has anchored the work has become a symbol of lament, for lost children and lost languages. After the marbles have come to a stop (yet another image: death and the silencing of language), the soprano sings 'O voice, O instrument / repeat, repeat!' – as neat an encapsulation of the musical techniques in play as one might hope to find – before a final duet of soprano and retuned violin. This time, apart from the minor third (sung twice to the word 'mother' and once to the word 'tongue'), the melody is not closely related to the one that began the movement. More complex, it articulates three descending scales from a high A or A♭ to the F a tenth below, a written-out weeping to which the violin can only sound its minor third drone and a pair of crotales placed upon a timpani skin add wavering, teardrop-like touches. The voice ends with four beats – ten notes in all – on the voiced velar nasal 'ng'.

Produced deep within the body by using the back of the tongue to obstruct the flow of air through the vocal tract, this is the most occluded of all English consonants. At the work's end, even this most widespread of languages 'winds up sounding like an endangered indigenous dialect', as the *New Yorker* critic Alex Ross (2014) puts it. 'Having echoed the origins of language, Lim suggests, at the close, a language becoming extinct'.

Example 3.20 *Mother Tongue*, movt III, bars 138–44

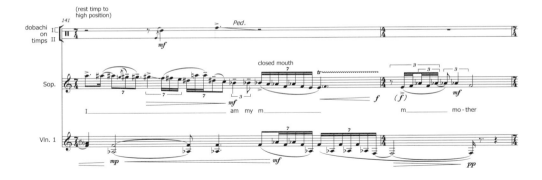

Tongue of the Invisible (2010–11)

As we noted in Chapter 1, Lim began in 2010 a period of association with the Cologne-based ensemble Musikfabrik. The first product of this was the hour-long song cycle *Tongue of the Invisible*. Revisiting a musical relationship first explored in *Voodoo Child*, it pairs the voice (in this case baritone) with piano and ensemble. Written for Musikfabrik's twentieth birthday, it was first performed on 25 June 2011 at Westdeutsche Rundfunk in Cologne, with baritone Omar Ebrahim, pianist Uri Caine and conductor André de Ridder. The involvement of Caine, a jazz specialist, was suggested to Lim by de Ridder, and his abilities as an improviser became central to the work's conception.

Tongue of the Invisible returns to Lim's ongoing fascination with Sufi thought and culture, setting for the first time the poetry of the renowned fourteenth-century Persian poet Hafiz (Khwāja Šamsu d-Dīn Muhammad Hāfez-e Šīrāzī, 1315/17–?1390). His pen name, Hafiz (or Hafez) refers to someone who has memorized the Quran; in one of the semi-mythical stories attached to Hafiz's life, this is a task he is believed to have accomplished at an early age from listening to his father's recitations. He is also believed to have learnt by heart the complete poetry of Rumi, alongside whom is he one of the most admired poets of the Sufistic tradition.

A particular feature of Hafiz's poetry is its extensive use of puns, in which words and images simultaneously convey both human and mystical meanings: his frequent descriptions of love, for example, often described in terms of union with the Beloved, are equally erotic and spiritual. As we have just seen in the examples in *Mother Tongue* of rolling marbles or the soprano's cello, Lim's music is full of sonic equivalents to such puns, and this idea of simultaneity – specifically the simultaneity of physical and spiritual ecstasy – is fundamental to *Tongue of the Invisible*.

Hazif's artful punning makes translation of his poetry notoriously difficult: his words' meanings are not easily captured by the linear organisation of a poem on the page. To get around this problem, Lim commissioned a new translation ('In the Time of the Rose') from the poet and director Jonathan Holmes, who created a 7x7 grid of translated lines across which the reader may trace their own chains of association. For each of the five movements that feature the voice – numbers I, III, IV, VII and VIII – Lim followed wandering paths across the grid to create her text, making longer or shorter strides between squares, returning to some more than once, ignoring others completely, and creating loops, eddies and a dense ball of knotted and entangled threads.

Related to the fluid and multivalent meanings of Hafiz's poetry is *Tongue of the Invisible*'s most characteristic musical feature: its blending of notated music and improvisation. While a lot of the score is fully notated in Lim's typical manner, almost every page features some element of improvisation or performance freedom. These can range from comparatively limited instructions to ornament with or on the given pitches to almost completely open scoring. An example of the latter is the piano solo that makes up movement VI, whose complete notation is given in Example 3.21. Indeed, while the other instrumental parts, notably those for oboe, violin and percussion, all feature indeterminate passages, the piano's is almost entirely improvised.

Example 3.21 *Tongue of the Invisible*, movt VI

There is no completely free improvisation, however. Lim provides various prompts that are intended to elicit a response to either notated or external materials. In order of their increasing distance from the written score, these prompts fall broadly into five categories of indeterminacy:

(1) Materials that are scored at that moment. This is the largest category and includes all those examples where some parameter(s) of the music is/are determined and presented in sequence, while another or others is/are left open. Examples include instructions to ornament freely around a given pitch sequence, instructions to play given material within a certain period of time (time bracket notation) or with free rhythm, graphic notations indicating glissandi etc, and instructions to vary freely the timbre of a drone pitch.

(2) Materials that are performed elsewhere in the ensemble at the same time. In these examples, the musician is not given any material but is instructed to enter into a dialogue with or respond to the notated music of one or more other players.

(3) Materials that have been used earlier in the work. Like category (2), the musician is not given any material at that moment but must improvise using material from a specified passage or movement they have played earlier, as in Example 3.21. In this way they enter into a dialogue with themselves and their own memories, displaced in time.

(4) Materials that are collected in the pitch table in the work's preface. The preface to the score includes a 7x7 grid of pitches (and small pitch collections). In these examples, the musician might have to improvise a melody that traces a path through that grid (analogous to the paths Lim traced through Holmes's Hafiz translation), or to use the grid's pitches to add ornamentation.

(5) Improvised birdsong. This occurs twice in the work, most prominently in the first movement and then again (briefly) in the seventh. Here, only the spirit or character of the improvisation is determined, although on the first occasion Lim also asks that the pitch table is used as a guide, making this an extension of category (4) (Example 3.22).

Example 3.22 *Tongue of the Invisible*, movt I, bars 57–62 (wind and piano)

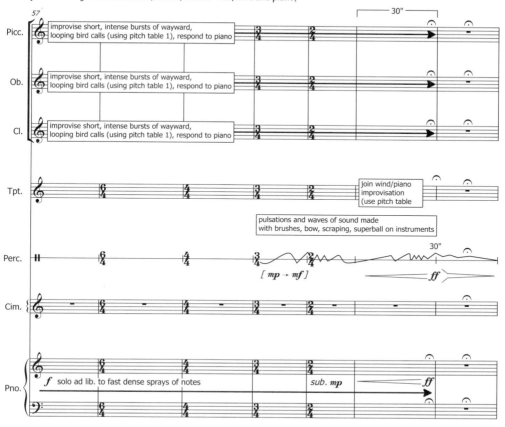

The work begins with a long 'tuning' passage lasting around five minutes, in which the instruments are introduced in cumulative fashion before the first entry of the voice. This prelude illustrates not only a number of these categories of improvisation or indeterminacy but also how they determine forms of interaction and creativity between and amongst the musicians. Example 3.23 shows the second page of the score; that is, minutes three and four of the prelude. The double bass sounds a pedal on the open D string, which it is to play (following a text instruction on the previous page) with changes of bow position, pressure and speed to create 'subtle waves of sound'. Although relatively modest in its scope, this is an example of indeterminacy category (1): the pedal pitch (and its duration) is determined in the score but alterations to its timbre are left free. In the same category are the bracketed notes and chords for brass and wind, although here it is pitch and timbre that are controlled while duration and rhythmic placement are relatively free: the bracketed notes are to be played at any time within the marked bar, somewhat like Cage's time-bracket notation. In combination, these two layers create a harmonic 'bed' for the more elaborate parts, but this is not passive or neutral, but rather continually flickers and changes in response to improvised adjustments in timbre and rhythmic coordination. The more soloistic parts must therefore continually listen to and respond to this unpredictably rippling texture even as they stand apart from it.

Example 3.23 *Tongue of the Invisible*, movt I, bars 7–11

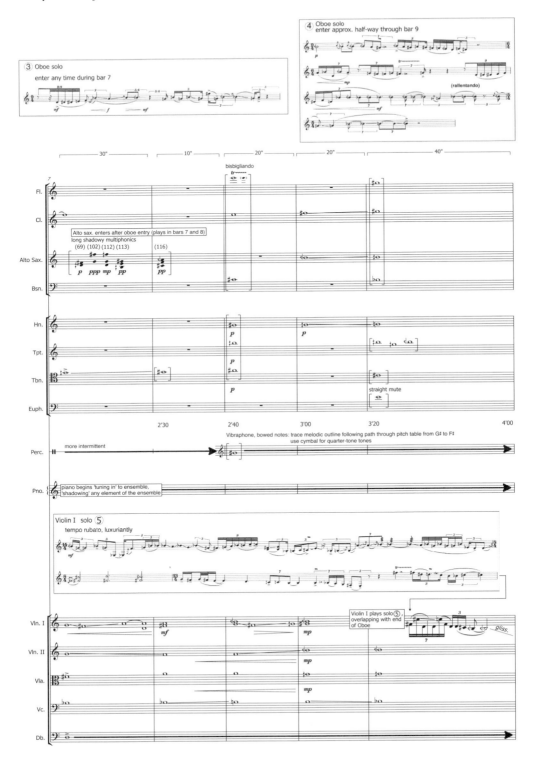

120   The Music of Liza Lim

Although they are more complex, the solos for oboe and violin also belong to category (1): their content is notated in detail but their position in time is somewhat undetermined. The two oboe solos (marked 3 and 4) are given time brackets ('any time during bar 7'; 'approx. half-way through bar 9'), while the violin solo begins some time before the end of the oboe's second. Although each instruments' solos are similar in notation, they play different roles in relation to the ensemble. The oboe is relatively free-floating: as long as it begins its solo within the generous timeframe given, it does not need to worry about coordination with other musicians; in terms of ensemble dynamics, it has to deal only with matters of balance and pacing (which is not to say that these are not important, especially in such an indeterminate context). The violin, however, must play a more integrated role. As well as controlling balance and pacing, it must also overlap its entry with the oboe's second solo (a matter of mutual listening and communication) and, with its final glissando, provide a signal for the unison attack between several instruments that takes place on the first beat of the next bar. Although still somewhat free in terms of duration (it is marked 'tempo rubato, luxuriantly'), it is also suspended between two timepoints that are critical for the rest of the ensemble – the oboe's second solo and the ensemble attack at the start of page 3.

The increased precision and coordination between the entry of the oboe's first (number 3) solo and the end of the violin's mirrors the overall trajectory of the prelude, a process of 'tuning' that outwardly expands the ensemble from the double bass's D pedal and increasingly coordinates its members. For these first few minutes the piano and percussion improvise a version of the same 'tuning' process. Following an instruction on page 1, the percussionist 'tunes' by briefly sounding each of their instruments in turn. Although they do so at their own pace, they must also blend with the rest of the ensemble and contribute to the overall sense of growth and entanglement. On page 2, the pianist enters in much the same way, but with the additional instruction to 'shadow' other members of the ensemble: an instance of category (2). Where the percussionist began the first page somewhat independently, by the second page the pianist is more tightly woven into the ensemble texture. For the second half of this page the percussionist abandons the tuning process to trace a melodic path through the pitch grid on vibraphone and cymbal: an instruction that is more determinate with regard to pitch and timbre but still indeterminate with regard to the rhythm or sequence of events (within the limitations of the pitch grid). This example of category (4) grants the percussionist a secondary soloistic role that is simultaneous with but rather different from those of the oboe and violin, and whose relationship to the rest of the ensemble is less precisely determined.

A different set of relationships is established in movement V. Apart from the piano solo of movement VI, this is the one in which indeterminacy is furthest to the fore. It takes the form of a miniature concerto grosso for oboe, percussion and strings. The oboe's solo part is in nine sections, of between two and seven bars. These are notated inside separate numbered boxes (compare the last movement of *How Forests Think*), to be played in sequence but freely placed in time and with pauses between each. This is a form of category (1) indeterminacy similar to the oboe and violin solos at the start of the first movement, and indeed the oboe's part here draws on similar material. The percussionist accompanies with brief 'commentaries' (category (2)), using fingers and brushes on drums, cymbals and cowbells. Their part is unnotated except for the eighth box, which is written out; an attacca hand drum solo (improvised) connects the eighth and ninth boxes, and the percussion continues to improvise using the hand drum until the end of the ninth box. Beneath these two solo parts, the strings improvise an accompanying 'garland' using a sequence of nine pitch collections, played very quietly and based upon the stylistic, rhythmic and gestural qualities of the oboe part (category (2), although with aspects of the pitch-grid reference of (4)).

Passages like these two illustrate the role of 'distributed' creativity in the performance of *Tongue of the Invisible*: that is, a process of co-creation that replaces the hierarchical relationship of composer to performer with a more cooperative, collaborative model of equal partners. In itself this is nothing new: composer-performer collaboration has been a feature of concert music since the aleatory and open-form experiments of the 1950s avant-garde, and in many forms of music outside the concert hall it is the norm. What is striking about Lim's approach in *Tongue of the Invisible*, however, is not that she gives creative agency to her players – like Cage does, for example, in his *Concert for Piano and Orchestra* – but how she enmeshes it within a larger aesthetic project.

In their study of the distributed creativity of *Tongue of the Invisible* – and the collaboration with Musikfabrik by which it came about – Eric Clarke, Mark Doffman and Lim note how themes in Hafiz's poetry invited a 'structural openness' to the process of composition by which the ensemble performers might 'in some way "live" the spiritual ideas rather than merely [represent] them'; indeterminacy is not used, therefore, in opposition to composition, but as a way to activate or enable 'different "threshold states" in the performers that might resonate with the world of the poetry' (Clarke, Doffman and Lim 2013, 633). They identify three main concepts in Hafiz's poetry that are explored in Lim's music: 'attunement', 'bewilderment and entanglement', and 'ecstasy' (635). The five categories of musical indeterminacy that I list above cannot be straightforwardly mapped onto these, but instead open pathways by which those concepts might be realised. Category (2), for example, might pair with the concept of attunement, for example – two or more instruments meeting one another in a dialogue. But likewise, an improvised response to another player might lead to bewilderment or entanglement in the form of diverging or contrasting music. Similarly, a melodic pathway chosen through the pitch grid (category (4)) might merge acoustically with the rest of the ensemble, but in itself it is a form of entangled wandering; 'rather than belonging to a single thematic category', Clarke, Doffman and Lim observe, 'most sections of the work are characterized by overlapping and interacting attributes, played out simultaneously'. In this way, Lim's familiar fluid aesthetic is realised at the level of performer–performer, performer–composer and performer–score interactions.

It is notable the extent to which Lim's choice of text drives her aesthetic approach to *Tongue of the Invisible*: the pattern of Hafiz's poetry – not only its themes of longing and union, but also its wandering structure, punning wordplay, improvised webs of connection and branching, entangling threads – informs the pattern of Lim's setting. This might also be said of all the works in this chapter: that in her works for voice, Lim is not interested in setting works for their imagery or their drama, but instead uses texts to establish guiding concepts in much the same way as she approaches writing for a particular instrument. Her music is not completely without word-painting – Hafiz's drunken night time wandering between temple and tavern is amply represented in the meandering paths of *Tongue of the Invisible*, for example – but far more important is the creation of a musical analogue, as opposed to a setting, of those texts.

References

Brindeau, Véronique (2005). 'Parole et musique, entretien avec Liza Lim'. *Accents* 27 (October/December). English translation available at https://limprogrammenotes.files.wordpress.com/2011/08/mother-tongue-lim-interview-with-veronique-brindeau.pdf.

Clarke, Eric, Mark Doffman and Liza Lim (2013). 'Distributed Creativity and Ecological Dynamics: A Case Study of Liza Lim's "Tongue of the Invisible"'. *Music & Letters* v94 n4: 628–63.

Lim, Liza (2005). *The Quickening, 2004–05* [programme note], https://limprogrammenotes.wordpress.com/2011/07/31/the-quickening-2005/.

Rosman, Carl (1999). 'Wie gelähmt die Zunge, Fieber unter der Haut … Prozesse in Liza Lims *Voodoo Child*'. *Musik & Ästhetik* v11: 30–47.

Ross, Alex (2014). 'Singing in Tongues: Two Song Cycles by Liza Lim'. *The New Yorker*, 21 April.

Endnotes

1 Conversation with the author, June 2020.

2 Lim originally had a different poem in mind and the work was to be called *Diabolical Birds* (Rosman 1999). That title was later given to a different work, however, for piccolo, bass clarinet, piano, violin, cello and vibraphone (1990). This was recorded by Ensemble für Neue Musik Zürich on Hat[now]Art 148 (2000) but was later withdrawn.

3 Details taken from: https://en.wikipedia.org/wiki/Guqin_playing_technique.

4 These designations are my own. Interestingly, the fact that the genders commonly ascribed to them are the inverse of the genders of the children to whom the respective works are dedicated harmonises with the principles of balance enshrined by *yin* and *yang* rather than undermines them.

5 Although it was at this point very nearly extinct, Yorta Yorta, the language of an Aboriginal people from northeast Victoria, has since been revived. Sixty-two speakers were identified in the 2016 census. The fragility of languages like this is due to assimilationist colonial policies that forbid people from practising their own language and culture, with the purpose of destroying those Indigenous societies. The romantic trope of a 'dying culture' is a legacy of those policies, the work of language revival is an important counter to Western notions of helplessly conquered Indigenous peoples. (Adapted from email correspondence with Lim, August 2021.)

6 In June 2021 N|u had only one surviving native speaker.

7 This example – so critical to the themes of the work – may in fact represent the midpoint of the diagram, where the two axes cross.

8 Moments of such melodic clarity are rare in Lim's music. A short passage in the middle of *The Heart's Ear* is an earlier example; a later one is the use of the actual nursery rhyme 'Twinkle Twinkle Little Star' in her piano concerto, World as Lover, World as Self. This quotation is associated with the campaign to release the four-year-old Tharnicaa Murugappan and her family from an Australian detention centre, where they have been held since Tharnicaa was nine months old. The song is a favourite of Tharnicaa's.

Chapter 4

Music for installations

Installations have been a feature of the visual arts since the late 1950s, when the American artist Allan Kaprow began making what he termed 'environments' – large-scale artworks that extended beyond the plinth or the gallery wall to occupy entire spaces. As other artists started to explore similar ideas, such works came to be known as 'installations'. Conceived as all-encompassing experiences, installations often make use of sound, film and lighting, as well as objects (either found or made) and the architecture of the exhibition space itself. In contrast to sculptural or pictorial art, installations are not displayed alongside other works, but are complete, unified environments. Often viewers must walk around or through an installation in order to take in every aspect of it. There is usually not a single ideal viewing point, and an important aspect of installation art is the freedom this grants the viewer to take in the complete work at their own pace and in their own sequence.

Although installations frequently feature sound (indeed, Kaprow's first environment included five tape machines playing electronic sounds), the open-ended, non-linear form of installation art presents a challenge to composers of notated music. Traditionally written for listeners occupying a single, idealised listening position (whether in a concert hall or on hi-fi speakers at home) and passively attentive from the beginning of a work to its end, concert music is not naturally suited to the more active installation environment.

In the late twentieth century, however, less linear conceptions of music emerged from the serial, experimental and minimal practices of the 1950s to 1970s that paralleled the rise of installation art. Although John Cage's multimedia works, such as *Musicircus* (1967) and *HPSCHD* (1967–9), were not called installations at the time, they were important precursors; so too were the presentations of music and film created at the San Francisco Tape Music Center by Pauline Oliveros, Ramon Sender, Morton Subotnick and Tony Martin. More recently, other notated composers have turned to installation work. Yet the challenges remain of composing for a 'decentred' space with no single focal point (despite the presence of one or more live musicians), and no privileged route through the music (despite it being written down in a linear fashion).

Among her generation of composers – particularly those whose music is so highly detailed in its notation – Lim has contributed to an unusual number of installation works (see Table 5.1). Her relative comfort in this format speaks to the multi-perspectival and interdisciplinary character of her work. However, documentation of these ephemeral, site-specific creations is limited. This chapter focuses on the four installations she made with Domenico de Clario between 1994 and 1996: *Afterward: From a Tower (a translation)*, the two versions of *Bardo'i-thos-grol (The Tibetan Book of the Dead)*, and *The Cauldron – Fusion of the 5 Elements*. Documentation for these may be found in the book *The Intertwining – The Chasm*, published in 1998 by the Institute for Modern Art, Brisbane, which includes photographs, writings by the artists, site plans and other items. The CD that accompanies the book features extracts (lasting between five and thirty-three minutes) of music played during the two installations of *Bardo* in 1994 and 1995. However, no scores exist (or were made) for these works beyond broad instructions to the performers, who used these as a basis for improvisation, and no complete recordings are available. This makes detailed analysis like that found in the other chapters of this book impossible. With that in mind, this chapter leans upon the composer's own recollections as well as the materials contained in the IMA book and CD.

Title	Description[1]	Artist	Musician(s)	Location	Date
Afterward: From a Tower (a translation)	Seven-night vigil	Domenico de Clario	Jeannie van de Velde, Deborah Kayser, Andrew Muscat-Clark, Carl Rosman (voices)	Auburn Uniting Church, Melbourne	1994
Bardo'i-thos-grol	Seven-night performance cycle	Domenico de Clario	ELISION	Hillside Auto Dismantlers and Summerland Demolitions, Lismore, New South Wales	1994
Bardo'i-thos-grol	Seven-night performance cycle	Domenico de Clario	ELISION	Midland Railway Workshops, Perth	1995
The Cauldron – Fusion of the 5 Elements	Two-part meditation	Domenico de Clario	ELISION	Northcote Uniting Church, Melbourne (May) and Institute of Modern Art, Brisbane (September)	1996
Sonorous Bodies	Video installation with koto	Judith Wright	Satsuki Odamura (koto)	Brisbane City Gallery	1999
Glasshouse Mountains	Video, sculptural, sound installation	Judy Watson (artist), Michael Hewes (sound design)	Rosanne Hunt (cello)	Institute of Modern Art, Brisbane	2005
TON	'scena' for mobile sculptures, audience and musicians	Sabrina Hoelzer (concept), Volker Maerz (artist)	ELISION	Elisabethkirche, Invalidenstrasse, Berlin	2008
Escalier du Chant	Architectural interventions with performance; 'songs' by twelve composers, incl. Lim	Olaf Nicolai	Neue Vocalsolisten Stuttgart	Pinakothek der Moderne, Munich	2011

Table 5.1 Liza Lim: installation works

Domenico de Clario

Born in Trieste, Italy in 1947, the artist Domenico de Clario immigrated to Australia in 1956. After studies in architecture and town planning, painting, lithography and art at the University of Melbourne (1966–9), the Accademia di Belle Arti di Brera in Milan (1967–8), the Accademia di Belle Arti di Urbino (1968) and the Preston Institute of Technology Melbourne (1973–5), he taught art at the Royal Melbourne Institute of Technology from 1973 to 1996.

Among de Clario's colleagues at RMIT was the architect Peter Corrigan, who in 1993 worked with Lim on the stage design for *The Oresteia*. Through him she was introduced to de Clario at his installation *Components of an Expression Machine*, which was installed at three sites around Melbourne in 1993; *The Oresteia*'s director Barrie Kosky was also there. Meetings like these, Lim says, were characteristic of the close-knit Melbourne arts scene at the time, in which poets, artists, musicians and directors were all friends and neighbours of each other. Such a free-flowing cultural milieu enabled and inspired the multidisciplinary character of Lim's early works like *The Oresteia* and *Garden of Earthly Desire*. It also fostered the willingness to just try things out that led to *Afterward, Bardo* and *The Cauldron*, and that is ELISION's principal *modus operandi*.

Prior to his collaborations with Lim, de Clario had developed an artistic practice working with lights, non-gallery spaces, long durations and principles derived from south Asian spiritualism and meditation. His sites were chosen, and sometimes accessed, in a guerrilla-like fashion: abandoned and off-limits places within the city, whose spiritual energies he would map out using coloured lamps (in the sequence red, orange, yellow, green, blue, violet, white) according to the seven chakras of Hindu tradition: sacral/root, spleen, solar plexus, heart, throat, brow and crown. Once a site had been chosen, nothing was disturbed. Nothing was moved, altered or cleaned up. De Clario simply placed his lamps in such a way as to reveal (through gradations of colour, intensities of light and shadow, and more elusive associations with the spiritual and the emotional) something already there that was otherwise hidden, a process Lim describes as witnessing. The installations made with Lim drew on the same techniques and principles; as the two artists write, 'The basic premise of these projects was a belief that the "work" was already in existence, in the invisible "essential" world. Our task was to bring it forward, to work with catalysts for manifesting it in the visible, "experiential" plane' (de Clario and Lim 1998, 19).

Afterward: From a Tower (a translation) (1993)

The origin of *Afterward: From a Tower* is 'From a Tower' by the Italian poet Eugenio Montale, from his collection *Afterward*, published in 1956 as part of the volume *The Storm and Other Things*. Inspired by this text, of which he made his own translation into English, de Clario created in October 1993 a light and performance installation at his home in Northcote, Melbourne. The second, larger version of *Afterward*, with Lim as co-creator, adds a musical component that brings together sound, text, light and architecture into a unified conception, guided by Montale's words.

As a location for this second version, Lim and de Clario chose Auburn Uniting Church, in the Melbourne suburb of Hawthorn, a few streets away from where Lim lived at the time. Designed by the young architect Alfred Dunn and built in 1888–9, the church is constructed in the Lombardy Romanesque style exemplified by eleventh-century buildings such as Parma Cathedral and the Basilica of Sant'Ambrogio in Milan, and it is distinctive for its banded red and brown brickwork and for the bell tower on its southwest corner.

This tower is one of the tallest features in the area, offering commanding views from Melbourne's CBD to the west to the Dandenong Ranges to the east. It is narrow and may be climbed by a series of wooden staircases and ladders. Small landings between these stairs divide the tower into seven ascending levels, which de Clario aligned with the seven chakras. Coloured lights at each level, in the sequence described above, marked out these seven stages, with the red sacral chakra at the bottom of the tower and the white crown chakra at the top.

In creating music for the installation, Lim found a sonic analogue to de Clario's 'witnessing' lights in Alvin Lucier's experiments with the resonant frequencies of rooms. She noticed that the resonant frequency of the tower corresponded to the fundamental pitch C. By setting a microphone to feedback inside the tower, she was able to activate that fundamental frequency whenever anyone entered the space, thus audifying, as it were, its hidden acoustic properties. The microphone was placed in the room just below the observation deck, in the violet brow chakra. (The crown chakra above it could be accessed by a precarious ladder up running up through the wooden ceiling.) Four singers occupied the same landing. Instructed to tune to the resonant frequency, they would then improvise upon the partials of that harmonic spectrum, using the Italian syllables of Montale's poem as a guide, and thus giving a physical body to the sound and its overtones.

Afterward was installed from Palm Sunday on 27 March 1994 to Easter Sunday on 3 April. Performances were given at 5:56pm on the first Sunday, marking the rise of the full moon over Melbourne, and at 11:57pm a week later, marking the setting of the half moon. For the first performance, the singers drew on the first half of Montale's poem, and for the second one they drew on its second half. In between the two performances the lights and microphone of the installation remained switched on and received many visitors throughout the week; Lim and de Clario sat on the ground floor of the tower every evening. 'It was significant during Holy Week that the space was activated and people who had long not visited or had never been inside popped in and told us all kinds of stories about their lives and the area', Lim says. 'This, for me, was always the most moving part of these projects and Domenico's practice – that the offering of "witness" really did activate something in the place and people: the church as pilgrimage point again, the meaning of place and time to people, and so on.'[2]

In its straightforward conception – without any of the visible intricacy or craft by which we usually define the work of composition – *Afterward* caused Lim to think about her own identity as a composer. 'It's so simple, anyone can do it, of course,' she explained to me. 'But what the work is, is not any of those things. It's the experience that happens when people came to this tower that had not been entered for a very long time. And extraordinary numbers of people just rocked up, because they were attracted by this beautiful light. And it was about storytelling, this permission, this space in which people felt they had permission to share very intimate stories about who they are and what was meaningful to them. That was the work.'[3]

Bardo'i-thos-grol (The Tibetan Book of the Dead) (1994 and 1995)

Crucially, Lim knew the four singers who performed *Afterward* very well: a year before, Jeannie van de Velde, Deborah Kayser and Andrew Muscat-Clark had all sung in *The Oresteia*. Indeed, the sixth scene of that opera, which makes use of overtone singing, was written specifically for Muscat-Clark.[4] Kayser is one of Lim's most frequent and inspirational performers, a school friend from PLC who she has described as her 'soul sister' (Lim n.d.). Carl Rosman ('my spirit animal') she also knew through ELISION; although principally a clarinettist he also performs as a vocalist (most notably in Richard Barrett's *interference*, in which a solo contrabass clarinettist is also required to sing over a five-octave range). Like a jazz bandleader, Lim extracted the material of her work out of the relationships she already had with her musicians: 'It's just made as a consequence of longer pathways', she says, an observation that might also be made of many of her notated works.

This simultaneous witnessing of performing individuals and the site itself is developed in the two creations of *Bardo'i-thos-grol (The Tibetan Book of the Dead)*, featuring and co-created by members of ELISION. In 1994 the work was installed at two adjacent wrecking yards in Lismore, New South Wales: Hillside Auto Dismantlers and Summerland Demolitions. A year later it was installed at Midland Railway Workshops in Perth, as part of the Festival of Perth. On both occasions the work comprised seven two-hour performances spread across seven nights, drawing upon the same sequence of colours and chakras as used for *Afterward*. Each performance began an hour or two later than the last, so that while the first one started at sunset on the first day, the last ended at sunrise on the seventh. For Lismore, the musicians were Carolyn Connors, Kayser and Muscat-Clark (voice), Jennifer Curl (viola), Rosanne Hunt (cello), Tim O'Dwyer (saxophones) and Rosman (clarinets), with sound engineer Jim Atkins. For Perth, they were Hunt, Kayser, Muscat-Clark, Chris Lockhart Smith (cello), O'Dwyer and Rosman, with Michael Hewes (sound). Except for night three, which on both occasions was given to a solo by O'Dwyer, the full ensemble was involved on each night, with different members of the group serving as the focus of that performance.

For both installations, each performance was given in a different part of their respective sites, following a roughly circular route through seven locations. Audiences coming on any night were led progressively through the areas in which performances had already taken place, with coloured lighting still in place, so that the sense of a continuing journey was clear. Over the course of its realisation, therefore, the work traced multiple overlaid cycles: from sunset to sunrise, through the days of the week and the seven chakras, and around a circuit around a defined space and amongst an ensemble of soloists.

Like *Afterward*, *Bardo* also took account of the time between performances when listeners were not attending and when no music was being made. In this case, this time comprised the six approximately twenty-four periods between the end of one performance and the beginning of the next. In Lim and de Clario's conception these periods are the bardos, or 'betweens', which, in Tibetan Buddhism, mark the soul's transitional states between death and rebirth. *The Tibetan Book of the Dead* describes six of these, which in *Bardo'i-thos-grol* correspond to the six periods between musical performances; in this way the Book is not set as a narrative drama but is used as a set of structural principles that generate the form of the work. Audience members were thus invited to continue experiencing the piece during their daily lives over the work's week-long duration – or, conversely, to incorporate their lives into its unfolding. As de Clario has described it, 'By extending the inclusive framing as widely as each of us can, the "work" allows us an opportunity to re-define the seamlessness of the art-experience/life-experience landscape. The "work's" potential is not activated until the moment the audience participates by walking through the chakra-sites and, later, by venturing back into each life-frame' (de Clario and Lim 1998, 39). Many audience members attended more than one of the week's performances and so had a sense of this continuity and transition between life and work; a few braved the cold night-time temperatures and experienced the work across its entirety.

One of the most important decisions in making the two *Bardo* installations was choosing the sites: the more emotionally resonant the site, the more powerful the work could be. The two chosen locations were dramatically evocative and thematically connected to the subject of death and rebirth. The wrecking yards in Lismore were chosen with the help of Lyndon Terracini – currently artistic director of Opera Australia but at that time artistic director of Northern Rivers Performing Arts, which he founded in 1993. NORPA supported the work's first installation and Terracini knew the owners of the two yards. 'They were just fabulous people who didn't know what we were doing but were really open', says Lim. A large part of the appeal of using the yards was the chance to witness the stories that were preserved in the piles of junk being dismantled and sorted for reuse or recycling. At the car wreckers, many of the cars were just simply old, but some, very sadly, had been involved in accidents, and the potency of these objects for capturing stories was very powerful. 'It was a big site', recalls Lim.

> The musicians would just wander, exploring the site and finding these bashed-up cars, and they would find children's toys, just awful, poignant stories held there. This is why the Bardo was so relevant, because you're looking at people's memories and stories, and the passage of life and death. And they're recycling as well, so it's rebirth. The house-wreckers' yard was a demolition yard, and you had huge expanses of windows and doors and toilet fittings, it was all there. And again this sense of people's lives. Seeing doors with notches where people have marked their kids' height, thinking about how many people have entered and exited … hugely poetic. And then these things waiting to be recycled into their next life: you see how the site was such an important part of the meaning of the work. For people who came, because they were just from the local area, that was very meaningful because this was part of their history.[5]

Midland Railway Workshops in Perth was the first railway workshop in Western Australia. Originally located in Fremantle it relocated to the eastern Perth suburb of Midland in 1904, where it occupied a vast 250-acre site, manufacturing engines and rolling stock for the Western Australian Government Railways.[6] In 1994, despite a year of protests, the workshops were controversially closed by the Western Australian state government, with the loss of more than 700 jobs.[7] In 1995, the site was as if frozen at the last moment of its working life: 'people had just walked off the job and left their stuff exactly as it was', recalls Lim. 'So again, there was this sense of an in-between space containing such powerful life moments and energies.'[8]

Nevertheless, the relocation of the work required a re-imagining of its meanings. As de Clario writes:

> The entire Workshops can be perceived as the physical body: the steel mesh compound in which the *Bardo* takes place can be perceived as the 'essential' body within; the specific Workshop buildings and their associated former functions act as the Chakras – [Root Chakra/red/generators; Spleen/orange/water-towers; Solar Plexus/yellow/coppershop/hearth; Heart/green/panel shop; Throat/blue/sand-shed; Brow/violet/steel-shop; Crown/white/Powerhouse]; the performers as the Indestructible Drop that carries 'clear-white of awareness-transmitting substances' (transmutation point energies). The chants/sounds/colours carry the manifestations of this indestructible drop through their vibratory rates as they increase in frequency from chakra to chakra, from the red, (lowest in frequency) to the white (highest). Finally the audience provides the *Ida-Pingala* energy current as they walk through the Chakra pathway. (De Clario and Lim 1998, 47. Punctuation as in original.)

'¬*Ida-Pingala*' is a reference to the paired currents of energy that in yogic teaching form a loop connecting the seven chakras up and down the body: *Ida* (female, moon, *yin*) and *Pingala* (male, sun, *yang*). These energies were instigated by the two electrical generators that formed the location for the first night of the installation, and completed their circuit with the two giant compressors, which once provided high pressure air to the whole site that formed the site of the seventh night.

The music for both installations of *Bardo'i-thos-grol* took the form of extended ensemble improvisations (or solo, in the case of O'Dwyer's night three performances) based on Tibetan chants drawn from the *dbyangs-yig*, or songbook, of seventy-nine chants used in tantric rites and written down from memory by the Lama Senge Norbu of the *Karma-pa* Buddhist sect.[9] These chants were to be used in a seven-day ritual similar to that of *Bardo'i-thos-grol*: '"When performed in succession the songs contained in the book were begun at midnight and would end, after numerous repetitions, seven days later." … As the texts of the *yang-yig* often appeal to various terror deities and the songs become part of the "terror rites", the night is the most appropriate time for their performance' (Kaufmann 1975, quoting Lama Senge Norbu).

The scores chosen from the *dbyangs-yig* served as prompts for improvisational exercises out of which the music for the installation was developed, and each selected chant was connected to what de Clario and Lim felt were the particular energies of each stage of the work. When they were working on *Bardo*, Lim and ELISION based themselves in Byron Bay, a centre for alternative and spiritual lifestyles in New South Wales. This cultural context fed into the process of creating the work: yoga and meditation exercises were used in rehearsals, as well as intense listening and tuning techniques. There is a parallel here – as there is in *Afterward* – with the Deep Listening practices of the American composer Pauline Oliveros (1932–2016), although Lim did not know much of her work at the time.

Extracts from four of the resulting improvisations are preserved on the CD that accompanies *The Intertwining – The Chasm*.[10] The performances are raw, primal, magma-like. In their slow evolution and amorphous shape, they are superficially very different from Lim's notated music. Yet they share a similar fixation on penetrating, deconstructing and reforming sound. The recording of O'Dwyer's night three solo ('Invocation: intensely sad song to all protectors of religion') from Perth unfurls an unbroken stream of rapid, descending figures that over the course of five minutes progresses from a lyrically bubbling brook to a high-pressure jet expelled from the highest register of the instrument. 'Song invoking demons and devils; prayer song to Mgon Po suppressing evil', a twenty-four-minute extract from night five in Perth, begins with long vocal drones by Rosman and Muscat-Clark, featuring overtone singing and extreme depths of range. These are picked up by Lockhart Smith's cello, which explores new dimensions to the sound, while adding harder breaks and punctuations within it with changes and rearticulations of the bow. After seven minutes the voices add new pitches; this precipitates a slow relinquishing of the original drone and the occupation of a different sonic territory of higher, scratchier sounds led by the cello. Towards the end of the recording, the sustained sounds begin to fracture – now led by O'Dwyer's saxophone – into points and short bursts of sound, maintaining the chant-like texture and geological pace of change, but reconfigured across a different musical texture, as though the original deep voices have been turned inside out.

The longest extract, the thirty-three-minute 'Mantra song concerning offerings', features the complete ensemble recorded on night six of the Perth installation. It begins with a strident bass clarinet solo reminiscent of the long *dungchen* trumpet used in traditional Tibetan music, which moves (like O'Dwyer's night three extract, above) from the instrument's lowest to highest registers. When they enter, cellos and voices begin a long sequence of listening and tuning around Ab. Around the twelve-minute mark this centred sound begins to unravel into separate threads that slowly coil around each other like smoke, and which continue in this way until the end of the recording.

As the extract proceeds, the players stretch the space within which they maintain their attunement to one another and to their environment, finding points of connection beyond the shared Ab and between different pitches, timbres and figurations. This structural principle provides a point of contact between the music of *Bardo* and Lim's notated music. In our previous analyses, we have come to see Lim's works in terms of spaces defined by a number of different parameters (ranges of timbres, pitches, instrumental relations and so on) whose boundaries are explored and stretched over the course of the composition. To take an example we have discussed in detail, *Mother Tongue* is – on one level at least – an expression of the space created by the axes of voice and instrument, and semantic and non-semantic text. Different moments within it are expressions of different points on that two-dimensional map. While these moments are distinct in themselves, they also reflect the overall conception of which they are part, just as one mountain also expresses the range to which it belongs, or one painting connects with the others with which it is exhibited. Likewise, the improvised threads followed

CHAPTER 4: Music for installations   133

by each of the *Bardo* players reflect different configurations or expressions of the central resonance or attunement of players and environment, turning a single starting pitch into long lines of sound, *Kadenzklangen* on the scale of whole movements. As the music unfolds, the complete potential of these points is revealed.

The challenge of creating and sustaining a two-hour improvisation was fundamental to the form of each performance within *Bardo*. As the improvisations proceeded, fatigue would become a factor, until late into the performance a breakthrough would be reached. The physical struggle is essential to the revelation that follows. 'It's very different from "Here's a thing that you perform"', Lim explains. 'It's very experiential: here's a journey that we're going through, and each person brings whatever they have. And the presence of the audience was very important, the fact that people came night after night into the freezing cold.' One such moment is captured in the recording of 'Song of compassion' from night four of the Lismore performance, a spell-binding aria improvised by Deborah Kayser and accompanied by Jennifer Curl and Rosanne Hunt that is made more remarkable by the knowledge that it was created between midnight and 2am in a remote demolition yard on a cold September night. It is impossible to recreate the full impact of moments like these – you really did have to be there, huddled around the fire with your hat pulled down over your ears. But something of their magic, and that of the whole of *Bardo*, can still be heard in performances like this, moments when something entirely unexpected arises from the coming together of artists' lives and friendships, long rehearsal processes, the preservation of memories and the innate resonances of a site.

The Cauldron — Fusion of the 5 Elements (1996)

The third and final collaboration between Lim and de Clario stretched still further the ideas of discontinuous cycles, long duration performance and site-specific ritual. A two-part performance work staged on two full moon nights, *The Cauldron* comprised a fourteen-hour performance from sunset to sunrise on 3 May 1996 at Northcote Uniting Church, Melbourne, and a twelve-hour performance from sunset to sunrise on 27 September 1996 at the Institute of Modern Art, Brisbane. The performers were Kirsten Boerma (voice), de Clario (retuned electric piano), Kayser, Lockhart Smith and Rosman for the May performance, and Kayser, Lockhart Smith, O'Dwyer and Rosman for the September one, with de Clario and Lim performing a movement ritual.

The title comes from a hexagram of the *I Ching* known as the cauldron, a vessel for alchemical change, for fusing elements, or for generating physical and spiritual nourishment. As de Clario and Lim further explain:

> *The Cauldron* is the I Ching's image of alchemical transformation and guides a cyclic process of integration of five phases of energy – described as water, wood, fire, metal, earth. When the dimension of time is taken into account, the interaction of these five elements can be seen to take place not on a linear plane but, rather, within a spherical vortex (cauldron).

In the hexagram, the first dark line (yin) [the broken line at the bottom of the figure] moves upwards through the light [unbroken] lines (yang), returning again to the dark at the fifth place and moving towards the light at the top of the hexagram. Thus over the six lines of the hexagram a spiral movement is described in which a continuing cycle of change is brought to life by the alteration of polarities. The property of the spiral's path is that the movement of return is also the continuation. The spiral is a continuum whose ends are opposite and yet the same. It contains the phases of contraction and expansion. (de Clario and Lim 1998, 62–3)

The overall conception of *The Cauldron* was more complicated than either *Afterward* or *Bardo*. The performance at the IMA, for example, incorporated several features in addition to the players and lighting. In one corner of the room was an illuminated 'tabernacle space' representing the five elements; this was connected electrically to a '5-element matrix-chandelier' suspended in the centre of the room. Also at the centre, on the floor, was a 'lunar clock' divided into twelve hours, around which the performers moved over the course of the night. Every hour the lighting circuit was dimmed, demarcating 'junctures of stillness' similar to the dividing concept of the bardos in *Bardo'i-thos-grol*. The music comprised improvisations upon different sounds associated with the five elements.

Linking and structuring these various elements was a complex symbolical and numerological system based upon Chinese astrology and the *I Ching*: the dualism of yin and yang, the five elements and five major organs of the body (kidneys, liver, heart, lungs and spleen), the six healing sounds of Taoist meditation and six lines of the hexagram, and the twelve hours of the clock. On top of this, the musicians made use of microtonal scales provided by Lim based on a Chinese tuning system of twelve modes of five notes each, numbers linked explicitly to the lunar months, the hours of the clock, and the number of elements.

Looking back, Lim remembers these performances as 'really, really hard'.[11] This is partly due to the durations involved, but also, one might guess, because of their less elegant conceptualisation in comparison to *Afterward* and *Bardo*; she thinks of *Afterward* as 'the best of those pieces, because it was the simplest!'. And while the first two installations were less about the performances than they were about how they framed an experience (over the course of a week) for those people who saw them, the long duration of time (and geographical distance) between the two halves of *The Cauldron*, as well as the intricacy and length of the performances themselves, somewhat diluted this feature of the work that Lim found most attractive.

After *The Cauldron*, Lim moved to Queensland and she and de Clario produced no more work together. De Clario continued to work with ELISION, making work with O'Dwyer in particular. And the group staged further installation projects, seeing them as a valuable way to generate creative partnerships with other artists: important examples include *Opening of the Mouth* and *DARK MATTER* by composer Richard Barrett, with the artists CROW (Richard Crow) and Per Ingo Bjørlo, and *TULP the body public* by composer John Rodgers and artist Justine Cooper.

Impact

Lim's creative process always begins with the people who are in the room: their qualities, skills and personalities; the things they can make their instruments or voices do; and their relationships to the composer and to each other. Although she is unlikely to have had this metaphor in mind when making the installation works of the mid-1990s (the ground-breaking research by biologist Suzanne Simard that inspired the term 'wood-wide web' was not published until 1997[12]), the entangled webs out of which these works are made are mycelial in form: dense networks of connections across which creativity and responsibility are shared and which make use of and transform what is available to them (soil, plants, climate; people, instruments, spaces). Like a fruiting fungus, Lim's work grows from such ecologies. This way of working is radically different from that of the stereotypical composer creating their work in isolation and then finding the resources to bring it about: compare the tuning and listening practices of the de Clario installations with those of Stockhausen's *Stimmung*, a composition that is by comparison placed fully formed into its environment rather than allowed to emerge from it. Lim's works arise as thought from 'a process of growth', rather than as the end products of a project (Ingold 2013, 20–21).

The four installation projects with de Clario came out of an extended process of co-creation, a way of working she found extremely satisfying. 'It was so fulfilling to make this work where there was no score, or a very minimal score', she says. 'You worked directly with the musicians, just as a choreographer might with dancers, making the work *on* and *with* people. My role as a composer was as a listener, a dramaturg – that's working well, let's do more of this, let's see how we can extend that – providing that kind of discussion. It was making, as opposed to doing the pre-scored thing.' Yet the success of these experiences challenged her self-identity as a composer: 'It moved and reached audiences in a way that I hadn't experienced before because of the pilgrimage and meditation aspects of the work . . . I wondered what place is there for the string quartet or the orchestral work?'[13] Although she now lists the de Clario works under her own name, for several of them she used her Chinese name as a way of avoiding any audience pre-conceptions.

In an interview with the composers James Saunders and Christopher Fox conducted just three years after *The Cauldron*, Lim revealed something of how she felt her artistic identity changing. 'After these experiences', she says, 'the question that arose for me was how, in the context of notated pieces, I could continue to "offer a space" in which musicians could have that kind of quality of attention to the moment.' She offers three tools she has used in her work to increase attention and engagement: silence (either across the whole ensemble, or within an ensemble, when one instrument becomes a soloist); continuously transforming, non-delineated sounds that require precise control of nuance; and different ways of regulating or 'tuning' pitch and rhythm (Saunders and Fox 1999). We might find such features, or something like them, in all her work, but since the late 1990s they have come to the fore: the latter two in particular align with the dynamic heterophony that we first explored in relation to *Inguz*, a work composed towards the end of the de Clario collaborations and co-dedicated to the cellist Chris Lockhart Smith, one of the players who had been instrumental in their realisation.

Other elements in Lim's music may also be traced back to this time. *Tongue of the Invisible*, in particular, owes both its extended sections of guided improvisation and the concept of attunement (especially the long drone passage with which it begins) to ideas developed in *Afterward* and *Bardo*. More generally, the concept of witnessing that Lim and de Clario established as a core aesthetic principle has remained a part of her work: compositions from *Invisibility* to *An Elemental Thing* have at their heart a desire to illuminate and reveal an instrumentalist and their instrument in raw, unmediated form. Her work *Machine for Contacting the Dead* (1999–2000) for chamber orchestra, commissioned by Ensemble Intercontemporain, takes its title from a series of installations de Clario began making in 1990; it is also the title of a catalogue essay from the *Components of an Expression Machine* installation at which he and Lim first met. Finally, it was de Clario who introduced Lim to the poetry of Rumi, one of the most enduring of all influences on her work.

Other installations

Although Lim has since worked on installations with other artists, none has required quite the same reinvention of her compositional identity or practice. In subsequent cases, a notated composition (either specially written or drawn from existing works) has been presented within a multimedia context of videos and/or sculptures without a long process of co-creation between performers and artist. A legacy of the earlier works is that such a fundamental rethinking was no longer necessary.

In 1999 Lim made *Sonorous Bodies* with the Australian artist Judith Wright for the Third Asia Pacific Triennial of Contemporary Art in Brisbane. In this instance, Lim wrote a new solo composition, *16 Touches of the Zither* for *koto*. Like *Burning House* of a few years previously, this was performed by Satsuki Odamura and written using traditional Japanese notation. Around Odamura's performance, Wright installed eight video projections that expanded upon the resonances of the music. 'Rather than deliberately trying to make equivalences between things, we've been taking "sideways glances" at what each other has been doing', is how Lim described her working partnership with Wright (Saunders and Fox 1999). *Sonorous Bodies* was later installed at the Hebbel Theatre, Berlin in 2001.

Glass House Mountains (2005) was made with the Australian Waanyi artist Judy Watson and explores the landscape and cultural heritage of the Glass House Mountains, a group of thirteen volcanic hills on Queensland's Sunshine Coast. Lim contributed a graphic score that was performed by the cellist Rosanne Hunt. Of all Lim's post-1990s installations, this is the one that grants the greatest freedom to the performer, although it is still not as fully improvisatory as those earlier works. As well as Hunt's playing, the installation incorporated sound and video field recordings, sculptures, video, floor- and wall-pieces made from volcanic soils, and projections of topographical drawings.

As part of the 2008 Maerzmusik festival in Berlin, at which Lim was a featured composer, she created *TON* with the director Sabrina Hölzer and the artist Volker März. Installed in Berlin's St. Elisabeth-Kirche, März constructed a giant mobile of human figures, each clinging to a trapeze while trying to go about their daily lives: a surreal, Kafka-like image of a disabled but persisting population. Lim contributed four solo works played by members of ELISION – Genevieve Lacey (Ganassi recorder), Richard Haynes (clarinet), Tristram Williams (trumpet) and Benjamin Marks (alto trombone) – that served as a kind of soundtrack while audience walked among the swinging figures. Three of these solos ¬ *weaver-of-fictions* (Ganassi recorder), *Sonorous Body* (clarinet) and *Wild-Winged One* (trumpet) were extracted or developed from *The Navigator*, which had been Lim's compositional preoccupation of the previous twelve months; all three may be played as standalone works. The fourth, *Well of Dreams* was composed specifically for *TON* and at the time of writing may only be played within that context.

Lim's most recent installation project is *Escalier du Chant* (2011), a conception of the German artist Olaf Nicolai installed at the Pinakothek der Moderne art gallery in Munich. Lim was one of twelve composers invited by Nicolai to compose a capella songs that could be sung on the gallery's large central staircase.[14] Songs were performed on one Sunday a month throughout 2011. The date of performance for each song was determined, but not the time: the singers would decide when to sing, concealing themselves first among the members of the public walking up and down the stairs. Lim contributed the three intertwining songs for soprano, mezzo-soprano and bass-baritone *3 Angels*. Following Nicolai's request to include reflections on current political events, Lim set texts by the French feminist author Hélène Cixous, from *The Writing Notebooks* (2004), and newspaper reports of the death in 2009 of the Iranian protester Neda Agha-Soltan. The performers were Neue Vocalsolisten Stuttgart, and Lim's songs were sung on 25 September and 30 October.

References

Bertola, Patrick and Bobbie Oliver, eds. (2006). *The Workshops: A History of the Midland Government Railway Workshops*. Crawley, WA: University of Western Australia Press.

de Clario, Domenico and Liza Lim (1998). *The Intertwining – The Chasm: Installation-Performance Works 1994–96*. Brisbane: Institute of Modern Art.

Ingold, Tim (2013). *Making*. London: Routledge.

Kaufmann, Walter, ed. (1975). *Tibetan Buddhist Chant: Musical Notations and Interpretations of a Song Book by the Bakh Brgyud Pa and Sa Skya Pa Sects*. Bloomington: Indiana University Press.

Lim, Liza (n.d.). 'Liza Lim', ELISION Ensemble website, https://elision.org.au/soundhouse/liza-lim/.

Saunders, James and Christopher Fox (1999). 'Interview with Liza Lim'. Available at: james-saunders.com/interview-with-liza-lim/.

Sheldrake, Merlin (2020). *Entangled Life: How Fungi Make Our Worlds, Change Our Minds, and Shape Our Futures.* London: Bodley Head.

Endnotes

1 Taken from the composer's website, https://lizalimcomposer.com/works/other-projects/.

2 Correspondence with the author. September 2021.

3 Conversation with the author, August 2021.

4 Lim's association with Muscat-Clark went back even further than this: she studied with him at Victorian College of the Arts and he sang the countertenor part in the performance of *Blaze* with which she began her ELISION career in 1986.

5 Conversation with the author, August 2021.

6 The location was used again by ELISION in 1997 for the installation of Richard Barrett's *Opening of the Mouth*, made with the artist CROW.

7 A history of this closure, and of the Workshops themselves, may be found in Bertola and Oliver (2006).

8 Conversation with the author, August 2021.

9 These chants are collected, transcribed and analysed in Kaufmann (1975).

10 A short video on ELISION's YouTube channel also documents some of the performances from the seventh night at Lismore: https://www.youtube.com/watch?v=uYWBri5fLSM.

11 Conversation with the author, August 2021.

12 For a history of research into mycorrhizal networks, see Sheldrake (2020, 165–93).

13 Conversation with the author, August 2021.

14 The other composers were: Tony Conrad, Georg Friedrich Haas, Georg Katzer, Samir Odeh-Tamimi, Enno Poppe, Rolf Riehm, James Saunders, Rebecca Saunders, Elliott Sharp, Mika Vainio and Jennifer Walshe.

Chapter 5

Music for orchestra and large ensemble

We have referred frequently to the importance of lines in Lim's music: lines of melody and heterophony, wandering paths, branches, mycelial threads, and so on. But we can take this analysis one step further, borrowing another observation from Tim Ingold. That is, that the presence of a line implies either a surface on which it is inscribed (Ingold calls these lines 'traces') or a space through which it moves (Ingold calls these 'threads') (Ingold 2016, 42–4). Being composed of lines, therefore, Lim's music is also composed of the surfaces or spaces across or through which those lines are drawn.

Ingold goes on to observe that in practice, threads can easily become traces and traces become threads (Ingold 2016, 54). He offers the crafts of knitting, embroidery and lacework as examples of where this happens, but Lim's use of musical lines and threads could be another. The thread-like monodies of *weaver-of-fictions, Invisibility, Axis Mundi* or *bioluminescence* are really paths across landscapes of instrument construction and history. The dynamic heterophonies of *Inguz* or *The Heart's Ear* turn lines into spaces, traced along the dimensions of pitch, rhythm and timbre. An ensemble of instruments – *Garden of Earthly Desire, Ronda, How Forests Think* – is a constellation, whose points may be joined in numerous ways, following lines of gesture, timbre, construction, acoustics and so on. Even the line between a voice and a piano, as in *Voodoo Child*, for example, is actually a surface across which any number of connections might be drawn. The text of a poem may appear to be another form of line, but in *Mother Tongue* it becomes a plane formed by the intersection of voice and instrument, sound and word; in *Tongue of the Invisible* an embroidery fabric, through whose holes a thread can pass from any point to any other. Finally, the line of a sound itself, its unique *Kadenzklang*, can be cracked open and drawn out into surfaces of shimmering pulsation (*Songs Found in Dream*) or spaces of profound attunement (*Bardo'i-thos-grol*).

In Lim's works for orchestra and large ensemble, the sheer number of instruments makes the space through and across which her lines are drawn more audible. So often, Lim's music begins from the idea of a thread, drawn out and extended from the personality

140   The Music of Liza Lim

and character of a musician and her instrument. That thread can become complex and multidimensional, woven around itself and others, transforming and penetrating, tying between and wrapping around; but it is almost always there. This may be why, even among her orchestral works, Lim has felt most comfortable with concertos, or at least works with a significant solo component. As well as those in this chapter, her other works for orchestra and large ensemble include *Machine for Contacting the Dead*, for twenty-seven musicians including bass/contrabass clarinet and cello solos; the recorder concerto *The Guest* (2010); and the piano concerto *World as Lover, World as Self* (2021). Even those works that aren't explicitly concertos feature crucial important parts. *Pearl, Ochre, Hair String* begins with an important solo cello part (for which, as we have said, *Invisibility* served as a study); likewise, *Sappho/Bioluminescence* is woven around a solo flute.

Even so, as a composer whose language depends so much on fluid, rapidly fluctuating relationships within and between instrumental lines, Lim has found the cumbersome juggernaut that is a modern symphony orchestra a challenging medium. Her list of works from before 2010 includes seven compositions for large orchestra, but three of these – *Cathedral* (1994), *Sri Vidya – Utterances of Adoration* (1995) for choir and orchestra, and *The Tree of Life* (2001) – have been withdrawn. Two more are less than ten minutes long, both written as part of Lim's residency with the Sydney Symphony Orchestra: *Immer Fliessender* (2004), commissioned as a 'companion piece' to Mahler's Ninth Symphony; and the fanfare for orchestra *Flying Banner (after Wang To)* (2005). And a sixth, the longest of those mentioned thus far, *Ecstatic Architecture* (2002–4), commissioned by the Los Angeles Philharmonic for the inaugural series at the Frank Gehry-designed Walt Disney Concert Hall, has also effectively been withdrawn. Although this last was, at the time, Lim's most high-profile international commission (it is inspired by the shapes and physicality of Gehry's spectacular, stainless steel-clad building), it is a work with which she has never felt completely satisfied. In an interview with Gordon Kerry, given towards the end of her Sydney SO residency, Lim described the question of orchestral writing as having to do with 'how to activate a large mass of sound without losing the detailing of colour and gestural nuance that has been so central to my musical language' (quoted in Kerry, 2009: 37).

Nevertheless, in 2010 Lim fully embraced the orchestra with two major works: *Pearl, Ochre, Hair String*, the culmination of her focus on Aboriginal 'shimmer'; and *The Guest*, one of many works inspired by the poetry of Rumi. More recently still, the orchestra has occupied a central place in the form of the monumental *Annunciation Triptych*, the first part of which, *Sappho/Bioluminescence*, we briefly encountered in Chapter 1. It is intriguing to note that this increasing comfort in the orchestral medium has paralleled a widening of the frame and a loosening of the connections within Lim's music, which began with *The Quickening* and was developed further in *Tongue of the Invisible* and *How Forests Think*.

As well as Lim's only pre-2010 extended work for symphony orchestra still in her catalogue, *The Compass* (2005–6) for flute, didgeridoo and orchestra, the present chapter

CHAPTER 5: Music for orchestra and large ensemble   **141**

considers three works for large ensemble: *The Alchemical Wedding* (1996) for chamber orchestra, *Speak, Be Silent* (2015) for violin and fifteen musicians, and *Extinction Events and Dawn Chorus* (2017) for twelve musicians.

The Alchemical Wedding (1996)

Lim's first work for large ensemble was composed towards the end of her period of collaboration with Domenico de Clario discussed in the previous chapter; it received its premiere at the Melbourne International Festival on 30 October 1996, a month after the second part of *The Cauldron*. It was a joint commission by ELISION and Frankfurt's Ensemble Modern, and Lim's initial thoughts were guided by the union of two ensembles, one Pacific and one European. The work's title comes from a symbol used by medieval alchemists: the marriage of Red King and White Queen, a union of opposites (masculine/feminine; sun/moon; active/passive; fire, earth/air, water; etc), as well as the perfect combining of sulfur and mercury that in some interpretations would create the Philosopher's Stone.

For further inspiration, Lim also turned to Rumi, to whose work de Clario had recently introduced her. Her programme note includes the following lines by the Sufi poet:

> They're lovers again: Sugar dissolving into milk.
>
> Day and night, no difference. The sun is the moon:
>
> An amalgam. Their gold and silver melt together.
>
> This is the season when the dead branch and the green
>
> branch are the same branch.

The ideas expressed in Rumi's poetry and by the image of the alchemical marriage extend into Lim's instrumentation. To her large ensemble of Western instruments, she added parts for *erhu* (a Chinese two-stringed fiddle) and *angklung* (a West Javanese percussion instrument made of tuned bamboo tubes suspended from a frame). These are instruments with lineages separate from each other and from the Western tradition, and Lim's composition poeticizes forms of union and longing between them by highlighting their differences and finding ways for them to connect with each other musically.

The Alchemical Wedding may be divided into seven sections, marked by changes of tempo and/or prominent changes in character:

> I, bars 1–32: Western instruments only. Opening contrabassoon solo, beginning in the almost sub-musical depths of its range, provides the basis for the ensemble music that follows.
>
> II, bars 33–76: Contrabassoon switches to standard bassoon and begins a new solo. This is soon accompanied, first by *angklung* and then other instruments. Erhu plays but remains in the background; the *angklung*'s percussive rattles are the focus of this section.

III, bars 77–116: *Erhu* solo emerges out of the end of section II. It becomes the focal instrument, and the ensemble music adapts around it, with greater emphasis on stringed instruments, glissandi, etc. Towards the end of the section *angklung* comes once more to the fore.

IV, bars 117–52: Low wind and tom-toms begin a new section form which *angklung* and *erhu* are once more absent. Towards the end of the section, however, unexpected connections arise: first a pairing of erhu with contrabassoon, then of *angklung* with strings.

V, bars 153–83: A section in which prominent pulsing patterns offer a way in which both *angklung* and *erhu* may merge with the Western ensembles.

VI, bars 184–204: Preceded by a pair of harmonic glissandi for French horn, section VI is the work's climax, achieved at the trumpet's high, melodic solo at bar 196 and carried through to its penetrating Eb at bar 204 (with Eb clarinet).

VII, bars 205–end: The Eb is held over by strings, harp and lower brass as the energy and tension accumulated in section VI fall away. Melodic fragments in the winds precede the last entry of the *angklung*, which initiates a decelerating pulse to conclude the work. The sense of finality is broken, however, by one final wisp of melody from the *erhu*, 'as if continuing on … '.

These seven sections outline a loose dramatic arc, from the introductions of Western ensemble, *anklung* and *erhu* in turn, to their mixing and mingling, to a climax and then to a falling away to the end. However, this stereotypical narrative of conflict and resolution does not precisely capture the form of the work.

As well as the opposition/combination of instruments and ensembles, the other principal feature of *The Alchemical Wedding* is its use of melody, a feature which it shares with *The Heart's Ear*, Lim's other major Sufi-inspired work from this period. The long solo for contrabassoon with which the work begins establishes the principal melodic materials. As other instruments join, this melody variously fragments, branches or multiplies to create an ongoing musical texture that is always changing yet always retains a familiar DNA. Example 5.1 shows the end of the contrabassoon's solo and the entry of the bass clarinet, the first instrument to join it. Note how the instruments interlock across the pitches F and Eb to create an almost seamless relay of melody and expand the threads of instrumental colour.

Example 5.1 *The Alchemical Wedding*, end of bar 1 to bar 5

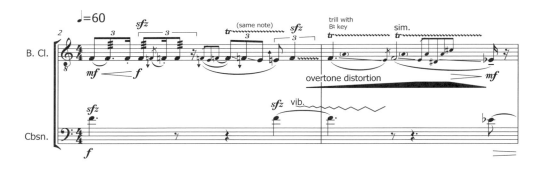

Two melodic motifs are of particular importance through *The Alchemical Wedding*. The first (A) is a broadly descending motif that begins on F and turns on the E and E♭ below it. A version can be seen in the contrabassoon part, beginning with the high F crotchet; the first three bars of the bass clarinet and contrabassoon duet make variations on this. Further versions of this motif, a slinkily descending idea that shifts freely between major and minor modes provides much of the work's melodic texture. The emphasis on F also serves to create a focal harmonic pitch.

The second motif (B) also begins on F but leaps up a fifth from this to C before developing its own descending, turning shape. This is the motif bracketed in the contrabassoon part. Although this motif is heard less frequently than the first, it is no less important, and Lim seems to reserve it for moments of structural significance. Its first appearance marks the end of the contrabassoon's solo, and near the end of their duo bass clarinet and contrabassoon play the same motif in unison, before the percussion and other winds enter.

Example 5.2 *The Alchemical Wedding*, bars 10–12

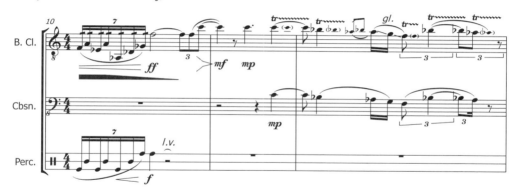

Apart from three Chinese opera gongs the first section of the work involves wind instruments only and is comprised of heterophonic variations and developments of these two motifs. F frequently recurs as a point of departure or coalescence for the overall texture, but it is nevertheless highly varied and detailed, in Lim's familiar polyphonic style.

The second section begins with the bassoon stating a version of motif (A), in which it is joined first by flutes and *angklung*. This is the *angklung*'s first entry, and in its left hand it doubles quite closely the bassoon. The right hand, however, adds a dissonant or colouristic counterpoint of a B and C tremolo – a sound quite foreign to the texture so far – that help establish the instrument as both part of, and somewhat separate from the rest of the ensemble.

Example 5.3 *The Alchemical Wedding*, bars 33–7 (bassoon and *angklung*)

The *erhu* enters a few bars later, but in this section it is the *angklung* that is prominent and around which the music is shaped. Drawing on the *angklung*'s distinctive capabilities, the music for Western instruments makes frequent use of tremolos and runs of grace notes (which on the *angklung* are played with a harp-like sweep of the hand). The percussion, meanwhile, focuses on bamboo chimes and guiro, instruments whose sound is similar to the *angklung*'s. Nevertheless, amongst these different points of connection are variations on the (A) and (B) motifs, whose melodic character borrows more from the *erhu*'s soundworld than the *angklung*'s. Example 5.4 shows an example of the latter, played by bassoon. Beginning from a point of contact with the *angklung* through tremolo/trilled Cs, the bassoon follows motif (B)'s drooping downward curve with support from the other winds in the form of contact pitches and from the violins in the form of general, descending melodic outline.

Example 5.4 *The Alchemical Wedding*, bars 60–61

At the end of the section, the *erhu* enters prominently. It briefly plays with the *angklung*, in a duet that brings both instruments together for the first time but highlights the distance between them. Playing the same notes, D and E♭, the difference in timbre and playing technique is emphasised between the *angklung*'s rapid percussive attacks and the *erhu*'s sinuous, sustained melodic line. The latter controls the third section of the music. Although the accompaniment to the *erhu*'s initial solo is closer to the dry percussive sound of the *angklung* – an extraordinary combination of harp, bamboo chimes and *angklung* itself – this gives way to brass (using wa-wa mutes) and string writing that is closer to the Chinese instrument in idiom. At one point Lim even makes an improbable pairing of *erhu* and trombone.

Example 5.5 *The Alchemical Wedding*, bars 88–91

Although the music of Example 5.5 shapes itself around the *erhu*, it also shows how all the instrumental types or groups continuously merge and diverge amongst each other, complicating the distinction between line and space. We noted in our earlier discussion of *Garden of Earthly Desire* how even in her earliest works Lim created connections between instruments along the plane of timbre. In *The Alchemical Wedding* we can see such connections extending across several planes at once. While the *erhu*'s timbre clearly relates it to the other string instruments, its melodic shape and use of portamenti connects it with the trombone. Its focal pitch of F provides a layer of connection, and it is from this that the *angklung* emerges, its contrasting timbre then being picked up by the trilling *sul ponticello* violins at the end of the example.

Passages like this, in which small networks of connection are made and remade over the whole ensemble through the parameters of pitch, contour, timbre and rhythm, occur continuously. Example 5.6 shows a rich instance, taken from section V. As the pulsing chords of *erhu* and Western strings taper down to a narrow five-note cluster and handed over to the dry percussion of *angklung* and harp. In bar 164 the erhu seemingly branches off entirely, joining the piccolo and clarinet's rising flurries, but a bar later is drawn into the harp and *angklung*'s pulsing, having traced a path between two musical layers and three instrumental groupings.

Example 5.6 *The Alchemical Wedding*, bars 161–6

CHAPTER 5: Music for orchestra and large ensemble

Lim describes *The Alchemical Wedding* as being constructed around a 'spine' of melody, 'from which "wings" of different transparency and density billow' (Lim 1996). As we can see, that melodic spine incorporates certain recurring motifs and processes of variation. However, these looping or transforming processes do not suggest directional forms of recapitulation or development: while one can hear the return of motifs, and while occasionally they are deployed at moments of structural significance, there is never a sense of departure or return, of a forward-moving narrative. Even the final – presumably conclusive – statement of motif (B), as the work winds down towards its end, is transposed a minor third higher than all the others.

None of the different statements of motifs (A) or (B) are definitive, and so there can be no movement or development towards or away from them. Instead, the melody wanders, crossing different planes of pitch, timbre or rhythm but always remaining in motion. Ingold's comparison between seafaring and transport offers a useful way to think about this. While transport is simply a means by which to get from one point to another – that is, travel *across* the sea – seafaring entails a life spent *at* sea, in which the journey rather than the destination is the point (Ingold 2016, 79). Similarly, rather than connect particular harmonic or structural points – as melody tends to do in more historical or traditional contexts – Lim's melody wanders *among* her instrumental groupings, creating the music's shape and structure from out of itself. In *The Alchemical Wedding* the ensemble 'map' over which the melody moves covers a wide terrain from Indonesian bamboo percussion to Chinese fiddle, with all points of the Western chamber orchestra in between. Pitch relationships and recurring melodic motifs make up, as we have seen, some of the possible paths among these different coordinates, but so too do relationships of timbre, rhythm or playing technique. Any dimension of one instrumental line may be cracked open and fitted to any other.

This spatialised, multi-dimensional, wandering conception of melody is related to the dynamic heterophony that we first identified in our discussion of *Inguz*, composed in the same year as *The Alchemical Wedding*. It is also connected to the improvisation techniques Lim and ELISION had recently explored in *Bardo'i-thos-grol*. Heterophony is a way of creating musical lines that are similar in some respects (say, pitch) while different in others (say, rhythm or timbre); the dynamic aspect in Lim's music simply means that those relationships of similarity and difference are continually changing. In *Bardo'i-thos-grol*, the heterophonic process was primarily a way of thickening or dividing the drone or melody into multiple versions of itself. In our discussion of *The Heart's Ear* in Chapter 2 we called this 'bending' (see Example 2.13). In *The Alchemical Wedding*, however, melodic lines bend inwards as well as outwards, creating moments of convergence as well as divergence that relate to the themes of longing and desire expressed in Rumi's poetry and in the image of the alchemical wedding itself. Longing comes from a desire to be connected, but to activate that desire you also need distance or difference. In *The Alchemical Wedding* the 'distance' between instruments from very different cultures creates the dynamic energy that motivates the music.

While the structure of *The Alchemical Wedding* suggests a typical dramatic shape, the work in fact avoids easy conclusions. Although the different instrumental groups do find ways to co-exist, and indeed to nourish the kinds of music they can make, they remain separate in their identities. This is not, as it may seem at first, an assertion of heroic individualism – the individual standing strong against the buffeting forces around them – but in fact the opposite: with no clear 'victor', as it were, at the end of her work, no singular goal, Lim maintains the state of longing. Even at the very end of the work, when the melody seems finally to have been obliterated or exhausted, the *erhu* picks up a new thread, 'as if continuing on …'. Wandering desire is an end in itself.

The Compass (2005–6)

The largest work to come out of Lim's residency with the Sydney Symphony Orchestra in 2005 and 2006, *The Compass* is written for large orchestra with didgeridoo and solo flute (playing piccolo, flute and bass flute). The central thread in this case is drawn from the didgeridoo and its player, the virtuoso William Barton. One of the world's leading didgeridoo players, Barton has for many years sought ways to blend and juxtapose Indigenous and Western musics: one of the first major results of this ambition was Peter Sculthorpe's *Requiem* (2004) for chorus, orchestra and didgeridoo, which begins with Barton, playing solo, walking up to the stage to join his European colleagues. *The Compass* belongs to the series of works Lim composed between 2005 and 2010 that are informed by Aboriginal culture and aesthetics. The presence of the didgeridoo is the most obvious manifestation of that in this work, but as we would expect Lim's engagement, like Sculthorpe's, goes much deeper than cheap cultural crossover.

Barton grew up on a cattle station in the Mount Isa region of northern Queensland. His uncle, an elder of the Wannyi, Lardil and Kalkadunga people taught him the didgeridoo; his mother, Delmae Barton, is a renowned singer, songwriter and poet. To begin the work, Lim and Barton wrote a chant in Barton's ancestral language, using a Kalkadunga–English dictionary to aid translation:

> Ja Whydoo Ka InneWoodjan Woodjan Woodjan
> Oul Gordee Wuroo Wuroo
>
> (Heart sits in the land
> Fire, fire, fire
> A river of stars)

As Gordon Kerry notes, Lim's setting of these words, with which *The Compass* begins, shares several features with traditional Aboriginal melodies, including a downward, stepwise movement that begins high in the singer's range, and frequent repeated notes (Kerry 2009, 41). Acting as reverberations of the main note, these pulsing articulations are related to the Aboriginal concept of shimmer (see also *Songs Found in Dream*, Chapter 2); the melody's downward compass across a tritone and its concluding A are important to the work's (Western) concerns with harmonic structure.

Example 5.7 *The Compass*, bars 1–6, solo didgeridoo (doub clapsticks and voice)

After the first line of the solo chant is repeated, the orchestra begins to enter, one instrument at a time; the cumulative emergence of the full ensemble is similar to that at the start of *Tongue of the Invisible*, but the respective energies are very different. In the vocal work, the goal is attunement, a way of gathering the instruments together and drawing them onto a single line. It is as if they have all arrived at the performance space from their homes or the street and are slowly warming up and coming into sync with each other. In *The Compass*, as Example 5.8 shows, the opposite is the case. There are points of contact, and possibly even attunement, between chant and orchestra: see the low and high Bs in the bassoons, the contrabassoon's low C♯, and the oboe and cor anglais' B and then A. However, the bassoon's Bs are separated by three octaves (neither the same octave as Barton's voice) and are distorted in sound by harmonics and *smorzato* (diaphragm pulsation) effects; the oboe and cor anglais play in rising sevenths rather than descending tones (the oboe adds multiphonic trills, too); the contrabassoon sustains its C♯ far beyond that of the chant, turning a unison into a dissonant, cleaving effect. There are other points of departure too. The rhythm of the voice's C♯–B appoggiatura at the start of the example is reflected in the timpani and tom-tom parts, but this rhythm seems to develop into a thread of its own with the piano's entry (whose low B loosely ties it to the pitch of the chant as well), which is further reinforced rhythmically by the percussion. And so on. The general effect, then, is less one of attunement and movement inwards or towards, but of movement that branches outwards and apart.

Example 5.8 *The Compass*, bars 12–16

Lim has spoken of *The Compass* as a form of 'branching song', in which each branch develops increasingly intricately from the initial chant. It falls into four broad sections. The first is most directly governed by the chant. Around first Barton's voice, and then his didgeridoo playing, the orchestra works through transformations, extensions and elaborations of the chant across a geological scale. At bar 90, just over four and a half minutes into the work, a sudden collapse onto a pedal E played by tuba and bassoons initiates a central section led initially by the solo flute. As the music becomes increasingly sibilant and/or perforated, the timbres of breath noises, stuttering repeated notes, trills and ocean drums become increasingly prominent.[1] A sort of climax to this second section is reached at bar 145, when the entire orchestra plays pitchless breath noises in unison, 'like giant wings opening and closing', interspersed with moments of 'frozen stillness'. The effect is similar – although enacted on a much greater scale – to that in the fourth section of *Songs Found in Dream* (see Example 2.21), a work composed at approximately the same time. Lim describes this passage as a 'translation of an amazing "silent dance"' that she saw performed by Aurukun people from Cape York, and draws a connection with Chinese music that we encountered earlier in relation to *The Quickening*, 'where the breathing of instruments, the sounds-in-between sounds, are as important as a melodic phrase'.

This climactic passage is framed by duos between the two solo instruments (they are the only ones that do not play the 'breath-music' at bar 145). In its aftermath the orchestra restlessly attempts to reform itself before settling once more on an E pedal. The texture here is of an orchestra dissolved, however: the brass's bold assertion of E fades without developing, while drones on A, Ab and B are sustained only by the eerie sound of bowed piano strings. Through interrupted fanfares and other fragmentary interjections the orchestra continues while, triggered by staccato trills from the solo piccolo and then tinnitus-like high string chords, the texture is gradually overtaken by percussive clicks, clacks and other ratchet-like sounds. These run through a number of iterations – including clapsticks, cabassa, string pizzicato and whirling windwands (an instrument similar to an Aboriginal bullroarer) – before settling on the sound of metallic insect toys. The didgeridoo builds a solo of increasing ferocity while every member of the orchestra takes their own insect clicker, creating a forest of cicadas before the work comes to a sudden and final stop.

Lim's image of a 'branching song' also calls up the didgeridoo itself. As usual, Lim's compositional process grew out of the particular acoustic, aesthetic and cultural qualities of the instrument. A didgeridoo is, somewhat like the bassoon of *Axis Mundi*, a resonating wooden tube – in this case literally a tree trunk or branch, hollowed out by termites. Unlike the bassoon, however, the didgeridoo does not produce sound of its own (via a reed), but amplifies the sound of the player's voice (like a trumpet) via vibrating lips, singing, speaking or other vocalisations. These are what create the instrument's characteristic range of howls and hoots over a fundamental drone. Central too are rhythms derived from spoken Indigenous languages, meaning that playing the didgeridoo is a form of singing, continuous with vocal chant. Furthermore, the instrument's irregular bore means that its resonances occur at different frequencies to those of an equally tempered instrument. As in *Axis Mundi*, Lim feeds this quality into her music: her orchestral writing makes use of use of microtonal intervals that align the two more closely together; she also emphasises the low instruments of the orchestra (especially winds and brass), inverting the usual hierachy of melody and bass – Lim has spoken of the didgeridoo gathering the low instruments of the orchestra to form a kind of 'meta-didgeridoo' (Kerry 2009, 42). Barton uses two instruments in the work, with fundamental pitches of A and C (these are the two lowest instruments he owned at the time), and these fundamental pitches serve as pedals around which the work is structured. He begins with the A instrument, switches to C at the start of the second section and returns to A before his final solo, giving the work a ternary form on the basis of its underlying harmony. (The use of minor third relations as a basis for the work's harmonic scheme comes directly out of Barton's instruments; it is intriguing that this is shared with *Mother Tongue*, composed at around the same time.)

Examples 5.9 and 5.10 illustrate contrasting relationships between didgeridoo and orchestra. In the first, they are in sympathy with one another, the orchestra creating a mass of heterophonic strands from the soloist's music: see in particular the rhythmic conjunction of didgeridoo and contrabass clarinet in bar 33, which itself interacts dynamically with the rhythms of bass clarinet, trumpets, tuba and percussion. Meanwhile, the didgeridoo's A fundamental is reinforced by the contrabassoon, bassoon and (from bar 35) clarinets. In the second example, didgeridoo and orchestra are rather more separate. Piano, strings, tuba and (to an extent) contrabassoon construct a complex form of drone, while upper brass, winds and piano overlay a dense staccato texture. The didgeridoo itself, however, plays independently, adding dingo and horn calls of its own that are sonically, rhythmically (and indeed culturally) unrelated to almost anything else in the orchestra. What is significant about these two examples, which are only a few bars apart from each other, is how the threads of Western orchestra and Indigenous didgeridoo can weave around and among each other while retaining their own independent characters; Lim is not interested in either 'Westernising' the didgeridoo or 'Indigenising' the orchestra.

Example 5.9 *The Compass*, bars 32–7

Example 5.10 *The Compass*, bars 44–8

CHAPTER 5: Music for orchestra and large ensemble 159

From these two examples we can also see some features of Lim's orchestral style. While the polyphonic style of her chamber music is apparent, this is realised in thicker strands of instrumental families (note the grouping of wind and brass in Example 5.9, for example) that may themselves be internally heterophonic, turning lines into spaces. Nevertheless, we can also see moments where this family-based organisation is allowed to break down, as in the links passed between trumpets and viola, and then cello and bass clarinet, in Example 5.10. As always, there are few absolutes in Lim's music, and any systemisation exists only to be cracked open and stirred about. What the orchestra does allow is a much wider sonic palette, particularly in the lowest registers from which the music of *The Compass* grows.

The words of the opening chant introduce another thematic thread, that of the concepts of earth, fire and stars, which Lim relates to different aspects of the music. The first two belong to the Chinese concept of Wuxing, or the generative cycle of the five elements: wood into fire, fire into earth, earth into metal, metal into water, water into wood, and so on. In the Wuxing cycle, too, fire and earth are the elements that bridge the cycle from wood (didgeridoo) to metal (flute). In this way the Chinese concepts of Lim's heritage interpenetrate with Barton's Aboriginal ones. Earth represents stability, a balance of yin and yang, rootedness, and drawing together. Fire is the element of transformation and dynamism.

Lim's solo instruments of didgeridoo and flute bring these first two elements together: the didgeridoo sings the songs of Aboriginal lands; its sound is grounded in fundamental resonances. Although the flute is related acoustically to the didgeridoo – it is another wind-blown tube, capable of a great flexibility of sound – it is also significantly different, made of ore melted by the action of fire, capable of rapid and dynamic movement. The two instruments together define what Lim calls 'the edges of the orchestral frame' – another space – which we may define in terms of register, culture or construction material. Several of the most significant moments in the work are when flute and didgeridoo play together and mutually influence and shape one another. In a duo that takes place midway through the work, the flute can be seen to adopt elements of didgeridoo playing, using the instrument as a resonator for a variety of vocal sounds.

Example 5.11 *The Compass*, bars 151–63

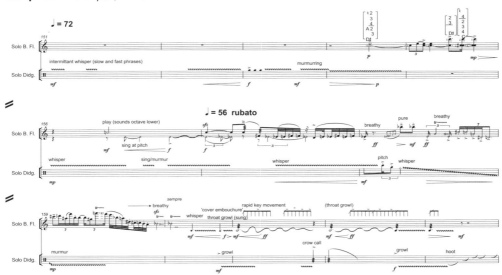

Although the third element, the stars, is related to the first two ('woodjan' in Kalkadunga also refers to starlight), it speaks to a cosmic rather than earthly realm: the 'river of stars' is the Milky Way. Lim chooses a slightly tangential route to depicting this, however, through the sound of multitudes of insects. This may seem unorthodox at first, until one considers that there is a shared pattern between stars and insects: both belong to extra-human worlds; both exist on life cycles far beyond our own; and both are characterised by masses or swarms of individual points. There are links too with the didgeridoo, an instrument that is made by the actions of burrowing insects is also a means of connecting (metaphorically, at least) earth and the heavens.

The insects/stars are represented at the end of *The Compass* by the sound of 'insect clicker' toys – small tin boxes that make a clicking sound when squeezed. Every member of the orchestra (apart from low brass and winds, and solo didgeridoo) has at least one. Lim gradually introduces these over the last few pages of her score, erasing each instrumental family at a time until only the didgeridoo – playing now a fierce, highly rhythmic solo – remains, surrounded by a veritable storm of clicks. It is surely not a coincidence, given the elemental symbolism running through the work, that it should end with another duet between metal and wood.

The insect clicks are also integrated into the musical language of the work. As an instance of musical shimmer – albeit one carried to a new level of intensity – they emerge as a consequence of the different kinds of percussive repetition that have been heard throughout, from pulsing breath-music to hissing ocean drum. Yet their origin, like every other thread from which the work is made, is once more in Barton and his instrument: man, musician, heritage, language; wood, insects, breath, body. Having sung his opening chant and before he plays his didgeridoo for the first time, he rattles a clapstick against the body of his instrument: a small-scale, wooden, human equivalent to the galaxy of tin-metal insects at the work's end. The gesture is more than simply musical: it references the boomerang roll, used in Aboriginal music to signal the start of a new section. So it is that beginning and end are wound together in a single thread. Is this the compass of the title? The line that has guided us across the map of the orchestra, from beginning to end, from earth to heaven? *The Compass* may conclude with a variation of Lim's favoured 'fade into noise', but this time it had always been there; rather than evaporate away, it becomes more solid as all else disappears and we reach for the stars.

Speak, Be Silent (2015)

'What is a concerto but a work that is somehow about "sounding together" and "sounding apart"; it is a form that deals in unison and separation', says Lim of her concerto for violin and chamber orchestra, *Speak, Be Silent* (Lim 2015). Once more, a work for large ensemble – here solo violin and an ensemble of fifteen musicians – has provided Lim with an opportunity to explore the relation between a single instrumental thread and its tracing across a large musical mass. Written for Ensemble Contrechamps and the violinist David Grimal, *Speak, Be Silent* received its premiere in Geneva in September 2015, conducted by Michael Wendeberg.

Although *Speak, Be Silent* is a concerto, it is based upon an unusual relationship between soloist and accompanist. As in *The Alchemical Wedding*, differences of instrumental timbre and tradition create states of 'longing' between instruments, across which movements towards union and separation may be dramatized. In this case, the sonic differences between the soloist and ensemble are heightened and at times even exaggerated: the music of *Speak, Be Silent* is sonically more heterogeneous than *The Alchemical Wedding* or even *The Compass*. Rather than connect instruments and instrumental groups to each other via smooth steps or small increments, such as we have seen in *The Alchemical Wedding* (see, eg, Example 5.5), Lim sets herself a deliberate challenge by contrasting her soloist with a very un-violin-like ensemble that is dominated by brass, piano and abrasive percussion, opening wide the space through which it threads.

Crucial to this ensemble sound is the woodblock: a pitchless, dry, wooden percussive instrument at the furthest reach, one might imagine, from the string-based, quasi-vocal melodic sound of the violin. The foregrounding of woodblock in *Speak, Be Silent* anticipates by a couple of years that instrument's solo role in *An Elemental Thing* (and its importance as we will see in the opera *Tree of Codes*), but its origins go all the way back to Lim's earliest compositional training. In an article about *An Elemental Thing* and a masterclass video with Speak Percussion she has described how, as a teenager, she was set a composition task by the Australian jazz musician Brian Brown to write a piece for woodblock and trumpet, the challenge being to combine these two very different soundworlds (Lim 2021; see also Speak Percussion 2016). Even at fifteen, Lim approached the problem by finding ways for a trumpet to sound like a woodblock or vice versa; some of these solutions are presented in her video with Speak Percussion. One interpretation of all the music she has written as an adult is that it is about finding ways in which contrasting sounds, instruments and materials can be transformed through their relationships with one another.

Sufism is also and once more an important inspiration, and Lim prefaces her score with a poem by Rumi:

> Just remember when you're in union,
> you don't have to fear
> that you'll be drained.
> The command comes to speak,and you feel the ocean
> moving through you.
> Then comes, Be silent,
> as when the rain stops,
> and the trees in the orchard
> begin to draw moisture
> up into themselves.

Rumi's poem references connection and union, but it also emphasizes the ecstasy that comes at a moment of change or transition: from an ocean passing through you to moisture being drawn up through roots. It is the moment of fullness just before breathing out, a child's weightlessness at the top of a swing, the first contact of bow hair with string. This kind of motion – inward and outward, to and fro, there and back again – determines the overall shape of the work.

The three movements of *Speak, Be Silent* describe an arc from closeness (or union) to maximal differentiation and distance and back to gradual reconnection. This in-and-out shape is drawn using two principal lines. The first is the use of pitch centres, rather like we have seen in, for example, *Mother Tongue* and *The Compass*. The work's principal pitch centre is F: the first movement gradually destabilises and eventually moves completely away from this, the second operates almost entirely without it, and the third gradually restores it. The second line is that between violin and woodblock. This is introduced midway through the first movement; in the second the contrast and connection between the two is the principal musical device; and in the third they are brought into an incomplete union with one another.

Speak, Be Silent begins with a 'tuning' passage that immediately recalls the opening of *Tongue of the Invisible*. Brass and Thai gong establish the pitch F, to which the remaining instruments tune themselves, freely embellishing around it. When they fall silent, the solo violin does the same (it plays throughout with its fourth string loosened by a tone to F). Unlike *Tongue of the Invisible*, however, this pitch centre serves as a point of departure rather than of arrival. I will call gestures like these 'de-attunements', in contrast to the attunement of *Tongue of the Invisible*. Example 5.12 shows the first example of this. It is relatively reserved but establishes some important features. First is the introduction of Eb as a counterpart to F, functioning rather like the dominant does to the tonic in tonal music. Second, it articulates a unison ensemble texture that will become a feature of this work. The particular rhythm here will return at an important juncture later in the work.

Example 5.12 *Speak, Be Silent*, Movt. I, bars 3–5 (wind and brass)

The next sounding of the F pitch centre (bars 6–8) focuses on solo violin and shows an increased level of deviation. The violin employs a high degree of distortion and violin, Thai gong, harp and piano share tremolos and various forms of glissando; the piano's Fs are prepared with screws to produce a gong-like sound.

As this passage illustrates, de-attuning (like attuning) is not necessarily related only to pitch but refers to a wider alignment of musicians and music across several possible parameters. Another way to think of it might be as a cousin of dynamic heterophony, but greatly magnified: we can conceive of the subtle coordinations and deviations of two heterophonic musicians as small-scale forms of attunement and de-attunement.

Several times over the opening pages of the work the F is restated with increasingly elaborate de-attunement, passing further into the background as the departures from it move increasingly into the foreground. By bar 49 it has almost completely disappeared from view. This is also the point at which wooden percussion is introduced for the first time; up to now the percussionist has played only gongs (with the occasional reinforcement of a muted pedal bass drum). The ensemble writing, which so far has been somewhat melodic/polyphonic, becomes pointillistic in preparation for the sounds of ratchet and guiro at bar 52. These two instruments play in dynamic heterophony with the solo and ensemble violins, while harp and piano add further accents. Only the harp sustains the F pitch centre, and at bar 56 it switches to an E♭, joining the soloist and upper strings. F is not heard again until the upbeat to bar 73, when it is played in unison by the whole ensemble – an instance of the rhythmic unison texture first heard in bar 3. Example 5.13 shows this in reduction; again, the guiro plays alongside the ensemble, here following precisely its rhythm.

Example 5.13 *Speak, Be Silent, Movt. I*, bars 72–3

This initiates a fast climactic passage based around unison melodic runs and rapid pulsing notes, a final de-attunement that blurs the entire ensemble into one shimmering mass. It is in this passage the woodblock is heard for the first time, a logical step on from ratchet and then guiro. The movement ends with a short series of cello and double bass pedals – F♯, B♭, A♭ – over which the solo violin searches uncertainly for a way to conclude. Alone and thoroughly de-attuned it cannot settle anywhere.

The middle movement is less than half the length of the outer two but contains many of the work's most consequential moments. Beginning from the same E–D♯ seventh with which the first movement ended, the violin begins another restless solo. Any sense of pitch centre is notably absent now, likewise any other stability of rhythm or timbre.

Example 5.14 *Speak, Be Silent, Movt. II*, bars 88–90

After four bars the violin is joined by the ensemble, playing a relatively stable A♭ ninth chord with added fourth and augmented fifth. The voicing of this chord resembles a harmonic series, with perfect octaves and fifths at the bottom and dissonant notes more closely spaced towards the top, giving the music a quality reminiscent of the spectral music of Gérard Grisey or Horatiu Radulescu. Two more 'spectral' chords like this are used in this movement, at bars 101 and 115, but this is the most consonant of the three. The stability of this chord is resisted by the violin, however, Instead, it reaches out to the guiro with its grainy *molto sul tasto* distortion at bar 93. The guiro responds in kind a bar later.

Example 5.15 *Speak, Be Silent*, Movt. II, bars 92–4

166   The Music of Liza Lim

When the ensemble chord dies away, the violin begins a second solo. This time it is joined by both guiro and wood block (played with a rasp stick to align it with both the guiro's perforated sound and the bowing action of the violin). The second 'spectral' chord – a stack of sevenths and tenths with some quartertone alterations – begins when they finish playing. Violin and wooden percussion are now clearly separate entities from the rest of the ensemble. Within this chord the percussionist plays a soft roll on Chinese cymbal; as the chord slowly melts, they switch to a woodblock tremolo while the violin sustains a high C. At bar 111 this tremolo grows to a rhythmic pattern and, using woodblocks and rasp sticks of their own, the wind players take up this rhythm in startling fashion in the form of a woodblock chorus.

Example 5.16 *Speak, Be Silent, Movt. II*, bars 111–14

The rhythm they play is identical to that of bar 3: the effect is that of a negative, or the 'upside-down' of the bar 3 instrumental 'chant'. What was a moment of attunement, unified and close, melodic and sustained, has become an extreme of de-attunement, sparse and distant, percussive and interrupted. Buzzing F octaves on harp and prepared piano at the end of this short chorus make explicit the link to the work's opening.

With this moment of greatest estrangement from its accompanying ensemble, the violin is momentarily completely destabilised. It hovers over a third 'spectral' chord, this time played only by strings, before tearing into a final sweep of triple forte distorted harmonics whose only companion is the ratchet, woodblock and guiro, whose rasping sounds it most closely emulates, and which bring the movement to a close.

CHAPTER 5: Music for orchestra and large ensemble   167

Example 5.17 *Speak, Be Silent, Movt. II*, bars 119–22 (solo violin and percussion)

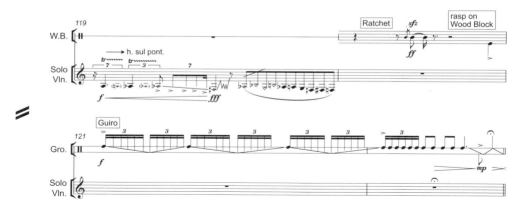

The final movement begins once again with the solo violin. Now, however, it seems surer of itself, as though the outburst with which it ended the second movement has brought some clarity. Although there is work still to do, its gestures move more towards attunement than away from it. The first bar of the movement, shown in Example 5.18, for example, drives towards (even if it never quite rests upon) a pitch centre on D.

Example 5.18 *Speak, Be Silent, Movt. III*, bar 123

The swing back to re-attunement is a long process: the second movement took us far from where we had begun. The distances to be travelled along the lines of both pitch centre and instrumental timbre are signalled by the ensemble. Over the first few pages of the movement, the harp bows an E♭ pedal (later joined by bowed piano), the most important of the secondary pitch centres. The ensemble accompaniment is dominated by percussion and brass, the two instrumental families from which the solo violin is most remote.

At bar 148 the string players do enter, but now they too are playing woodblocks, and they soon work in antiphonal chorus with the wind's woodblocks. Otherwise isolated, the violin seeks ways to attune itself with these groups. In bars 152–3 it creates a bridge between string woodblocks and hand drum. In bars 161–2 it joins harp and piano (whose Fs are prepared, remember) in a melodic articulation of the strings' woodblocks. And in bars 163–5 it enters into a more complex relationship with different parts of the ensemble. In bar 163 the violin's quavers work against the woodblocks' triplets. Its circular and sweeping bow movements, however, align with the guiro in bars 164 and 165. In the second half of bar 164 the crotchet pulse of the violin's low Fs link up first with the harp and then (in the next bar) with piano; these rhythms in turn are synchronised with the bassoon and saxophone's woodblocks and, on the second beat of bar 165, with the guiro's semiquaver groups. Across parameters of pitch, rhythm, timbre and gesture, a web of connections is created that makes something coherent out of this unusual ensemble.

Example 5.19 *Speak, Be Silent, Movt. III*, bars 163–5

As the wind and strings return to their usual instruments these connections are further explored, particularly through pulsing and *moto perpetuo* passages in the midst of which the pitch centre F is also gradually restored. From bar 197 it is taken up by a series of instruments, beginning with piano, then trumpet, solo violin, harp, Thai gong and, at bar 219, double bass, which provides a pedal beneath an unwinding *moto perpetuo* violin solo. At bar 231 oboe, violin and solo violin sound a melody based on the pitches F, E♭ and D. They are joined by the piano and the woodblock, which synchronises with their regular quavers. After some digressions to a D♭ pedal, F is once more firmly restored and at bar 248 woodblocks and F pedal are heard together. Now, though, what was a woodblock chorus is dispersed, its rhythm spread pointillistically across the ensemble.

Example 5.20 *Speak, Be Silent*, Movt. III, bars 248–50

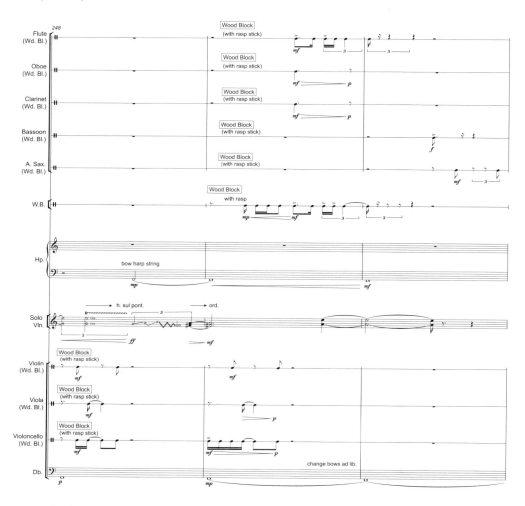

With the woodblocks having passed out of view, the solo violin brings the work to a close. Over a pedal F sustained by double bass and bowed harp it plays an expressive melody based upon a rising scale. Gradually this scale grows until in the penultimate bar it reaches a full octave; with this final melodic step from E♭ to F the work comes abruptly to an end, the reunion of soloist and ensemble having been finally achieved.

Example 5.21 *Speak, Be Silent*, Movt. III, bars 262–4

Extinction Events and Dawn Chorus (2017)

Extinction Events and Dawn Chorus is an appropriate point on which to end our discussion of Lim's concert music. Although her style and aesthetic has continued to develop after this, notably with the abovementioned piano concerto, the music theatre work *Atlas of the Sky* and the *Annunciation Triptych* for orchestra, in many ways *Extinction Events* is a consolidation of everything we have considered up to this point, and a springboard towards the music that has come after it. It was commissioned by the Wittenertage für Neue Kammermusik and the APRA AMCOS Art Music Fund and is dedicated to Ensemble Klangforum Wien, who gave its first performance at Witten in April 2018.

Although I have mentioned before (see discussion of *Koto*, Chapter 2) that there is a political and ethical dimension to Lim's musical aesthetic, it is rare for her music to engage directly with external issues: the three vocal songs *3 Angels*, written for *Escalier du Chant* on feminist texts by Hélène Cixous and reports of the death of Neda Agha-Soltan, are the only explicit instance we have encountered so far. The framing of *Extinction Events and Dawn Chorus* – as a response to man's destruction of the environment, and in particular the pollution of the oceans with plastic waste – is therefore unusual.

Characteristically, however, such images of pollution and destruction are neither represented nor lamented, but are analysed for their patterns, just as if they were instruments or texts. Lim focuses on the vast collections of plastic that have ended up in the world's oceans and have been gathered by circulatory currents (known as gyres) into five giant, swirling patches of rubbish and pollutants. The musical images of circling and rotation, prominent in *Ronda – The Spinning World* but present in many other works, are thus made central to *Extinction Events*. As the gyres turn, plastic is drawn into them and then ground together to create smaller and more dangerous particles, which enter the food chain and pose an existential threat to life on Earth. Plastic itself takes thousands of years to decay: if the Ancient Egyptians had had plastic, Tutankhamun's discarded coffee cups would still be with us. The ocean debris from just a few decades of plastic production will be with us for centuries.

These features of plastic – its durability, its circulation in ocean gyres and its pulverisation into microplastics by the actions of those gyres – form the basis for the guiding principles of the work. Plastic also features prominently as a musical object. In the first movement, a large sheet of cellophane is used as a percussion instrument. In the last, a one-metre plastic pipe is attached to the contraforte[2] to deepen its range to the edge of human audibility.

At the heart of the work is a seemingly innocuous instrument: the waldteufel. A waldteufel ('forest devil') is a handheld percussion instrument comprising a small friction drum whose string is attached to a rosined stick. With the string under tension, the stick can be turned to create a cracking, popping sound rather like the croaking of a frog as the friction of the string causes the drum skin to vibrate. With the stick held, the drum can also be whirled in a circle to create a smoother buzzing or whirring sound, a little like a ratchet. This small instrument thus shares many of the features of rotation, slippage and granularity that also make up the pattern language of the ocean gyres. With a string, a skin and a wooden soundbox, a waldteufel shares characteristics with several instruments in the ensemble, most notably the violin, and these allow for various lines of musical connection to be drawn through the conceptual space.

Extinction Events and *Dawn Chorus* is in five movements: 'Anthropogenic debris', 'Retrograde inversion', 'Autocorrect', 'Transmission' and 'Dawn Chorus'. The first threads the sound of the waldteufel among three main 'found' materials, forms of musical waste circling in the great gyre of sonic culture: a transcription of the song of the Hawai'ian Kaua'i 'ō'ō bird; fragments from Lim's violin solo *The Su Song Star Map*; and allusions to historical music in the form of the first few bars of Leoš Janáček's late-Romantic piano suite *On an Overgrown Path*. All of them are representations of degradation, loss and abjection. The Kaua'i 'ō'ō's mating call will never be answered: the recording is of the last of its species; it lives on only online. Su Song's chart predates Western astronomy by five hundred years, but its achievement has been erased by history. The Janáček – which was described by its composer as comprising reminiscences 'so dear to me that I do not think they will ever vanish' – but is altered almost beyond recognition.

The last of these is heard first at the start of the work. Lim draws on the opening bars of the first piece of Janáček's suite, 'Naše vačery' (Our Evenings). Over a piano pedal on B♭ (sustained using an Ebow), horn and trumpet play a version of the descending chromatic inner voices of the original, warped and distorted in rhythm and intervals. Lim further instructs her brass players to play with half-pressed valves (the diamond noteheads) to create a sound that slips unsteadily between tone and noise.

Example 5.22 *Extinction Events and Dawn Chorus*, 'Anthropogenic debris', bars 1–2

The liquid, dissolving brass are followed by the dry, grainy sound of a low waldteufel. Although the two are connected by the concept of slippage, sonically they appear at this moment far apart, creating a pleasing alternation of textures and posing an opening question that will be resolved later in the work. This field of contrasting sounds is sustained by the entry of flowing piano (with its own version of the brass's opening motif) and grinding cello, followed by oboe, bass clarinet and pizzicato double bass. At bar 16 a pair of interlaced repeat marks are introduced, cutting across another statement of the descending Janáček scale in the manner of a skipping CD. As we have seen in Chapter 1 (*The Su Song Star Map*) and Chapter 2 (*Ronda – The Spinning World*) repeats like these have become a significant feature of Lim's music since the mid-2010s. In *Extinction Events* they serve several poetic functions. First, the loop is one of many images of circling used in the work, related to the controlling idea of the ocean gyre. Second, a loop disturbs the forward motion of time. If it is repeated exactly, time is becalmed; if it is very short or cuts unexpectedly into a phrase it creates a sense of glitch or of failure. Third, it introduces stickiness or friction to the flow of time: like the pops of the waldteufel's string as it rubs against its stick, time catches in these repetitions and seems to have to work a little harder to move forward, an input of grinding energy that is released as sound. Finally, repetition gives a spatial quality to the passage of time, allowing linear motion to be folded, cut or shifted. Lim describes this aspect of the technique in tactile terms, borrowing a language of handicrafts that recalls Ingold's description of the transformation of lines into surfaces: 'There's something very materially satisfying about bracketing off the flow of the music in this way—it feels like folding time, or cutting a small section and sewing it into a new position, or knitting pockets into the music's unfolding' (Lim 2020).

Example 5.23 *Extinction Events and Dawn Chorus*, 'Anthropogenic debris', bars 16–18

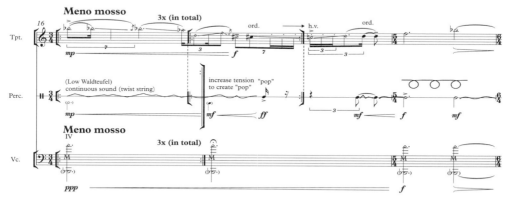

Over the next few pages, as the Janáček scale and glitching loops continue to play a part, the grainy sound of the waldteufel is developed around the ensemble, with wind underblown bassoon multiphonics, muted piano harmonics, spring drum, brushed bass drum and other such sounds. These are all preparations for the dramatic entry of the violin at bar 37. Amplified and playing at the back of the hall, the violin enters with a pedal on the E quarter-sharp below middle C (the lowest stopped note possible on her retuned instrument). Applying strong bow pressure, she creates a highly distorted, granulated noise marked 'like an oracle' on the score – a sort of mystical, non-verbal ventriloquism. The sound is audibly like that of the waldteufel, and the partnership between these two instruments will become one of the most important features of the work; for now, the waldteufel has found a sonic partner within the ensemble. When the pedal comes to an end at bar 47, a spinning high waldteufel, played by the bass clarinet, takes over, while multiphonic low strings, half-valve brass and scraped percussion increase the palette of related timbres. At bar 57, the violin enters into a heterophonic duet with the percussionist's medium waldteufel.

Example 5.24 *Extinction Events and Dawn Chorus*, 'Anthropogenic debris', bar 57

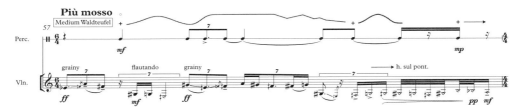

This short duet triggers most of the other musicians to take up their own waldteufels in a chorus of ratcheting, swirling sounds that recalls the woodblock choruses of *Speak, Be Silent*. As they do so, the violinist makes her physical entry, walking from the back of the hall to the stage, dragging with her a large sheet of cellophane, which is passed over the heads of the ensemble to the percussionist, who arranges it on a stand and rustles it in duo with the violinist, who is 'vary[ing] dynamic shaping against violin part'. The violinist here plays music extracted from *The Su Song Star Map*; the piccolo, meanwhile, enters with a transcription of the recorded call of the male Kauaʻi ʻōʻō, placed freely in time like the bird calls in *Tongue of the Invisible*. At bar 65, the combination of (recorded, extinct, transcribed) bird, internally looping violin, turning waldteufel and rustling plastic creates a gyre operating on several simultaneous timescales and drawing in drifting objects from across the natural and manmade worlds.

Example 5.25 *Extinction Events and Dawn Chorus*, 'Anthropogenic debris', bars 65–7

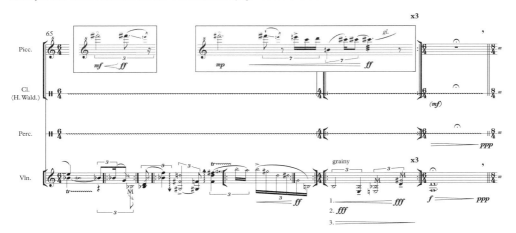

With the violin and plastic installed in the ensemble, the music turns towards the song of the Kaua'i 'ō'ō, taking up and developing ideas from the piccolo. Gradually, the clarity of this song degenerates and rasping sounds related to those of the waldteufel begin to return; the gyre continues to have an effect. A piano tremolo emerges out of the birdsong, then string multiphonics, then half-valve brass, the loose snares of a snare drum being bowed with a rasp stick and finally, at bar 97, a long ratchet crescendo. The final bars of the movement see an acceleration of the disintegration process, with the brass and lows strings playing allusions to the opening Janáček motif but distorted still further through *sul ponticello* playing, split tones and, in the case of the trumpet, extreme depth of register.

The second movement, 'Retrograde inversion', begins where the first left off. Starting with the same low F, the trumpet plays a solo in the bass clef, far below its normal, comfortable range. It begins with a rising scale that is almost literally a retrograde inversion of the 'Janáček' brass motif from the first movement, but although there are some pitch associations like this in the movement, its title is less 'an in-joke about Schoenbergian music theory' (Lim 2020) than a reference to the particular malleability of time in this movement, which makes great use of complex knots of repetition.

The first of these is in bar 5, after the trumpet's solo. The horn enters with a slightly altered restatement of the Janáček motif, but with two overlapping loops cut into it, while the trombone plays a repeating figure of its own (the third, written-out, repeat is varied). In this way the Janáček is not only brought into the pulverising gyre but also becomes one of its own making.

Example 5.26 *Extinction Events and Dawn Chorus*, 'Retrograde inversion', bar 5

A few bars later, an even more knotted tangle becomes a strange kind of fanfare.

Example 5.27 *Extinction Events and Dawn Chorus*, 'Retrograde inversion', bar 8

Loops of all sorts of kind proliferate through the movement. Some are complex, like the previous two examples; some, as at bars 12 and 13 – a two-bar repetition for the whole ensemble – are simpler. At bar 19 horn and trumpet play in written-out loops, a variation of the *moto perpetuo* idea we have seen elsewhere, with strings providing slight displacements, one decelerating, one accelerating.

As we have noted, the looping effect bears resemblance to the noise of the waldteufel and at bar 26 a new variation to its rasping sound is introduced in the unlikely form of a pair of whoopee cushions and a claxon. Although these obviously comic instruments represent a further degradation of the sound, they also provide a sonic link to the brass, which have been distorted by using half valves or, as with the trumpet at the start of the movement, playing in extremely low registers.

Example 5.28 *Extinction Events and Dawn Chorus*, 'Retrograde inversion', 26–8 (brass and percussion)

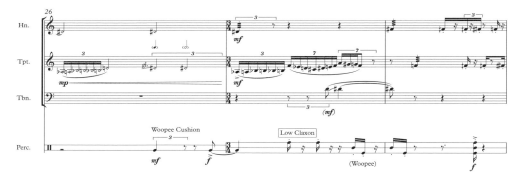

At bar 48 the cello and double bass take up a distorted 'grunting' sound in a written-out, bar-long repetition. At bar 51 they are joined by the trumpet and trombone playing their own distorted sounds, and three bars later by the contraforte. The overall texture – growling, grinding, flatulent – connects multiple sonic lines that run across the map of the work: the rasping waldteufel, the grinding 'oracle' violin, the rustling plastic, the whoopee cushion and claxon and, as we will see, the 'singing' fish of the final movement.

Example 5.29 *Extinction Events and Dawn Chorus*, 'Retrograde inversion', bars 54–6

To end the movement, cello and then violin solos drag the music up from this seemingly maximum point of disintegration. The violin's solo recapitulates last seven bars of *The Su Song Star Map*, a densely repetitive whirl of husky harmonics that narrow down to a single point; in the present whirling ocean context, the effect is rather like the water draining out of a bath, with the remnants of human history spinning backwards and downwards with it.

The third movement throws in another musical artefact – the sentimental late-Romantic harmonic style exemplified by Janáček and his peers. There are no specific allusions here, but the music is made up of disconnected chords, in lush, sonorous orchestration. Never forming a tonal grammar they are as if half-remembered, tarnished or crushed using layers of added dissonance, microtones, glissandi and noise. This movement shows a particular influence of the 'spectral' school of music associated with the French composers Gérard Grisey, Tristan Murail and Hugues Dufourt. (In its languid atmosphere there is a distant recollection, too, of the middle movement of *Speak, Be Silent*.) Several chords are decorated with florid, microtonally inflected arpeggios in a style reminiscent of Grisey's *Vortex temporum* (1994–6).

Example 5.30 *Extinction Events and Dawn Chorus*, 'Autocorrect', bar 4

At bar 10, the trumpet makes another statement of the Janáček scale motif, but this time with its intervals compressed to quarter tones and its rhythm stretched to three or four times its original length. Flute, oboe and bass clarinet add microtonal glissandi that approximately follow the music's line but in fact only distort it even further.

There is only one repeat in this movement, between bars 23 and 26. Because it is large, because it does not cut into the meter and because it involves the whole ensemble, this one feels less like a glitch than those of the second movement and more like a pause – although the climactic dynamic shape of this passage (an arpeggiated collapse down from fortissimo and then a swell back up again) is subverted by the retake, revealing the hollowness of its meaning as a gesture. Lim has said that in writing this movement she was 'interested in the possibility of referencing tonal materials as fictions – as found objects that continue to hold something of their historical aura even as they are warped and melted, plasticised and pulled in a few different directions' (Lim 2020).

The movement's final gesture is a perfect example, a root position A major chord in Mahlerian voicing, from double bass pedal to soaring solo violin five octaves above. However, the sound is muddied by the oboe's added ninth (B) and the bass clarinet's D three-quarter sharp. Over the next fifteen bars, to the end of the movement, this chord is further dirtied and altered without ever seeming like it has stopped; yet when the movement ends, a minute later, it is on a low Bb (with contraforte Eb), harmonically almost as remote from its beginning as it possibly could be, but a point to which this work is frequently drawn.

Example 5.31 *Extinction Events and Dawn Chorus*, 'Autocorrect', bars 31–3

CHAPTER 5: Music for orchestra and large ensemble 179

The fourth movement, 'Transmission', is the most unusual of the five. It is for a duo of violin and percussion, who move to the front of the stage to sit side by side at a small table, illuminated only by a desk lamp. This intimate, private space is somewhat removed from the large-scale ensemble setting so far. The violinist plays an instrument with a radical scordatura: the first string is tuned up a tenth(!) to B; the others are in fifths above this, but with the top two tuned down a quarter-tone. The percussionist meanwhile plays a snare drum that has been prepared in the manner of a large waldteufel: the usual drumhead is replaced with one pierced by a string of fishing line attached to a rosined stick. Twisting the stick creates a sustained sound; a rasp is used like a bow on the string to articulate attacks. Simply put, the rasping, ratcheting waldteufel, which in the second movement was aligned with the sound of low brass and in the first with the plastic-shrouded entry of the violin, is now reconceived as a rudimentary string instrument. The line of connection between the two instruments that was lightly drawn back then is brought into vivid realisation.

The form of 'Transmission' is that of a rudimentary instrumental lesson. The violinist plays short extracts (all of them derived from *The Su Song Star Map*), which the percussionist attempts to imitate. After the first attempt (clearly) fails, the second extract is rehearsed more carefully, with the violinist offering demonstrations of certain moments. Thus emboldened, for the third extract the two musicians play in unison, even though the music far exceeds the capabilities of the friction drum (Example 5.42). Finally, as if giving up – or perhaps bidding farewell – the violinist continues alone, repeating tiny fragments up to twenty times, the increasingly redundant repetitions serving to erase the instrument entirely.

Example 5.32 *Extinction Events and Dawn Chorus*, 'Transmission', letter C

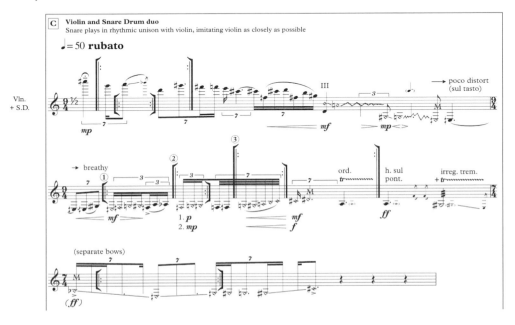

This remarkable movement is unique in Lim's music to date, yet it is grown from seeds we have seen elsewhere. The attempted unison of violin and friction drum is a form of heterophony, after all. And the fundamental conceit – of two radically different instruments finding common ground – is one we have seen many times. This is a variation on the idea of longing between *angklung* and *erhu* captured in *The Alchemical Wedding* but translated into the world of teaching. (It is not irrelevant to note that in the time between the two works Lim became an internationally valued composition teacher.) It is also connected to the anxieties about cultural survival first encountered in *Mother Tongue* and that inform so much of *Extinction Events* – a quixotic attempt to pass on knowledge and beauty in ever more challenging circumstances. And finally it is an expression of the guiding principles of slippage and degeneration (and of circling, in the instruments' repeating attempts to find a connection with one another) that Lim derives from the pattern language of ocean gyres.

At the end of 'Transmission', the percussionist turns off the desk lamp and the stage is left momentarily in darkness. When the lights rise again, they are kept low, 'as if at dawn, underwater' in the score's instruction. With the violin having failed to pass on what it knows, the fifth movement reaches towards a post-human form of music. It is a dawn chorus but not, as one might expect, of birds, but of fish. Like birds, fish 'sing' at changes of light; among the reef fish in the waters off Western Australia at least seven distinct choruses can be heard – surprisingly loud forms of buzzing, croaking and grunting. A work about the oceans and the destruction of the environment simply had to include these extraordinary sounds, and Lim's fifth movement, 'Dawn Chorus', is in large part a transcription of recordings made by the Australian marine biologist Rob McCauley and his colleagues.[3] Using windwands, kazoos and – of course – waldteufels, Lim is able to recreate with uncanny precision the sounds of dawn on the reef.

This last section joins others we have encountered in turning towards forms of white noise as a conclusion; this one is the most substantial of all (the movement lasts thirteen minutes, almost one third of the total length of the work). Noise here is not a static emptying-out of sound but a malleable compositional material that can be used to create contrasts, motifs and developments. Although there are a few additional elements, the movement is essentially a symphony of rasps, creaks and growls, a full realisation of the low grunting music we heard near the end of the second movement and a great magnification of the grainy sound of the waldteufel that has been with us all along.

CHAPTER 5: Music for orchestra and large ensemble   181

Example 5.33 *Extinction Events and Dawn Chorus,* 'Dawn chorus', bars 1–9

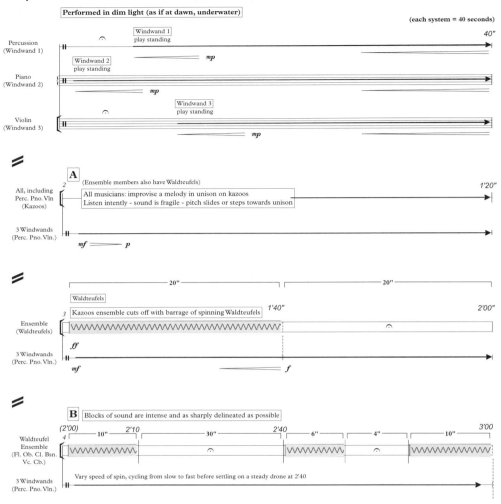

Lim has noted the comfortable fit of these sounds with her existing style – 'The distorted rasping and percussive sounds of the aquatic world already approach favoured elements of my musical language and so "realism" found an easy fit with musical abstraction' (Lim 2020) – and examples can be traced back to her very first professional work, *Garden of Earthly Desire,* which ends with the ensemble gently shaking an array of rattling objects (Example 2.5). Yet 'Dawn Chorus' depends upon many techniques and devices that have been developed in her music since then, and even in its apparently simple concept exemplifies the depth and variety of Lim's craft at the end of the 2010s. Example 5.43 shows some of these devices already: the freedom from metered rhythm represented by time bracket notation; the use of text instructions (rather than detailed notation) to describe generalised actions; asking musicians to play instruments other than their own (with the associated theatrical dimension); and the idea of attunement, represented here by the improvised unison kazoo melody (a new addition to the palette of buzzing instruments, related to the rudimentary sounds of whoopee cushion and hampered, half-valve brass). Even the introduction of more-than-human sounds has a precedent, in the cicada insect clicks of *The Compass*.

As the movement continues, other techniques that Lim has made her own are introduced. Horn, trumpet and trombone – instruments that have throughout been privileged with some of the most important material – introduce a variety of 'fish calls', repeated ad lib. from the third to the fifth minute. At the five-minute mark they switch to a sonorous drone (joined by contraforte) on B♭, another element that was not introduced into Lim's music for several years; the use of a prominent tonal centre as a way of tying together a large-scale form also dates from her later music.

Example 5.34 *Extinction Events and Dawn Chorus*, 'Dawn chorus', bars 9–12

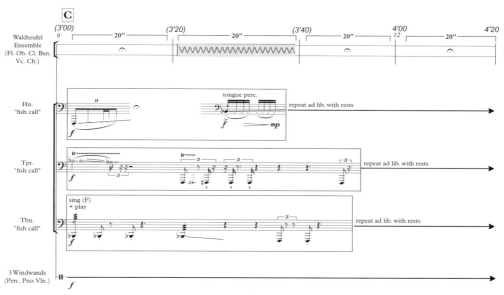

At six minutes, the flute, oboe, clarinet, horn, trumpet, percussion, piano and violin all take up their waldteufels once more, and as they spin them in one final chorus they leave the stage and walk through the audience (something we have seen previously with the brass in *Ronda*), reversing the entrance of the violin from the first movement. The remaining instruments – contraforte, trombone, cello and double bass – develop an improvised texture of fish calls in a manner that recalls the distributed creativity of the bird call chorus in *Tongue of the Invisible* (Example 3.29). Cello and double bass, moreover, use friction effects (forms of slippage once more!) including drawing a rubber superball mallet across the soundboard of the instrument to create strange, fish-like 'vocalisations' that resemble some of the techniques Lim developed for *An Elemental Thing*.

The last minutes of the work descend still deeper into the depths. While the cello detunes her lowest string to a deep bass B♭ the contraforte fixes the homemade length of pipe that will deepen her instrument to a low, low F (a plunge deeper than that with which *The Alchemical Wedding* began). This is a major third below the range of a piano and at a frequency of 22Hz is right at the edge of human hearing. It is a tone so low its waveform is experienced as a granular stream of pulses, more felt than heard. These last few bars are music that human ears can no longer understand, pointing to a future perhaps no longer meant for us.

Example 5.35 *Extinction Events and Dawn Chorus*, 'Dawn chorus', bars 42–4

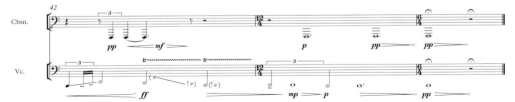

References

Ingold, Tim (2016). *Lines*. Abingdon: Routledge.

Keenan, Great (2016). 'Fish Recorded Singing Dawn Chorus on Reefs Just Like Birds'. *New Scientist*. 21 September, https://www.newscientist.com/article/2106331-fish-recorded-singing-dawn-chorus-on-reefs-just-like-birds/.

Kerry, Gordon (2009). *New Classical Music: Composing Australia*. Sydney: University of New South Wales Press.

Lim, Liza (2015). 'Speak, Be Silent (2015)' [programme note], https://lizalimcomposer.com/2015/06/11/speak-be-silent-2015/.

Lim, Liza (2020). 'An Ecology of Time Traces in *Extinction Events and Dawn Chorus*'. *Contemporary Music Review* 39, no. 5: 544–63.

Lim, Liza (2021). 'How to Make a Woodblock Sing: Artistic Research as an Art of Attentiveness'. In *Creative Research in Music: Informed Practice, Innovation and Transcendence*, edited by Anna Reid, Neal Peres Da Costa and Jeanell Carrigan. New York: Routledge.

Speak Percussion (2016). 'Online Masterclass 12: Liza Lim on Musical Dialogues' [video], http://soundsunheard.com/online-masterclass-12/.

Endnotes

1 An ocean drum is a drum containing metal beads that roll over its bottom head to produce a sound like ocean waves; a similar instrument was invented by Messiaen, who called it a geophone, for his work Des canyons aux étoiles.

2 An instrument similar to the contrabassoon but with a slighter deeper range. If a contraforte is not available a contrabassoon can be used instead.

3 Examples can be heard at Keenan (2016).

Chapter 6

Music for the stage

Lim's five works for the stage – the operas *The Oresteia*, *Yuè Lìng Jié (Moon Spirit Feasting)*, *The Navigator* and *Tree of Codes*, and the music theatre work *Atlas of the Sky* – are focal points along the line of her career marking, respectively, her early collaborations within the Melbourne arts scene, her engagement with non-Western cultural traditions in the late 1990s, the 'shimmer' period and her return to composition in the late 2000s, the ecological turn in her music of the mid-2010s, and her recent interest in heterogeneous and massed sounds. They also mark her most important collaborative partnerships with Australian and European ensembles: the first three works were written for and performed by ELISION, *Tree of Codes* was written for Musikfabrik, and *Atlas of the Sky* was written for Speak Percussion. This chapter focuses on *The Oresteia*, *The Navigator* and *Tree of Codes*. It also briefly discusses *Yuè Lìng Jié*, but to date only one scene from this opera ('Chang-O Flies to the Moon') has been recorded, making it hard to analyse at more length.[1]

All four operas are concerned with states of transformation and/or many-voicedness. Cassandra, the Apollo-possessed prophetess of *The Oresteia*; the goddess Chang-O of *Yuè Lìng Jié*, who attains immortality and takes control of her own story; in *The Navigator*, the erotically inspired division of Beloved and Navigator; and in *Tree of Codes*, the Son's transformation into his father in a world beyond death. Such states of transformation are typical of Lim's concert music – think only of the singing woodblock of *An Elemental Thing* or the ¬*erhu*-into-*angklung* becoming of *The Alchemical Wedding* – but in her operas they become sites for the dramatic transformation of character and narrative, and thus acquire a specific emotional dimension. In order for these transformations to take place, the emotional states of Lim's operas – revenge, self-actualisation, desire, grief – must be extremely heightened. This chapter therefore looks at some of the ways in which those emotional states are activated and some of the ways in which transformation takes place.

The Oresteia (1991–3)

Lim's first opera is for six voices, eleven musicians and dancer. It was first performed at Theatreworks, Melbourne, in a production directed by Barrie Kosky and designed by Peter Corrigan. ELISION were conducted by Sandro Gorli. It is a quintessential product of the young, adventurous, inter-disciplinary Melbourne arts scene described in Chapter 4 and in which Lim worked and found her voice after completing her studies: Kosky, who had directed the Australian premiere of Michael Tippett's *The Knot Garden* in 1989, originally suggested to Lim the idea of collaborating. He knew Corrigan through his work with the Gilgul Theatre, which Kosky had founded in 1990. Another young Melbourne-based artist, Shelley Lasica (b. 1961), was also known by the group and was engaged as choreographer and dancer. Among the singers, parts are written for the unique skills of Deborah Kayser (mezzo-soprano) and the countertenor Andrew Muscat-Clark; the other parts were sung by Jeannie van de Velde (soprano), Julie Edwardson (mezzo-soprano), Tyrone Landau (tenor) and Grant Smith (baritone). The ensemble is characteristically ELISION-esque: the line-up is similar to that of *Garden of Earthly Desire*, with the earlier work's harp and violin replaced by trumpet and trombone, and Stephen Morey's mandolin replaced by Cassandra Azzaro's *bağlama saz* (a Turkish lute similar to a mandolin).[2] Daryl Buckley's electric guitar is prominent, as is Rosanne Hunt's cello, although, as in *Garden*, Lim gives every instrument a moment in the spotlight.

The Oresteia is a chamber opera – Lim calls it a 'memory theatre' – in seven short scenes and lasting just over one hour. It is based on Aeschylus's trilogy *The Oresteia*, plus the missing satyr play *Proteus*. More a theatrical ritual around the House of Atreus's cycle of revenge killing than it is Aeschylus's story of the end of Trojan war and the birth of Athenian justice, the libretto, created by Lim and Kosky from Aeschylus's original Greek, Tony Harrison's 1983 translation and a Greek fragment by Sappho, radically compresses the trilogy into its iconic moments. The opera also tilts its focus away from the warring Agamemnon and his son Orestes to the female characters: Agamemnon's vengeful, power-hungry wife Clytemnestra; his prophetic lover and war-trophy Cassandra; his daughter Iphigenia, sacrificed to Artemis to aid victory against Troy; and the goddess Athena, who ultimately restores order.

Scene 1: 7 Positions of a Memory Theatre (Cassandra's Dream Song)

> *Seven archetypal figures are introduced: the Prophetess, the Furies, the Male-Female duality, the Mother, the Father, the Wanderer and the Divine. Alongside them are six 'objects of transformation': a net (with which Clytemnestra will ensnare Agamemnon and Cassandra), a hatchet (with which she kills them), an eagle/vulture (a combined image of Zeus and the Furies), a beacon (which proclaims the razing of Troy and the return of Agamemnon), the lion (Cassandra's image of Agamemnon in her prophecies), and the bed/bath/coffin of the husbands, fathers and sons of Troy.*

The opera begins with indecipherable cries of pleasure and pain – sobbing, laughing, gasping – before swiftly introducing the seven archetypal figures. The singers are not allocated fixed characters, but, as if the stage is magically charged, take them on when they step out of this pre-linguistic babble and into the performing space. Reflecting this restless, still-forming scenario, the music is heterogeneous in sound and style and jumps rapidly between characters and settings, as though flicking switches on a lighting board; the voices are, at this point, musical-visual ciphers, not yet characters in an ongoing narrative. To begin with, the first mezzo-soprano (as Prophetess) sings of the hell-net, accompanied by a culturally disjunct quartet of alto flute, *saz*, viola d'amore and *rin* (Japanese singing bowl) placed upon a timpani. Following this, the Furies are performed by a dancer, to an ensemble combining the piercing howls of electric guitar (played through a harmonizer to create a harsh, metallic timbre), oboe, clarinet, cello, double bass and the dry hatchet blows of a Thai gong.

Example 6.1 *The Oresteia*, Scene 1, bars 22–3

This texture is preserved to portray the duality of male and female, sung by countertenor, but without the winds or guitar. After this, the Mother is sung by the second mezzo-soprano to ululating music of high, staccato repetitions and tremolos. The Father is sung by the tenor in a strained, moaning voice accompanied by a more fragmented ensemble, punctuated with soft bass drum strikes, and the Divine is sung by the soprano 'with an unearthly brilliance', to the accompaniment of a florid oboe solo that picks up from the end of the Father's section. Between them the baritone, as the

Wanderer, interjects a sardonic, screeching falsetto accompanied with the whoops of a flexatone.

Example 6.2 *The Oresteia*, Scene 1, bars 53–62

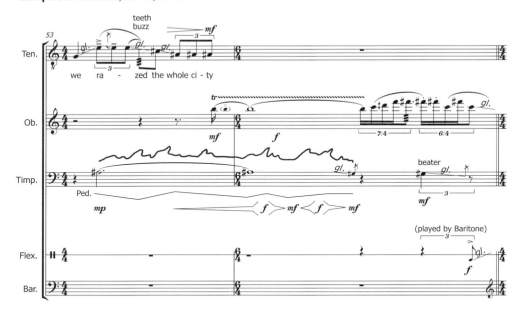

f) The Wanderer / (Bed-Bath)-Coffin

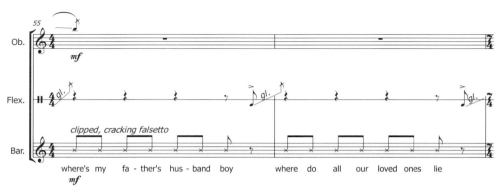

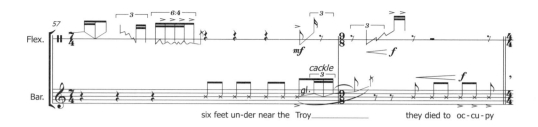

g) The Divine / Bed-Bath-Coffin

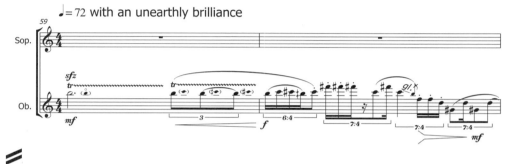

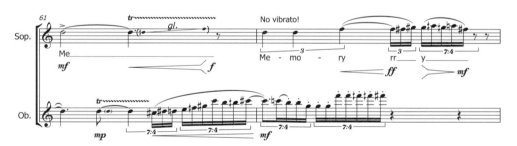

The scene ends with the return of the prophetic Cassandra, divided between soprano and first mezzo, and her unique accompanying quartet once more.

Scene 2: Memory Spills from the Split Skulls of Clytemnestra and Agamemnon

As they receive their death blows, Clytemnestra and Agamemnon's memories spill like blood the scenes of Aeschylus's story: the birth of Iphigenia to Clytemnestra; the 'blood wedding' of Iphigenia, staged by Agamemnon in order to enable his sacrificial killing of her to appease Artemis and aid passage of his troops to Troy; the herald announcing Agamemnon's return; the 'blood wedding' of Agamemnon and Cassandra; the carpet of blood-red tapestries Clytemnestra lays out for Agamemnon to walk upon; the birth of Orestes, during which Clytemnestra haemorrhages and Cassandra prophesies Orestes' murderous vengeance.

Scene 2 begins with a clattering, juddering motif, played twice, which seems to symbolise the deaths of Agamemnon (at the hands of Clytemnestra) and Clytemnestra (at the hands of Orestes).

Example 6.3 *The Oresteia*, Scene 2, bars 77–8

This motif is developed throughout this scene and recurs (with variations) at points elsewhere in the opera where murder or its consequences are suggested; I will call it the 'killing motif'. First, the tenor, in the role of Agamemnon, considers the prophecy that will lead to the 'battle hungry blood sacrifice' of Iphigenia. As the music repeats this blood-curdling shiver it is, for the moment, the sound that marks the beginning and end of the cycle of revenge.

A second thread is introduced by the cor anglais and strings, who develop a keening, quarter-tone melody parallel with but distinct from the killing motif. This 'birth motif' comes to the fore with Iphigenia's birth, sung by the second mezzo as Clytemnestra. When Orestes is born a few pages later, similar music returns. Within these two contrasting ideas – a staccato chopping and a smooth crying – Lim balances the competing forces of birth and death that drive the story of *The Oresteia* forward.

Example 6.4 *The Oresteia*, Scene 2, bars 92–5

Agamemnon musters himself to kill his daughter with a chant of 'the war effort wants it', a ghastly mantra that soon devolves into the homonymic repetition of 'whore/war', and then further still into the obscene cries of the Furies as the deed is done. A passage for percussion marks the 'blood wedding' of Iphigenia and Achilles, which Agamemnon uses as a pretext to bring her to the sacrificial altar, and includes strikes of the Thai gong that in the first scene marked the blows of Clytemnestra's hatchet.

Example 6.5 *The Oresteia*, Scene 2, bars 108–12 (countertenor and baritone)

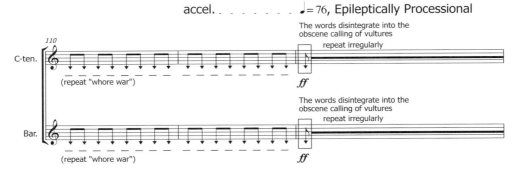

As Herald, the countertenor announces Agamemnon's return from Troy, but the joyful moment is tainted by echoes of the killing motif. As the Herald describes Agamemnon's victory, the motif morphs into an image of the desolation of Troy and the putrefaction of empire.

Example 6.6 *The Oresteia*, Scene 2, bars 137–42 (countertenor and baritone)

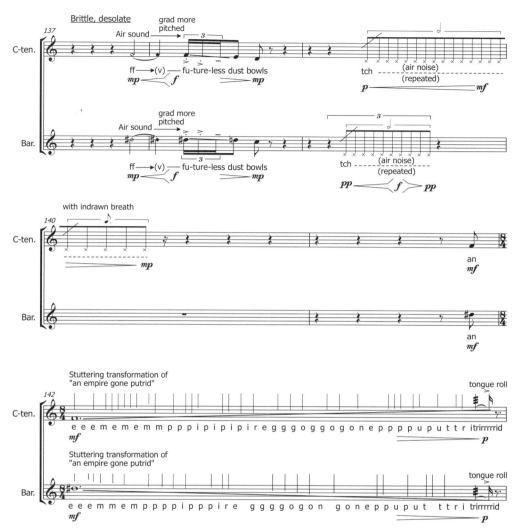

As Agamemnon walks the carpet of sacred garments that Clytemnestra has ominously laid out for him, the percussion plays music that, in its dry pulsation of guiro and rototoms, is a striking anticipation of the 'shimmer' textures of Lim's music more than ten years later.

As Clytemnestra, the second mezzo sings her own response to the carpet of blood red robes: they are symbols of the eternal cycle of bloody vengeance, 'the dyes of dark sea-red to stain all the garments this house has the wealth of'. Agamemnon introduces Cassandra – 'Trojan spoil, loot pearl' – and Clytemnestra turns her thoughts to Zeus, whose benevolence brings both the wealth of her house, and whose purpose she must fulfil. The meaning of that purpose is revealed in the bloody birth of Orestes that follows, out of which the voice of Cassandra speaks and prophesies the vengeance he will wreak:

'He'll come avenger blood-grudge fulfiller'. The music returns to the wailing labour cries of Iphigenia's birth, but now infected with the killing motif: birth and death wound together in one thread.

Example 6.7 *The Oresteia*, Scene 2, bars 188–92 (voices, oboe and alto flute)

The scene ends with the grainy sound of a ratchet, anticipating Cassandra's song in Scene 3 – a foreshadow of the rasping 'oracle' sound of the violin's entrance in *Extinction Events and Dawn Chorus*?

Scene 3: Cassandra — The Banquet

> *At the banquet to celebrate Agamemnon's return, Cassandra realises she is in the vengeance-reeking house of Atreus. In two ecstatic prophecies she foretells the deaths of Agamemnon and herself. On the roof she sees the gathering Furies. When she is finished, she vomits out the voice of Apollo, who has been speaking through her. Singing words by Sappho, she steps into the 'memory space' of Selene, the moon-goddess of prophecy.*

The opera's longest scene centres on Cassandra, sung principally by the first mezzo, but with aspects of her voice divided among all six singers. It begins with a return of the distinctive instrumental quartet that accompanied Cassandra in scene 1, and which heterophonically augments her vocal line. Here and elsewhere, timbre and instrumentation are used to signify different characters rather than melodic motives. Cassandra is joined by a chorus of the other five voices, who sing in Greek of where she has been brought to – 'The house of Atreus … a godless house echoing with dark secrets'. Cello and trombone are added to the instrumental ensemble, and their glissando lines – contrasting with the staccato plucking of the Cassandra-quartet – offer a throughline that can join all six voices together.

Cassandra's realisation of where she is ('a slaughterhouse streaming blood') is expressed in stuttering, retching, nauseous sounds of voices, unpitched, scraping strings, and percussion (guiro and rototom): grainy, scratching sounds once more aligned with prophecy and revelation.

Example 6.8 *The Oresteia*, Scene 3, bars 222–5

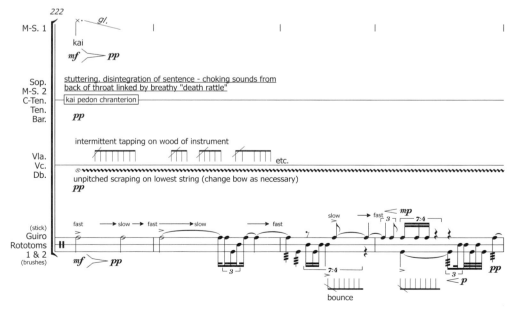

Her first prophecy is sung by all six voices, staggering their entries over seven graphically notated approximations of gesture – a very particular instance of dynamic heterophony. It is accompanied by the jangling rustle of a sistrum, a metallic rattle originating in ancient Egypt but also found in ancient Greece, with a sound somewhat like a tambourine and associated with religious or ecstatic rituals. It is an entirely new sound at this point in the opera, and so invests Cassandra's first prophecy with dramatic significance.

The first prophecy is followed by a 'bizarre madrigal', an almost completely a cappella passage for all six voices in which Cassandra sings of the dancing troupe of Furies waiting on the roof. Once more, the voices continually divide and come together in different configurations.

Example 6.9 *The Oresteia*, Scene 3, bars 243–5

Cassandra's second prophecy begins at bar 267 with a solo for piccolo, who vocalises the syllables of Agamemnon's name. Other wind and brass join, also vocalising: through their instruments they freely sound 'sharply gasped breath noise with intermittent high sucking sounds'. These two layers continue over the entry of the voices, who in graphically notated fashion enunciate Cassandra's words. The almost totally free distribution of her voice here suggests the psychological fragmentation that she is undergoing.

Example 6.10 *The Oresteia*, Scene 3, bar 276

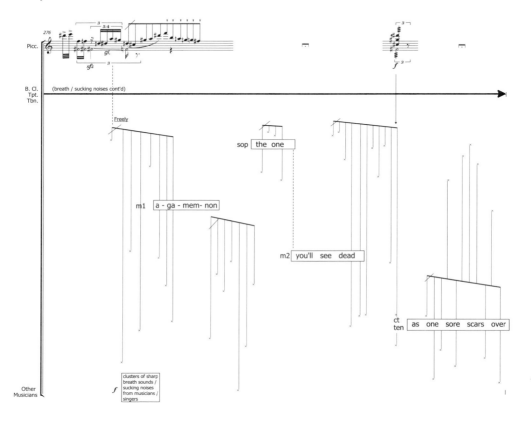

Using a shared prosthetic mouthpiece (made up of a flexatone with added jingles) to modulate the timbre of their voices, soprano and baritone sing of the Furies once more, who sing 'showering curses on the man who tramples on his brother's bed': the reference to a bed and the use of an adapted flexatone link this passage sonically to the Wanderer figure and bed-bath-coffin in Scene 1.

As the scene approaches its close, Cassandra sings her own 'death dirge'. Over an accompaniment of piccolo, *saz*, strings and sistrum (an instrumental grouping like her original quartet, augmented with instruments that have been connected to her subsequent prophecies), soprano, second mezzo and countertenor chant in Greek around the pitches of a second-inversion F major triad, supported by clarinet multiphonics on the same chord.

Example 6.11 *The Oresteia*, Scene 3, bars 309–10

Cassandra vomits out the voice of Apollo, who had given her the gift of prophecy. The prophetic sound of the piccolo, *saz* and sistrum ensemble is gradually replaced by the more piercing sounds of piccolo trumpet, trombone and clarinet, an inversion of the delicately plucked string sounds by which we have known Cassandra so far. At the scene's end, the first mezzo-soprano sings a solo aria accompanied by one chime of the rin, in which, now free of Apollo's influence, Cassandra enters into the memory space of Selene, the Greek moon-goddess of prophecy. Singing words by Sappho, she is centred as a heroine rather than murdered offstage, a farewell more lyrical and mournful than the one given her by Aeschylus.

Scene 4: The Furies

> *Agamemnon's funeral procession. The Furies cast a binding spell: the cycle of vengeance will continue. To the 'demented processional music' of Agamemnon's funeral, Orestes and Electra invoke their father's ghost: 'Time spatters the guilty. The living scratch open old scabs'.*

Scene 4 recalls some of the archetypes and figures from the beginning of the opera. The entry of the Furies is marked by a repeat of the metallic guitar bends of Example 6.1, before the baritone, as Agamemnon, sings a distorted plea to 'remember me' (a distant recollection of Dido's Lament from Purcell's *Dido and Aeneas*?). The dancer, who in Scene 1 represented the Furies, vocalises their binding spell as a kaleidoscope of expressions from grieved to orgasmic, from childlike to demonic,[3] after which the countertenor repeats the lament of the male-female duality, also from the first scene: 'Who'll bury, who'll sing, who'll mourn'.

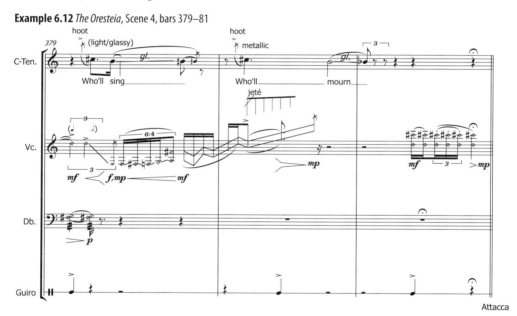

Example 6.12 *The Oresteia*, Scene 4, bars 379–81

As the instrument most closely associated with the Furies, the electric guitar is prominent throughout this scene. Between the vocal moments described above, it leads instrumental interludes characterised by glissandi, distortion and high pitch. As Agamemnon's burial rites are performed, it leads a 'demented processional music' (featuring the unusual sound of steel drums filled with water to produce glissando pitches) culminating in a virtuoso solo of fragmented, dissociated polyphony. The scene ends with a short cello solo that is like a hushed echo of the guitar's screeches.

Scene 5: Clytemnestra's Ghost

> *Clytemnestra pours libations to Gaia. She dreams of a snake suckling her breast – an image of her son, Orestes, who will one day kill her. With the death of Agamemnon,*

however, her dreams have – for now – reached their fulfilment. An accusing chorus lays the blame for all this bloodshed at the feet of Helen of Troy.

The cello that ended Scene 4 as a ghostly inversion of the Fury-guitar becomes the dominant instrument of Scene 5. The scene begins with the second mezzo-soprano, as Clytemnestra, singing a hymn to Gaia. As she does so, she plays a second cello, anticipating *Mother Tongue* of twelve years later. She only plays open strings and variation in sound is created through her bowing actions; for several bars she is asked to play with a circular bowing movement (the first time this appears in Lim's music); in another bar she must play long sliding gestures over the length of the C and G strings. As in the later work, circular bowing is associated with motherhood and childbirth, although nightmarishly in Clytemnestra's case as she dreams of a belly filling with corpses and a snake suckling her breast.

Example 6.13 *The Oresteia*, Scene 5, bars 442–9

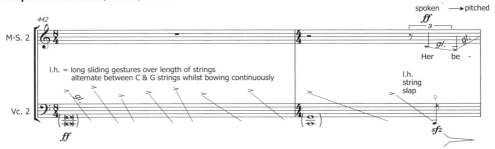

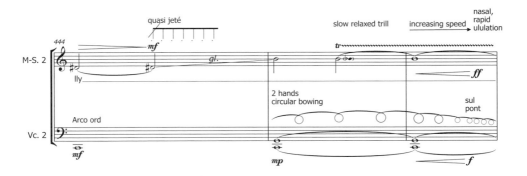

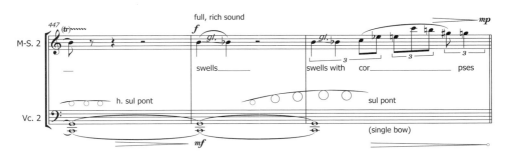

CHAPTER 6: Music for Stage   201

After a few pages, the mezzo is joined by the soprano, both in song and at the cello. While the mezzo bows on open D and A strings, the soprano lightly sweeps her hands in birdlike shapes over them, creating the sounds of harmonics. After an instrumental passage, and their double cry, 'Dream bitter womb', Clytemnestra, with the amnesia of a ghost, sacrifices Agamemnon in a duet with the ensemble cellist. A violent *jeté* strike on her own cello, just as she herself sings 'sacrifice', recalls the death blows of Scene 2, and the sacrifice of Iphigenia that set the opera's story in motion.

Example 6.14 *The Oresteia*, Scene 5, bars 501–2

With Clytemnestra joining the bloody vengeance cycle, a chorus of accusation swells against 'Helen, wrecker', its self-affirming insistence recalling Agamemnon's 'the war effort wants it' chant of Scene 2 (indeed, the baritone adds the telling words 'whore-war'): Clytemnestra's bloody motivation is the same as her husband's. Led by the second mezzo and tenor, all six singers begin to attack the cello with fierce percussive sounds. In a horrifying climax, the cello becomes a body, a victim and the site of violent, furious vengeance as Lim overlays sound, spectacle and drama within a single gesture. The singers' attacks only end as the cello is physically hauled away from them and out of reach.

Example 6.15 *The Oresteia*, Scene 5, bar 514

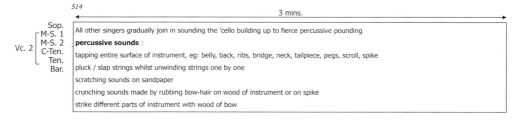

Scene 6: Apollo's Masque

> *Based on the surviving fragment from the satyr play,* Proteus, *the lost final part of Aeschylus's* Oresteia, *Apollo plays with the fates of Clytemnestra, Agamemnon and Cassandra. Orestes, having killed his mother in revenge for her killing of his father, is pursued by the Furies and comes face to face with the Gorgons.*

Scene 6 was written for Andrew Muscat-Clark, whose skill at overtone singing (a method of shaping the vocal tract to create different overtones over a fundamental pitch) would soon become such a feature of the de Clario installations.

Just two lines of *Proteus* survive: 'wretched struggling dove, on the wing for food / crushed by the winnowing fans its breast split open'. At the scene's start Lim sets these to a nursery-rhyme-like melody for unaccompanied countertenor. Before the melody is completely repeated, the other five voices unfold a distorted rendition that continues throughout the first half of the scene. As Apollo toys with the fates of Clytemnestra, Agamemnon and Cassandra, we must take this cruel child's play with the dying dove to be the god playing with the lives of mortals. The countertenor, meanwhile, takes on the voices of these three, singing their anguish over the increasingly malevolent chorus.

Example 6.16 *The Oresteia*, Scene 6, bars 528–33

The instruments enter in turn, their timbres (hi-hat, cor anglais, trumpet, guitar, etc) emphasising hard edges and heterogeneity. Tiny fragments of the melody enter the instrumental music – repeated emphases on A, F and E, for example, but the music of both instruments and voices is increasingly fragmented, even if elements of both text and melody remain. Eventually, the chorus degenerates completely into meaningless syllables, accompanied only by clattering percussion.

At bar 593 three statements of the killing motif played by the whole ensemble announce unmistakably the pursuit of Orestes. His encounter with the Gorgons (drawn from the very end of *The Libation Bearers*) is sung almost completely unaccompanied, making use of overtone singing: as Orestes confronts the horror and consequences of his actions, his voice is split in a manner that recalls Cassandra's. There is just one instrumental passage, for piccolo, oboe and sistrum, who seem to evoke the Gorgons' serpent hair. In Aeschylus's trilogy, this is the moment at which the eternal revenge spiral of the House of Atreus starts to come to a halt, and Lim's music has a quality of fading away and of climbing down from the horrors that we have witnessed. In its use of both overtone singing and tonal melody, the scene sets a template that will be revisited in the conclusions to *The Navigator* and *Tree of Codes*.

Example 6.17 *The Oresteia*, Scene 6, bars 616–22

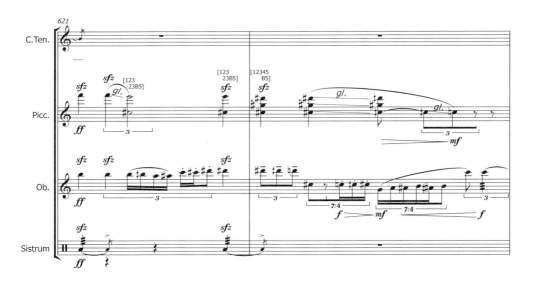

Scene 7: Athena's Trumpet

The third part of Aeschylus's surviving trilogy, The Eumenides, *concerns Athena's creation of a trial-based system, by which the house of Atreus's bloody cycle of vengeance is broken. Concerned less with the creation of the Athenian legal system than with the looping repetitions of the plot, Lim sets only three words for her final scene: memory, dream, fury.*

The short final scene of *The Oresteia* is scored for soprano, in the role of Athena, and piccolo trumpet. Their duet is conceived as a single line, in which the voice of the goddess and the unearthly brilliance of her trumpet are almost indecipherable; fanfare and song one and the same. The opera ends with both descending swiftly past the edge of their respective voices – the soprano into a violent exhalation of breath, the trumpet into a scale of half-valve notes and a flurry of deep pedal notes.

Example 6.18 *The Oresteia*, 'Athena's Trumpet', bars 647–51

Yuè Lìng Jié (Moon Spirit Feasting) (1997–2000)

Yuè Lìng Jié was commissioned by the Telstra Adelaide Festival and was first performed there in March 2000 (it was staged five more times between 2002 and 2006 in Melbourne, Berlin, Zurich, Tokyo and Brisbane). It marks a peak in the exploration of Chinese culture and thought that runs through Lim's music (and draws on her own Chinese heritage), beginning with *Li Shang yin* (1993) for soprano and fifteen instruments, through *The Cauldron* and *The Alchemical Wedding*, and on to later works such as *The Quickening, The Compass, How Forests Think* and *The Su Song Star Map*. It was written at the same time as Lim's other major engagement with Chinese culture, *Machine for Contacting the Dead*, a double concerto for bass/contrabass clarinet and cello inspired by the fifth-century BC tomb of Marquis Yi of Zeng that was discovered in 1977 and is one of China's most celebrated archaeological sites.[4]

The opera was written with the author Beth Yahp, like Lim another Asia-born Australian, whose Chinese-Thai parents moved to Australia from Malaysia in 1984. Her first novel, *The Crocodile Fury*, published in 1992, tells a story of Asian migrant experience in a world populated with ghosts and spirits. In preparation for writing the opera, the two women spent a fortnight in Malaysia researching Chinese opera, shamanic rituals and shadow puppet theatre in Kuala Lumpur and Penang. Of particular interest to them was the Hungry Ghost Festival, celebrated in the seventh month of the Chinese lunar calendar, during which spirits are believed to be released from hell to roam the earth and demand offerings, prayers and performances, and the opera's staging draws heavily on Southeast Asian street festivals like this. In Adelaide, the set was constructed on a barge on the Torrens River; the musicians performed both on the stage and in a 'shrine' behind the audience. Audience participation was important, as was the inclusion of food stalls, the burning of incense and the decoration of the river bank with lights and religious offerings: the work's performances were multi-sensory, festive occasions. Finally, the performance space was blessed by a Daoist priest prior to the first rehearsal.

There are four characters: the moon goddess Chang-O (soprano), the demon goddess Queen Mother of the West (dancing mezzo-soprano), the Archer Hou-Yi and the Monkey King (both performed by acrobatic baritone). The ensemble of nine instruments includes *erhu, koto* and two percussionists, the second of whom moves around the performance space. It was performed by Deborah Kayser, Melissa Madden Gray, Orren Tanabe and ELISION, conducted by Simon Hewett, directed by Michael Kantor and designed by Dorotka Sapinska.

Yuè Lìng Jié retells the story of Chang-O from a number of angles – a woman transformed into a goddess, a figure of nightmare, a wish-granting heavenly creature – and its seven scenes and two interludes draw on many Asian theatre traditions, including riddles, puppet shows, song contests and poetry. In the aria for soprano that constitutes Scene 6, Chang-O takes charge of her own story as she takes an elixir of immortality and completes her transformation. Her aria is accompanied by a striking quartet of bass flute, *koto*, cello and percussion (water gong, frame drum and *yunluo* or 'cloud gong'), whose timbral profile resembles that of the Cassandra-quartet in *The Oresteia*. Lim's technique of dynamic heterophony, developed in the mid-1990s, is markedly more evident here than it was in her first opera, and the music freely explores heterophonic relationships between voice and instruments. After riddles, a ritual burning of joss sticks (held by the audience) and a final release of the characters back into the spirit world, the opera ends with a 'swarming song' by Chang-O that is, Lim says, an attempt to recreate the sound of Deborah Kayser's heart chakra from *Bardo'i-thos-grol*.[5]

The Navigator (2007–8)

The Navigator was composed alongside the 'shimmer' works of the mid-2000s but instead of Aboriginal art and culture it takes inspiration from the Sanskrit epic the *Mahabharata* and Wagner's *Tristan and Isolde*. Lim describes its themes as 'Eros and Thanatos, Desire and Death, the gamble of love and war, and choices made between annihilation and creation' (Lim 2009). From the *Mahabharata* she borrows the dice game scene, in which King Yudishthira is duped into gambling away his wealth, his kingdom, his family and finally his beloved wife. The catastrophic aftermath of the game is where the opera begins, with The Beloved lost and abandoned. But within the gamble are also the two extremes of ecstasy and annihilation: an entwining of love and death that draws in the influence of *Tristan and Isolde*. The geometry of desire and longing in Wagner's famous 'Tristan' motif – in which elements that are moving past each other are momentarily held in tension, and then continue on their separate trajectories – informs the whole opera, and as tribute Lim inserts a reference to it at one point in her music. Lim has said that attending a performance of the prelude to *Tristan* by the Sydney Symphony Orchestra in 2004 (during the break she took from composing between 2002 and 2005) reignited her love of music (Leonard 2008), and in the years following she sought as many productions of the opera as she could, including revelatory productions by Peter Sellars and Bill Viola for Opéra National de Paris (2005) and by Barrie Kosky for the Aalto-Musiktheater, Essen, Germany (2007).

In an interview with the broadcaster Andrew Ford in 2009, Lim described the central concern of her music as a search for the 'ecstatic': 'some kind of ecstatic experience and transformation, you know where you are inside the sound, you're no longer separate from it, and I think when I'm writing music and then I'm listening to music, that is the kind of experience that I'm trying to make contact with. . . . I think there's a sense in which there's a dissolving of boundaries in some way . . . where the boundaries between your intellectual functioning, your kind of emotional world, your physical world, become kind of blurred' (Ford, 2009). Such a description of boundary-dissolving desire and ecstatic transformation will by now be familiar to the reader. *The Navigator*, however, is the work in which Lim most fully explores these ideas. The transformation of The Beloved into The Navigator in Scene 2 of the opera exceeds the arias for Cassandra and Chang-O already described in the extraordinary sensuality of its instrumentation (here bass recorder, Baroque harp and viola d'amore), and the opera is, even more than *The Oresteia* or *Yuè Lìng Jié*, shaped by the vivid contrasts of its soundworld.

The Navigator and The Beloved are sung by countertenor and coloratura soprano, respectively. They are accompanied by a chorus of three sirens (The Crone, The Fool and The Angel of History), sung by bass baritone, baritone and Baroque alto. The ensemble comprises sixteen musicians and includes a Baroque trio of Ganassi and Paetzold contrabass recorders, viola d'amore and triple harp (several strings of which are prepared with blu-tak or bray pins[6]), plus winds, brass, strings, percussion, electric guitar and electronics. The musicians also play small 'frog' guiros. *The Navigator* was commissioned by Brisbane Festival 2008, Melbourne International Festival of the Arts and ELISION, and first performed at the 2008 Brisbane Festival by ELISION, conducted by Manuel Nawri. The singers were Andrew Watts (The Navigator), Talise Trevigne (The Beloved), Philip Larson (First Siren/The Crone), Omar Ebrahim (Second Siren/The Fool), Deborah Kayser (Third Siren/The Angel of History). It has subsequently been performed in Melbourne, Moscow and in a concert performance at the Festival d'Automne, Paris.

CHAPTER 6: Music for Stage **209**

Prelude: Weaver of Fictions

Solo for Ganassi recorder.

The mood is set by Lim's evocative solo for Ganassi recorder, described in Chapter 1, which plays with tensions between sinuous melody and blazing multiphonics.

Scene 1: The Unwinding

> *The Beloved is bartered in a game of war, but in an act of resistance she morphs into her shadow twin, The Navigator. Escaping and unwinding with her are three Sirens – The Crone, The Fool and The Angel of History – who sing of the forces of blood, history and time.*

Scene 1 is announced by the noise of cicadas and the piercing howl of an electric guitar played through a tube screamer pedal. The juxtaposition of these harsh sounds with the gently erotic Ganassi recorder mirrors the thematic opposition of the opera. The sound of a heavily distorted guitar (to say nothing of the clicking of cicadas) may not immediately call to mind desire but, as in *The Alchemical Wedding*, Lim uses the juxtaposition of radically different instruments (with radically different histories) to activate structures of longing. The distance between them is essential to that structure: 'What is desire but a longing for that which is outside of one's reach – a trajectory of longing that moves to an impossible "vanishing point"? A triangular geometry is created in which the lover yearns to be one with "the beloved", yet also strives to maintain the distance that is the condition of the erotic … That is the paradox of the erotic – the attainment of desire cancels out desire' (Lim 2009).

Like the waldteufels of *Extinction Events and Dawn Chorus*, the sound of cicadas activates a network of sonic and cultural associations. Recall their role at the end of *The Compass*, where they are used as an instance of musical shimmer and a representation of the stars, and in the final movement of *The Quickening*, where they are associated with pregnancy and childbirth. (Remember, too, the 'Insects' sections of *Garden of Earthly Desire*!) Known for their long lifecycle (some species live underground as nymphs for seventeen years before emerging overground as adults) cicadas have been symbols of death and rebirth in Chinese culture for more than three millennia. In Plato's *Phaedrus*, Socrates describes how cicadas were once humans who, having allowed the Muses to enchant them into singing and dancing, forgot everything else and became 'pure beings of desire' (Lim, quoted in Gruchy 2007). They thus conjoin the opera's two main themes. The familiar singing of male cicadas is created either by using dedicated muscles to 'pop' the abdomen (which is hollow, to amplify the sound) or by rubbing it with their wings; its purpose is to attract a mate within the short window an adult cicada has before it dies. Many cicadas together – a vast chorus of desire! – creates a continuum of pulses across a harsh frequency spectrum. In *The Navigator*, Lim's instrumentation transforms this sound into a surface of interconnected timbres. Baroque harp, viola d'amore (with its sympathetic strings) and electric guitar (with distortion pedal) all include forms of buzzing or sizzling as part of their 'natural' sound production. Likewise the percussion set-up, which includes cellophane, sandpaper blocks, cabasa, guiro, rainstick, ocean drum, snare drum (with rasp stick and brushes), bass drum frame with beads, and sizzle cymbal. The other instruments can create a variety of cicada-like effects through specific techniques, including multiphonics, trills, tremolos, *sul ponticello* playing and so on, all of which are used frequently, as is the harmonic 'beating' that is created by close dissonances between them. Finally, the singers also make use of wacky whistles (see the last movement of *The Quickening,* Chapter 3) and a range of vocal techniques to add distortion to their voices. Together, these instruments and techniques invest the music of *The Navigator* with a particularly vibrant energy that is both sonically and symbolically connected to the lifecycle and symbolism of the cicada.

Example 6.19 *The Navigator*, Scene 1, bars 1–2

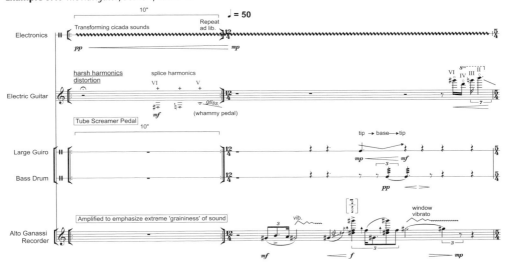

Although the recorder symbolises initially a melodic side of the music that is opposed to the cicada sounds, it is clear even from Example 6.19 that it mediates between the two, its characteristic vibrato containing elements of erotic sensuality and sizzling cicada. Amplified to emphasise their graininess, the dissonant multiphonics in bar 2 are similar in timbre to the guitar's distortion. Somewhat later in the scene, this duality is emphasised still further, as the recorder (continuing to draw on the music of the Prelude) plays alongside The Beloved while the strings and percussion play a contrasting cicada-like music. A few bars later, however, another passage repeated from the Prelude draws the recorder into that soundworld.

Example 6.20 *The Navigator*, Scene 1, bars 65–7

A long central passage featuring guitar, rasping percussion, electronic static, sandpaper blocks, wind breath sounds and more (Lim's 'shimmer' sounds brought into a new, emotionally heightened context) accompanies The Beloved's unwinding transformation into her 'shadow-twin', The Navigator. A last melodic aria for The Beloved, accompanied by recorder and alto flute, winds down into an a cappella passage for her and the three Sirens. The scene ends, however, with an aria for The Angel of History. Singing with a wacky whistle her voice channels the animal-insect-human-divinity of Walter Benjamin's Angel, condemned to give powerless witness to the inexhaustible wreckage of history. Lim's music here is some of the most remarkable of the opera. Written for Kayser, it extends the use of prosthetic mouthpieces introduced in *The Oresteia* and the use of the wacky whistle in *The Quickening* into a virtuoso display of polyvocality whose growling, shivering, screeching, distorted sounds are taken up across the ensemble, ending in a duet with trumpet (from which the solo *Wild Winged One* is partly derived). In *The Oresteia*

and *Yuè Lìng Jié* Lim had already written roles that showed off Kayser's extraordinary vocal skills, but here she exceeds both in honouring one of her longest-serving collaborators.

Scene 2: Sensorium

> *In a world of luminous illusion and suspended time The Navigator and The Beloved pursue an ecstasy of sensory discovery.*

The influence of Kosky's Essen production of *Tristan*, which Lim has described as 'a fugue of the senses' (Leonard 2008), is particularly apparent in this scene. Lim begins The Beloved and The Navigator's sensory exploration of themselves with music for the Baroque trio of recorder (here a contrabass Paetzold), viola d'amore and triple harp. The music is far from Baroque in style, however, and makes use of various extended techniques, including prepared harp strings and a multiphonic sweep technique for the recorder that bears comparison with Lim's didgeridoo writing in *The Compass*. Example 6.21 shows also how Lim uses heterophony to pass a musical line between the parts, pairing Beloved/recorder, recorder/harp, harp/viola and viola/recorder.

Example 6.21 *The Navigator*, Scene 2, bars 10–12

When The Beloved and The Navigator sing as a duo, they connect with each other and members of the ensemble in a similar way, creating a bundle of two, three or more threads that entwine around each other.

Example 6.22 *The Navigator*, Scene 2, bars 23–6

At bar 48, the strings enter, playing almost static chords – a rare example in Lim's music, but one that has precedent in this opera in the a cappella voices towards the end of Scene 1 (and that will return at the opera's end). From bar 52 The Navigator comes to the fore, partnered (as The Beloved has been with the recorder) with the cor anglais. Lim gives the cor anglais an explicit reference to Wagner's 'Tristan' motif at bar 63, but its yearning, descending chromaticism shapes the whole of this section, as Example 6.23 shows.

Example 6.23 *The Navigator*, Scene 2, bars 73–4

At bar 113 electronics and cabasa signal a return of the cicada music, against which The Fool, 'with the intensity/timbre of a muezzin call', sings riddles of loss. 'Rapture and rupture are twins', reply Beloved and Navigator, in unison. The scene ends with them singing images of binding and slashing together to heterophonic lines between oboe and viola d'amore that emphasise semitonal clashes, a recollection of the 'cleaving' idea described in Chapter 1 in relation to *The Four Seasons* and a striking example of word-painting.

Scene 3: Annihilation

> *The gamble between war and lover intensifies. The Sirens describe a desolate, frozen landscape in the aftermath of war. The Navigator, missing the presence of The Beloved, describes a dream of white violets.*

There are echoes in this scene of the desolation of Troy from Scene 2 of The Oresteia but played out on a much larger scale. After a short, drone metal-like guitar solo, the scene begins with the three Sirens singing of 'bone music under white stars'. The music is the antithesis of the erotically charged lyricism of the previous scenes: dry, percussive, without melody and almost without pitch. In the face of war, the ecstasy of 'Sensorium' is freezing over. The vibraphone and harp play descending scalar figures that emphasise dissonant, 'beating' reverberation rather than melodic movement; the winds play variants of pedal tones and multiphonics; and the strings play pulsing, *col legno jeté* figures that recall some of the 'shimmer' effects of, for example, *Songs Found in Dream*, but which might also be heard as a slowed-down version of the cicadas' song.

Example 6.24 *The Navigator*, Scene 3, bars 5–7 (strings)

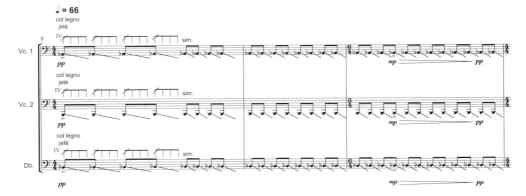

A melodic component is introduced by *The Navigator*, who at bar 18 sings briefly in duet with the tenor Ganassi recorder. But the first part of the scene belongs to the Sirens' desolate song. The Fool is joined first by The Crone, and then The Angel of History, their voices become increasingly distorted and animalistic. At the sight of a comet – prophetic omen, lonely ball of ice – the Sirens call upon The Navigator to name it. Hallucinating a dream of white violets, a glacier and the scent of The Beloved's 'elusive musk', The Navigator sings an aria to the accompaniment of the tenor Ganassi recorder (the recorder music here was extracted, adapted and extended by Lim to make the solo work *the long forgetting*, used in the installation TON). Navigator and recorder share their melody with tiny variations in pitch, rhythm and timbre: an example of dynamic heterophony employed to create a sensual, erotic charge.

Example 6.25 *The Navigator*, Scene 3, bars 108–11

The scene ends with a return of the animalistic Sirens, whose 'bone music' devolves into a recursive chant led by The Angel: 'the erotic bathings / of a man inside a woman / inside a man who makes love / with water, sings of a woman / inside a man inside a woman / who makes love with a comet / sings of a comet inside a glacier …'. Reflecting this final descent into time-unmoored delirium, Lim writes the last three pages of the scene in open form. Over an unpitched 'pedal' of electronic static and high woodblock – a cicada song denuded of its life and desire – The Angel recites her text freely. As she does so, selected words trigger percussive fragments performed by trumpet, Fool and Crone, which themselves build up to a maximum density of sound and then a sudden dénouement. 'Sings of a doubt so cold it breeds ice', speaks the Angel, alone, before another punctuation from the guitar leads us into Scene 4.

Scene 4: False Sail

Adrift and apart between ocean and sky The Navigator and The Beloved depth-sound for reunion, safe passage and arrival. The scene ends with a chorus of Navigator, Beloved and Sirens.

Scene 4 is divided between The Navigator and The Beloved, who sing solos in search of each other while the Sirens add commentary. Only at the end of the scene do all five voices come together. The scene begins with a loud, tutti instrumental chord of A and C♯ over an E♭ bass. This is related to Wagner's 'Tristan' chord (an F♯ in the treble would complete it), but Lim says that this is a coincidence[7]; the chord is derived instead from its 'spectralist' sonority (compare similar chords in *Speak, Be Silent*, for example). Its effect is to portray the inscrutable vastness of the ocean on which Navigator and Beloved drift in search of each other. The Navigator sings first, telling of the treachery of horizons: 'horizons flicker beg shift decay'. The Fool supports him: 'horizon and water could never be lovers / horizon adores only distance'. A second, much more dissonant instrumental chord (Ab–Bb–Eb–E♮–F–Eb–C–E♮) announces the entry of the first and second Sirens, whose chant outlining the predicament of Navigator and Beloved draws on this harmony.

Example 6.26 *The Navigator*, Scene 4, bars 27–30

When The Beloved sings, she is joined heterophonically by the alto Ganassi recorder. Her aria contains fragments from the opera's Prelude (particularly the dotted note descending triplet from its beginning; see Example 1.3), an indication of the enduring presence of Eros and desire. Other instruments are also drawn towards this thread, in particular the viola d'amore.

Example 6.27 *The Navigator*, Scene 4, bars 52–4 (Beloved, recorder and viola d'amore)

With The Beloved's words 'this sea I am embraces even treachery', the music takes a different turn. The recorder (and alto flute), which have supported The Beloved so far, are replaced by the sharper sounds of brass and reed instruments, which have previously been associated more often with The Navigator. The clarinet briefly becomes The Beloved's heterophonic partner, before passing the torch to the viola d'amore once more.

Example 6.28 *The Navigator*, Scene 4, bars 77–80 (Beloved, clarinet and viola d'amore)

This transfer signals the end of The Beloved's aria and the beginning of The Navigator's. As he sings, he too is drawn into unusual instrumental territory, and in a complete reversal of roles becomes partnered with the alto Ganassi. This pairing has none of the melodic affinity between voice and instrument that we have seen with The Beloved, however: still adrift on the ocean, Beloved and Navigator are as far apart as ever.

Example 6.29 *The Navigator*, Scene 4, bars 92–5

A return to the E♭–A–C♯ triad from the scene's beginning introduces the last section. The five voices sing together, standing firm against a roiling instrumental music of maximum heterogeneity. Eventually the brass break through; their chiming call becomes a run of chords for vibraphone, then harp and clarinet, and the Sirens look out for the sail that in the original Tristan story was supposed to signal the safe return of Isolde: 'blood sail or rainbow, illusion or shroud'. Gradually the music settles down into slow waves of sound and The Beloved and The Navigator are reunited before an ecstatic guitar solo brings the scene to an end.

Scene 5: Transfiguration

> *Arriving at a desert shore, Beloved and Navigator face only more challenges: the land is both barren and fertile. The only way forward is to choose between annihilation or creation.*

The key to the fifth scene is given towards its end as The Beloved sings of annihilation and creation as 'two rivers / whose thin divide / is a membrane's shudder'. This shudder, which divides death and desire (or acts as a passageway between them), is represented musically in a variety of ways. (It might also describe the cicada's song-producing organ.) At the start of the scene, rainstick, electronic static and sizzle cymbal provide suitably grainy percussion. This is enriched by low brass, wind and string pedal tones spaced in sevenths or ninths, whose slower frequencies create one form of acoustic vibration (compare with the low strings and contrabassoon at the end of *Extinction Events and Dawn Chorus*) while their 'beating' dissonant intervals create another. The Siren chorus, meanwhile, creates forms of vibration, first in their unison rhythm and then, as the second Siren briefly peels away from that, in the interaction between difference and similarity.

Example 6.30 *The Navigator*, Scene 5, bars 5–9 (Sirens)

As the scene continues, related effects are created by trilling flute, half-valve trumpet, *col legno* and *jeté* strings, and a range of other instrumental techniques, many of which will be familiar as musical representations of shimmer or, in Lim's later pieces, as representations of granularity or friction. In the present context they also relate to the death/desire sound of the cicada. The emphasis on the ecstatic that is the theme of *The Navigator* means that Lim tilts these sound-types towards the radiant or piercing (as opposed to, say, the drier percussiveness of *Songs Found in Dream*, or the softer 'breath music' dance of *The Compass*). Example 6.31 shows a more complex example from a little later in the scene. Beginning from the viola d'amore's pedal D, Navigator and viola d'amore spin out a heterophonic melody that both draws them together and pulls them apart. In bar 37 the viola d'amore adds a radiant ripple to the voice and in bar 39 it is the other way around. In bar 38, however, the viola d'amore seems to go somewhere entirely new, with a bow scrape (reinforced by the guiro) inside of which the Navigator sings a delicately turning figure.

Example 6.31 *The Navigator*, Scene 5, bars 34–9 (Navigator, viola d'amore and guiro)

As the scene continues, these oppositions – 'annihilation, creation / tide against tide', sing the Sirens – reach a climax with The Beloved's words quoted above. Against the percussive shuddering of cymbals, drums, harp and double bass she sings a melody whose trilling ornamentation threatens to tear it open. Note here the almost complete lack of pitch or rhythmic connection between instruments, as if the whole ensemble is shaking itself apart.

Example 6.32 *The Navigator*, Scene 5, bars 78–80

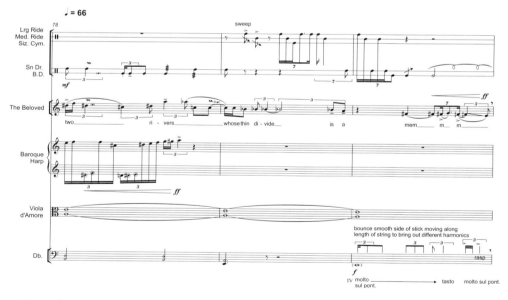

From here to the end of the scene, it is the sounds of annihilation and the desert that dominate. Beloved and Navigator, vocalising gasps and croaks more than song, are accompanied by a pitchless, distorted viola d'amore and the rustling and crunching of guiro and brushed drums, and then finally the massed sound of handheld frog guiros played by the ensemble.

Scene 6: The Binding

> *A dream in the womb. The Sirens guide a ritual of rebirth in which a cicada is placed on the eye of a foetus. The journey embraces its desire and chooses hope.*

But the opera does not end here. Out of the percussive sweeping of the frog guiros emerges the sound of a Jew's harp (played by the second Siren), and then the harmonic multiphonic sweeps of the contrabass Paetzold recorder (compare the beginning of Scene 2). The transformation is distinctively Lim-like, one parameter of the sound (here the physical sweep of the guiro) becoming a bridge to a different kind of sound. Threads connect and diverge. Out of nothing, something is reborn.

The first part of this scene concerns the ritual of rebirth. The Sirens sing modal chants in bare fifths and octaves, with interjections from The Beloved and The Navigator that contrast in both timbre and harmony.

Example 6.33 *The Navigator*, Scene 6, bars 43–4 (voices)

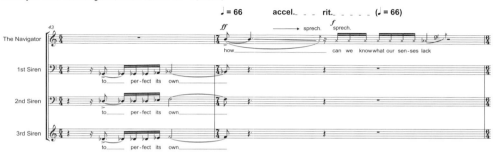

After several such alternations, The Navigator sings his own version of the chant, building on the pitch centre of B♭ that has been established by the Sirens. This pitch is taken up by harp and pizzicato strings (with the indication 'papery'). The rustling quality of this texture is enhanced by the addition of cellophane and the whispering of the first Siren before the guitar enters playing a slow flange effect/harmonic sweep on B. Cellophane and improvised whispering by the Sirens sustain the rustling effect against the guitar's forceful drone; together they are something like a cicada song separated into its constituent parts – a model of desire within desire. This climactic passage ends with Beloved and Navigator singing long, nasal melismas, another take on the cicadas' song, on the phrase 'tears open the membrane'.

Example 6.34 *The Navigator*, Scene 6, bars 72–3

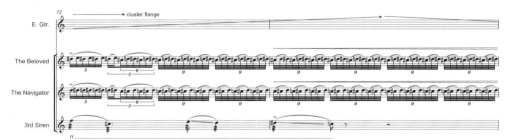

After a sudden stop, the second and third Sirens introduce a new element: a Sufi-like melody (marked 'ney-like timbre', referring to a type of Persian flute). They are joined by the first Siren and recorder, who adds a flourish of the 'Eros' motif.

Example 6.35 *The Navigator*, Scene 6, bars 80–82 (voices and recorder)

A large part for percussion, playing metal block, temple block, guiro, tom-tom, snare and bass drum, fractures the sonic and rhythmic homogeneity as the singers continue: the membrane torn open, the music fragments and divides. As the polyphony of the vocal and instrumental texture continues to increase, The Beloved and The Navigator add their voices too. Eventually, the music exhausts its energies and the voices come together for a final a capella chorus, sung in unison: 'the binding intimacy of breath / is named for joy'.

This final statement complete ('the single note that is ours / prolongs its shimmer / wave / within which all fear / dissolves'), the opera moves into its last section, a duet for Beloved and Navigator to at first an accompaniment of the three Sirens, and then gradually the full ensemble. For nearly three minutes the music's harmony is almost static. There are changes in harmony, but these are like changes in focus, as though the underlying chord were a rotating glass, refracting different parts of the spectrum. The principal harmonic notes, heard almost continuously throughout this section, are a widely spaced cluster of F, G and G♯, but around these other notes are added, emphasising both close dissonances (F♯, A, A♭, for example) and open fifths (C in particular), harmonic extremes that have both featured prominently in this scene, the one a dense, vibrant buzz, the other a calm, ritual resting place. While these and other 'ecstatic' colours are added by the instruments, the singers' music, particularly that of Beloved and Navigator, who are now completely entwined, becomes more and more breathlike, circling around an inhale-exhale repetition of 'opening / closing' before the music finally comes to a rest, with harp and recorder providing one final layer of slow shiver.

Tree of Codes: 'Cut-outs in time', an opera (2013–15)

Tree of Codes is based upon the eponymous novel by Jonathan Safran Foer of 2010. That book itself is based on *The Street of Crocodiles*, a collection of short stories by the prewar Polish author Bruno Schulz. Having herself written a piece called *Street of Crocodiles* for nine musicians in 1995 that is based upon Schulz's book, when Safran Foer's novel was published fifteen years later, Lim was compelled to compose a response of her own.

Lim's opera is, along with *Tongue of the Invisible*, one of two major products of her period of collaboration with Cologne's Ensemble Musikfabrik. It was commissioned by them, Oper Köln and HELLERAU – Europäisches Zentrum der Künste, Dresden. The development of the electronics part was supported by the ZKM Center for Art and Media in Karlsruhe and the FHNW Musik Akademie in Basel. The libretto is by Lim, based on *Tree of Codes* and Celina Wieniewska's English translation of *Street of Crocodiles*, with additional texts taken from Michel Foucault's *Madness and Civilisation* and Goethe's *Der Erlkönig*.

Tree of Codes was first performed in Cologne in April 2016, by Musikfabrik, with Emily Hindrichs (Adela), Christian Miedl (Son/Doctor), Carl Rosman (Mutant Bird/ clarinet) and performers from Company Numero23Prod, conducted by Clement Power, directed by Massimo Furlan and with dramaturgy by Claire de Ribaupierre; this production toured to Dresden in October 2016 and in 2018 a new production was made by Ong Keng Sen for the Spoleto Festival, USA.

Safran Foer's novel is not a new text but is extracted from Schulz's story collection. By cutting holes through the pages of Schulz's book, Safran Foer was able to remove words from that text and open holes through which parts of the pages beneath can be seen, creating new continuities of sense and story (hence *sTREEt OF CrocODilES*). The conceit of Lim's opera is that holes like these enable passage between different states and realities, and the creation of hybrid forms in between. Just as Safran Foer's book is as much sculpture as fiction, as much one author's text as another's, so Lim's opera is full of hybrids, liminalities and boundary states: a time between life and death, beings who are part human and part bird, plant or insect, and instruments that inhabit multiple sonic spaces. The brass play with double-belled instruments that enable rapid changes between different mutes, developed by Musikfabrik and first used by Lim in her solo for double-bell euphonium, The *Green Lion Eats the Sun* (parts of which are incorporated into the opera, along with parts of *Axis Mundi*, the other solo she wrote for Musikfabrik). The ensemble also includes a Stroh viola, a form of viola fitted with two amplifying horns (designed for the early days of recording) that is a visual and aural hybrid of brass and strings. Players also use birdcalls, woodblocks and other auxiliary instruments, and they all also interact at various times with an electronic soundtrack featuring Australian birdsong (recorded by the composer David Lumsdaine), environmental sounds, the engines of trail bikes and a sonification (by composer Manuel Senftt) of the magnetic field oscillations of the comet 67P/Churyumov-Gerasimenko.[8] Finally, a special part is written for Rosman, who performs as both singer and instrumentalist.

Act I: An Enormous Day of Life

Into a laboratory full of strange mutant life-forms enters the Father, a scientist. He is dead, but unknown to him his colleagues have turned time back to give him an extra day, a margin of secret time in which the boundaries between animals, birds, trees, humans and machines are dissolving.

The prelude to the opera (extended to more than six minutes in Musikfabrik's production) is based on recordings of Bell Miner birds made by Lumsdaine around New South Wales, whose isolated 'pips' are taken up and imitated by members of the ensemble. The way in which the music for instrumentalists and Mutant Bird (and finally Adela and the Son) emerges from this pre-linguistic, pre-musical soundscape resembles, on a much larger scale, the beginning of *The Oresteia* and the cicadas at the start of *The Navigator*, and establishes a magical sonic location enclosed within the quotidian. It speaks to one of the principal themes of Lim's oeuvre: the existence of an inexplicable, ecstatic realm hidden behind the veil of reality, and music's ability to mediate our access to it. In her instrumental music, reality is pierced by the physical presence of musicians' bodies and instruments; in *Tree of Codes* those tears – like the holes in Safran Foer's text – are the opera's subject. Only once this breach has been thoroughly established by the music, and by the singers' half-human, half-bird singing (Example 6.36), does the Father enter, his arrival of a piece with the strange hybrid world into which we are now drawn.

Example 6.36 *Tree of Codes*, Act I, bars 27–8 (Adela and Mutant Bird)

Act II: The Comet

> *Act II takes us back in time; it is divided into two scenes. In the first, a masked carnival fills the streets. A 'fatal comet' traces its path across the sky. Son and Adela wander through the crowds, he lost and anxious, she seductive and sensual. In the second scene, the Father is seduced by Adela. We learn of his idea of a 'generatio aequivoca', 'a kind of pseudofauna and pseudoflora, the result of a fantastic fermentation of matter'. The Father conjures mutant birds from the rubbish but they are destroyed by the crowd. Having conveyed something of his vision to his son – including 'a secret escape ... the back gate of the world' – he dies.*

Act II begins with a solo for Stroh viola, punctuated by brutal ensemble strikes (that evolve into music for hi-hat and tom-toms); these are the comet 'as fiery bird and portent' according to the score. The voices of Adela and the Son are drawn to the Stroh viola, however, in a loose bundle of wandering threads.

As she becomes more seductive, Adela is paired with an out-of-tune upright piano in music that is equally evocative of pre-war Berlin cabaret, Hafez's wandering desire and *The Navigator*'s shivering ecstasy.

Example 6.37 *Tree of Codes*, Act II, bars 39–41

The revelation of the Father's theories of species mutation is accompanied by suitably exotic and hybridised music: a 'sultry, subterranean and sexual' call and response between bass and sub-contrabass flute, who are joined by double-bell euphonium, playing music based on *The Green Lion Eats the Sun* that also, to begin with, references the 'pips' of the Bell Miner birds from Act I.

Example 6.38 *Tree of Codes*, Act II, bar 98

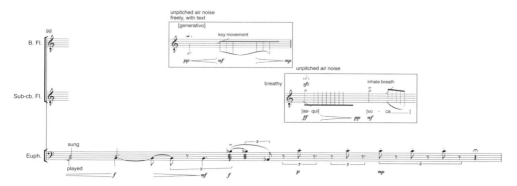

As the Father creates a flock of mutant birds, the instrumental music becomes increasingly bird-like (and less typically instrumental), with players using wacky whistles, toy instruments, vocalisation and other means to become something other than their usual selves. As he dies, they are reduced once more to almost silent whispering, muttering sounds.

CHAPTER 6: Music for Stage

Example 6.39 *Tree of Codes*, Act II, bars 256–8

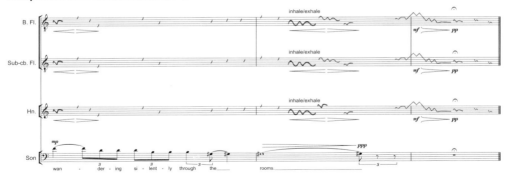

Act III: The Ventriloquist

In the sanatorium, the Son ventriloquises a conversation between himself and the Doctor, establishing the truth of his father's condition: at home he is dead but here is still alive, but does not know it. In this place it is possible to reactivate the past, to put back the clock. Adela sings a ballad – of the carnival, the mutant rubbish birds and the crowd that killed them. The Son sings a boat song, using words from Foucault's Madness and Civilisation: 'The mystics say / The soul is a skiff / Abandoned on the infinite / Sea of desire'. Adela sings a second ballad, this one based on Goethe's Der Erlkönig.

Act III begins with the recording of Comet 76P/Churymov-Gerasimenko. Alongside its buzzing, popping drone the brass play long pedal notes (the horn plays with a contrabassoon reed to create rich multiphonic chords, anticipating the bassoon's solo later in this act). In the Musikfabrik production this passage was staged as a funeral procession, and this act is concerned with the Son's acceptance of his father's passing. Alternating lines in English (as himself) and Polish (as the Doctor), he learns what has taken place.

Adela's first ballad introduces the tinkling sound of the kalimba, a West African thumb piano, which accompanies her song with triplet arpeggiations of a slightly detuned B minor sixth chord of B, D, F quarter-sharp, G♯ and B. They are joined by temple blocks and later strings, who play a harmonically static, pizzicato *moto perpetuo*. The simple harmonies, gently percussive timbres and 12/8 meter of this section contrast vividly with the funereal brass of the act's beginning and help resolve into childhood memory the tragedy of the carnival.

Example 6.40 *Tree of Codes*, Act III, bars 45–7

The Son responds with a 'boat song', in which he is joined by the bassoon, who plays a solo derived from the music of *Axis Mundi* but with glitches in which it gets caught on a repeating B♭–E dyad, like a thread becoming snagged on a nail. The bassoon solo ends with support from the double bass, which improvises slow harmonics that shroud the bassoon's own harmonic-filled line.

Example 6.41 *Tree of Codes*, Act III, bars 154–5

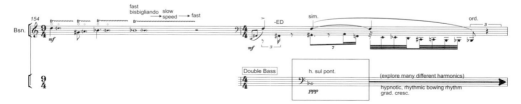

Goethe's tale of the 'Erl-King' – the story of a supernatural incursion upon nature, a ruptured boundary between the real and the magical, and the protective bond of a father and son – is obviously rich in suitable resonances, and Adela's aria is intended to provide some comfort for the Son: it draws on the sound of her first ballad, with kalimba and simple B minor harmony. However, the accompaniment is augmented by the sound of the first with the addition of a cello, which takes up (in fully notated form this time) the harmonics of the double bass just before. The lines of her English song are alternated with whispered ones from Goethe's poem, an act of ventriloquism that echoes the Son's ghastly conversation with the Doctor.

As Adela's aria continues, the nursery-rhyme texture is gradually overtaken by a reference to Schubert's famous setting of *Der Erlkönig*, in the form of a triplet piano pedal that recalling the shivering triplet octaves that begin Schubert's song. Veiled though it is, this reference is only slowly pieced together, as though it is coming into focus from Lim's previous music. We are a long way from the *Axis Mundi*/boat song music, but the transition takes place across a series of smooth steps: bassoon and double bass to cello; cello joins the ballad; ballad kalimba to piano; piano octaves gradually accelerate to Schubert's triplet quavers. Going one step further than Schubert, however, Lim further transmutes the piano into a chorus of rasping woodblocks, played by percussionist and wind (Example 6.42), that combines the sound of marching feet and angry voices with the rustling of cockroaches and the gesture of sweeping them away (Speak Percussion 2016). The translation of Romantic song into dry percussion prefigures the similar relationship between Janáček and waldteufels in *Extinction Events and Dawn Chorus*, and draws the act to a chilling close.

Example 6.42 *Tree of Codes*, Act III, bars 205–7

Act IV: The Tree of Codes

> *We return to the 'secret backstage area'. The Son considers 'the experiment of life' and the possibility of a transformed existence. As she did his father, Adela invites the Son to 'dip your face into that dusk / under the lid of a coffin'. Seduced by her words, and by what he has seen of his father's experiments, he passes behind the screen of reality, in search of 'a night that would not end'.*

The return to the setting of Act I is sonically signalled by a return of the Bell Miner pips. The last act is made of two contrasting musical threads, wound around each other. Both can be derived from the Miners' song. First are wild, abandoned gestures, like birdsong but expanded to include toy instruments, hybrid vocal and instrumental sounds, and recordings. As the Son follows the Father's path into human-animal hybridity, these sounds evolve from a pairing of Stroh viola and wah-wah French horn, like the cooing of doves, to a regression into childhood with the Son's frantic playing of toy instruments, the return of the Mutant Bird and, climactically, an explosion of concrete sounds including revving trail bike engines, slamming doors, children playing, babies crying and the sound of orgasm – all of them expulsions of energy at the edge of control. The second thread contrasts with these a harmonic stasis, manifest primarily in contemplative vocal writing, particularly for chorus. Sometimes the different musical threads are heard in sequence; at others, as in Example 6.43, they are heard simultaneously.

Example 6.43 *Tree of Codes*, Act IV, bars 92–5

Gradually, the chorus subdues the erratic and disturbed impulses of the bird-like music. The instruments fall silent; last are two piccolos (who play bird-like motifs) and then trombone, whose wah-wah B♭ pedal adds subtle colours to the chorus's chords. (There is an echo here of the overtone singing in the final sections of both *The Oresteia* and *The Navigator*.) Finally, in a reversal of the 'tuning' opening of *Tongue of the Invisible*, the chorus finds its way to this same B♭, tenors and basses settling on a repeating pattern of harmonics, a peaceful, chant-like resolution of the Miners' pips; a serene sink back into the pre-linguistic, animal place from which we began.

Example 6.44 *Tree of Codes*, Act IV, bars 138–40

Conclusion

Surveying Liza Lim's body of work is like trying to unravel a tapestry from a vast ball of brightly coloured threads. She is a restless artist, always moving, changing and exploring. Like fungal mycelia, her imagination probes forward and into, continually building new connections and new partnerships, nourishing itself with whatever it finds. And yet, it is possible to identify constant inspirations and preoccupations – her artistic DNA, as it were – as well as the technical and stylistic means by which she brings them about. The earliest works in her catalogue exhibit interests in the tactile and erotic, in multiplicity and richness, and in ritual and wildness, and these fascinations have expanded to include Sufism, Asian and Aboriginal cultures, forests and fungi, motherhood and female experience, desire, hybridity, and language. Lim's imagination translates all of these into ways of looking at the same thing. And what is that? It is a vibrant, generous, respectful and thrilling vision of a world of limitless variety in which everything is infinitely connected and vividly present.

Although I have only touched on it occasionally in these pages, female experience – of rhythm, desire, motherhood, transformation, difference and connection – is central to her work, and to her operas most of all. Lim has written recently about the frequent association in operatic 'mad scenes' of female voices with 'emotional volatility and loss of control'. Her words then might stand for her entire artistic project:

> Opera has often focussed on the woman's voice as a siren call – seductive, sexualised and dangerous. And actually, all power to that! The gendered valuations and devaluations of things variously called 'shrill', 'volatile', 'hysterical' – in other words, everything related to distortion – are for me a source of deep knowledge and beauty. For me, there's a basic truthfulness in noise, particularly the high intensity full spectrum kind, and the way it disrupts norms, the way it invades the body and blurs boundaries between things, the way ecstasy creates its own time and space and physicality. Noise creates force fields with which and within which one can conjure up presences. (Lim 2022: 206)

Lim's words highlight the renewal that can be found in the distorted, concealed and marginalised; they hail the necessity of disruption and disturbance as sources of pleasure and understanding; and they foreground the body and experience as sources of truth and knowledge. From a sound to a musician, an instrument to a culture, a word to a language, everything in her artistic vision is given dignity by what it can become. All we must do is listen.

References

Ford, Andrew (2009). 'Composer Liza Lim'. Broadcast interview, ABC Radio, 18 April 2009. Transcription available at https://www.abc.net.au/radionational/programs/musicshow/composer-liza-lim/3066934.

Gruchy, Jane (2007). 'Alchemical Journeys – Part Two: Liza Lim', *Resonate Magazine*, 17 December, https://www.australianmusiccentre.com.au/article/alchemical-journeys-part-two-liza-lim.

Leonard, Doug (2008). "Fugue of the Senses, Geometry of Desire", *realtime*, n85, http://realtimearts.net/article/85/9017.

Lim, Liza (2009). 'Interview with Jérémie Szpirglas (6 June 2009)'. Available at https://limprogrammenotes.files.wordpress.com/2011/08/interview-with-jc3a9rc3a9mie-szpirglas-festival-dautomne.pdf.

Lim, Liza (2022). 'Rifts in Time: Distortion, Possession and Ventriloquism in My Operatic Works'. In *Sounding Fragilities: An Anthology*, edited by Irene Lehmann and Pia Palme. Hofheim: Wolke Verlag, pp. 201–10.

Speak Percussion (2016). 'Online Masterclass 13: Liza Lim on "Tree of Codes"', [video], http://soundsunheard.com/online-masterclass-13/.

Endnotes

1 *The Oresteia, The Navigator* and 'Chang-O Flies to the Moon' are recorded on the three-disc set *Singing in Tongues* (HCR25CD, 2021), along with *Mother Tongue*.

2 Morey, ELISION's original mandolinist, had to give up playing in the early 1990s due to a hand injury, after which he became a linguist; see also Chapter 3. Azzaro was a student of his, but as a keen collector of instruments it was Morey who first introduced Lim to the sound of the *saz*. (Conversation with Lim, November 2021.)

3 This passage is not included on the available recording of the opera.

4 The tomb is noted in particular for containing a large number of musical instruments, including a set of sixty-four bronze bells.

5 The tomb is noted in particular for containing a large number of musical instruments, including a set of sixty-four bronze bells.

6 Bray pins are L-shaped wooden pegs that can be positioned to lightly touch the harp strings and so produce a buzzing sound (supposedly like the braying of a donkey); common in European harp design of the Renaissance and Baroque, they are an unsung predecessor of John Cage's piano preparations of several centuries later.

7 Conversation with the author, November 2021.

8 Recorded by the European Space Agency's Rosetta Plasma Consortium, this 'comet song' can be heard at https://soundcloud.com/esa/a-singing-comet.

Chronology

1966 Born in Perth on August 30 to Chinese-Bruneian parents. Her family moves several times between Australia and Brunei before settling in Melbourne.

1978–83 Boarder at Presbyterian Ladies' College, Melbourne, where she takes up the violin.

1981 With encouragement from her school teachers, takes private composition lessons with Richard David Hames, and later too with Riccardo Formosa.

1983–6 Undergraduate degree at Victoria College of the Arts, where she majored in violin.

1986 Formation of ELISION by a group of Lim's VCA student colleagues. Lim contributes *Blaze* (which she also conducts) to the group's second-ever concert.

1987 Studies with Ton de Leeuw at the Sweelinck Conservatory, Amsterdam, and a small number of private lessons with Brian Ferneyhough in The Hague.

1988 Master's in music at the University of Melbourne, where she subsequently teaches from 1988 to 1992.

1988 ISCM World New Music Days in Hong Kong, in 1988. Arditti Quartet play Lim's *Pompes funèbres*. Makes contact with Germany's Radio Bremen, who commission Voodoo Child (1989).

1989 First post-student work, *Garden of Earthly Desire*, premiered by ELISION and the puppetry group Handspan Theatre.

1990 Marries ELISION's artistic director and guitarist, Daryl Buckley.

1993 ELISION give the premiere of Lim's first opera, *The Oresteia*, at Theatreworks, Melbourne.

1993 Meets the artist Domenico de Clario.

1994–6 Collaborates with de Clario on a series of site-specific, long duration installations. De Clario also introduces her to the poetry of Rumi, which becomes a lifelong inspiration.

1995 Visiting lecturer at the University of Western Sydney.

2000 ELISION give the premiere of Lim's second opera, *Yuè Lìng Jié (Moon Spirit Feasting)*, at the Adelaide Festival.

2002 Completes her PhD at the University of Queensland.

2002–2004 Takes a three-year break around the birth and early years of her son.

2004 Attends a performance of the prelude to *Tristan und Isolde* by the Sydney SO, which helps her return to composing.

2004 Composes *Ecstatic Architecture* for the opening season of Walt Disney Hall Concert in Los Angeles.

2004 Wins the Paul Lowin Prize for Orchestral Composition for *Ecstatic Architecture*, and the Fromm Foundation Award.

2005 Featured composer at the Festival d'Automne à Paris, which commissions and see the premieres of several new works – *In the Shadow's Light, The Quickening* and *Mother Tongue* – that signal a new engagement with Australian Aboriginal culture and ideas.

2005–6 Composer-in-residence with the Sydney SO, composing among other pieces *The Compass* for didgeridoo, flute and orchestra.

2006 During research into the singing traditions of Yolngu women in northern Australia is invited to spend a week with the Yunupingu clan.

2007–8 Lives in Berlin as part of the DAAD artist-in-residence programme.

2008 ELISION premieres Lim's third opera, *The Navigator,* at the Brisbane Festival.

2008–2017 Professor of Composition at the University of Huddersfield, UK, where she also directed the university's Centre for Research in New Music (CeReNeM).

2009 Séverine Ballon gives premiere of *Invisibility* for solo cello at Huddersfield Contemporary Music Festival.

2010–2016 Collaborates with Cologne's Ensemble Musikfabrik, producing *Tongue of the Invisible* (2011), *Tree of Codes* (2016) and solo instrumental works.

2017 Wins Vocal/Choral Work of the Year (for *Tree of Codes*) and Instrumental Work of the Year (for *How Forests Think*) at the APRA AMCOS/AMC Art Music Awards.

2017 Appointed Professor of Composition at the Sydney Conservatorium of Music, University of Sydney.

2018 Premiere of *Extinction Events and Dawn Chorus* by Klangforum Wien. Wins the Don Banks Award for Music. Jessica Aszodi and Speak Percussion give the premiere of *Atlas of the Sky* in Melbourne.

2019 Appointed the inaugural Sculthorpe Chair of Australian Music at the Sydney Conservatorium of Music.

2021 Wins the Happy New Ears composition prize from the Hans and Gertrud Zender Foundation. Premiere of piano concerto *World as Lover, World as Self,* by Tamara Stefanovich and the Orchestre Philharmonique du Luxembourg.

2022 Premiere of *Annunciation Triptych* for orchestra by WDR Sinfonie-Orchester.

Further reading

Browning, Joseph, and Lim, Liza (forthcoming). 'Sonic figurations for the anthropocene: A musical bestiary in the compositions of Liza Lim', *Journal of the Royal Musical Association*.

Clarke, Eric, Doffman, Mark, and Lim, Liza (2013). 'Distributed creativity and ecological dynamics: a case study of Liza Lim's *Tongue of the Invisible*', *Music and Letters* 94, no. 4: 628–63.

de Clario, Domenica and Liza Lim (1998). *The Intertwining – The Chasm: Installation-Performance Works 1994–96*. Brisbane: Institute of Modern Art.

Ford, Andrew (1993). 'No beginning and no end . . . : Liza Lim'. In *Composer to Composer: Conversations about Contemporary Music*. London: Quartet Books, pp. 157–62.

Gruchy, Jane (2007). 'Alchemical Journeys – Part One: Liza Lim'. *Resonate Magazine*, 19 November. https://www.australianmusiccentre.com.au/article/alchemical-journeys-part-one-liza-lim.

Gruchy, Jane (2007). 'Alchemical Journeys – Part Two: Liza Lim', *Resonate Magazine*, 17 December, https://www.australianmusiccentre.com.au/article/alchemical-journeys-part-two-liza-lim.

Kerry, Gordon (2009). *New Classical Music: Composing Australia*. Sydney: University of New South Wales Press.

Lim, Liza (2009). 'Staging an Aesthetics of Presence', Search: *Journal for New Music and Culture* 6, http://www.searchnewmusic.org/index6.html.

Lim, Liza (2013). 'A Mycelial Model for Understanding Distributed Creativity: collaborative partnership in the making of "Axis Mundi" (2013) for solo bassoon', CMPCP Performance Studies Network Conference, Cambridge, 4 April 2013. Available at http://eprints.hud.ac.uk/id/eprint/17973/.

Lim, Liza (2020). 'An Ecology of Time Traces in *Extinction Events and Dawn Chorus*'. *Contemporary Music Review* 39, no. 5: 544–63.

Lim, Liza (2021). 'How to Make a Woodblock Sing: Artistic Research as an Art of Attentiveness'. In *Creative Research in Music: Informed Practice, Innovation and Transcendence*, edited by Anna Reid, Neal Peres Da Costa and Jeanell Carrigan. New York: Routledge.

Lim, Liza (2022). 'Rifts in Time. Distortion, Possession and Ventriloquism in My Operatic Works'. In *Sounding Fragilities: An Anthology*, edited by Irene Lehmann and Pia Palme. Hofheim: Wolke Verlag, pp. 201–10.

Rosman, Carl (1999). 'Wie gelähmt die Zunge, Fieber unter der Haut ... Prozesse in Liza Lims *Voodoo Child*'. *Musik & Ästhetik* 11: 30–47.

Rutherford-Johnson, Tim (2011). 'Patterns of Shimmer: Liza Lim's Compositional Ethnography'. *Tempo* 65, no. 258: 2–9.